D0467999

A CHRISTMAS CAROL

The Night That Changed the Life of Eliza Scrooge

A CHRISTMAS CAROL

The Night That Changed the Life of Eliza Scrooge

Adapted and Illustrated by
Rod Espinosa

DARK HORSE BOOKS®

president and publisher
MIKE RICHARDSON

designer
ALLYSON HALLER

editor
RANDY STRADLEY

assistant editor
FREDDYE LINS

Published by Dark Horse Books
A division of Dark Horse Comics, Inc.
10956 SE Main Street
Milwaukie, OR 97222

DarkHorse.com

To find a comics shop in your area, call the Comic Shop Locator Service toll-free at 1-888-266-4226

Library of Congress Cataloging-in-Publication Data

Espinosa, Rod.
Charles Dickens's A Christmas carol : the night that changed the life of Eliza Scrooge / adapted and illustrated by Rod Espinosa. -- 1st ed.
p. cm.
Summary: "The miserly Eliza Scrooge, is visited by the ghosts of the past, present, and future on one fateful Christmas eve"--Provided by publisher.
ISBN 978-1-59582-991-7
1. Christmas--Comic books, strips, etc. 2. Ghosts--Comic books, strips, etc. 3. Graphic novels. I. Dickens, Charles, 1812-1870. Christmas carol. II. Title. III. Title: Christmas carol.
PN6727.E86C47 2012
741.5'973--dc23
2012016661

First edition: October 2012
ISBN 978-1-59582-991-7

1 3 5 7 9 10 8 6 4 2
Printed at Midas Printing International, Ltd., Huizhou, China

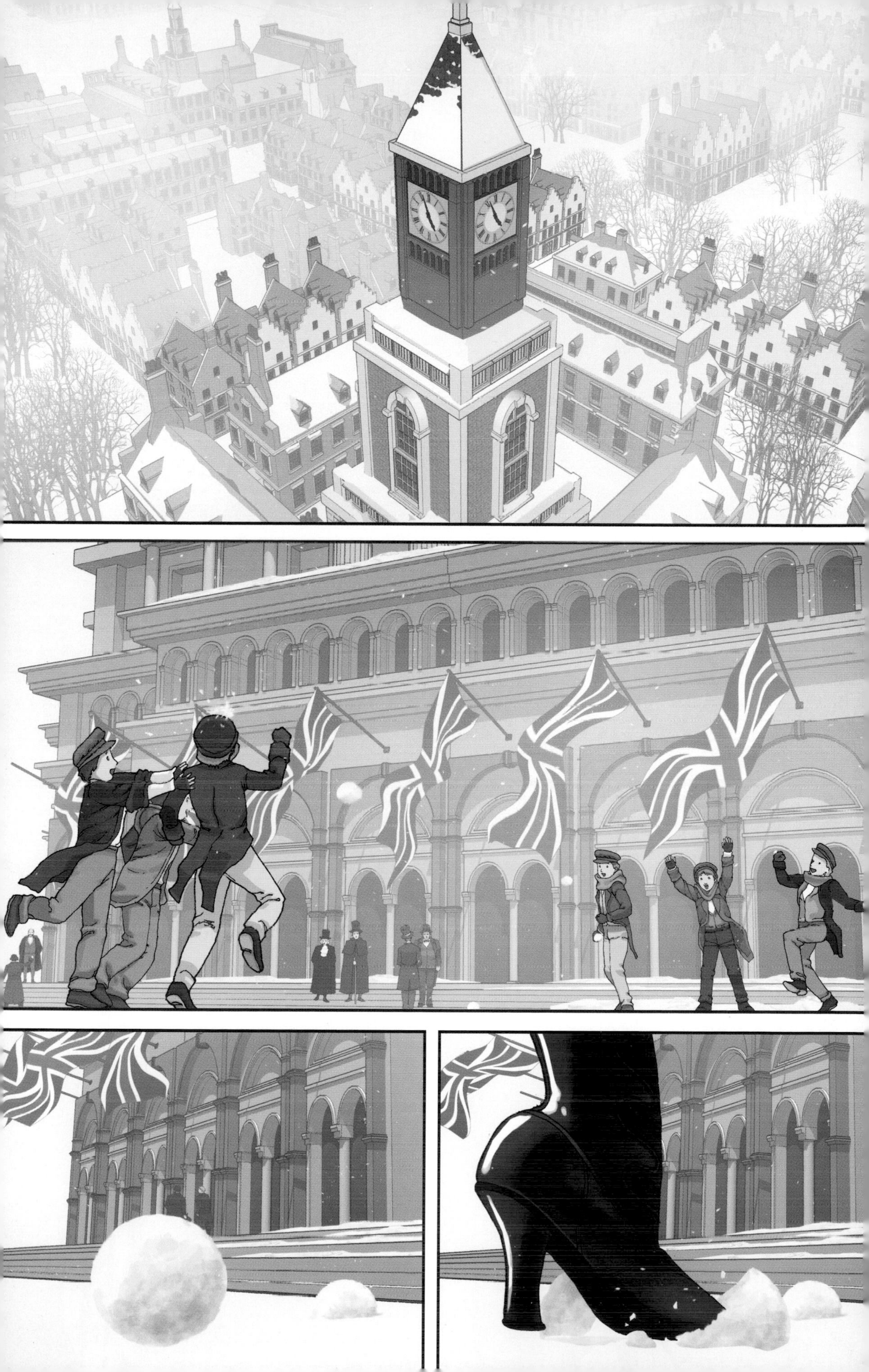

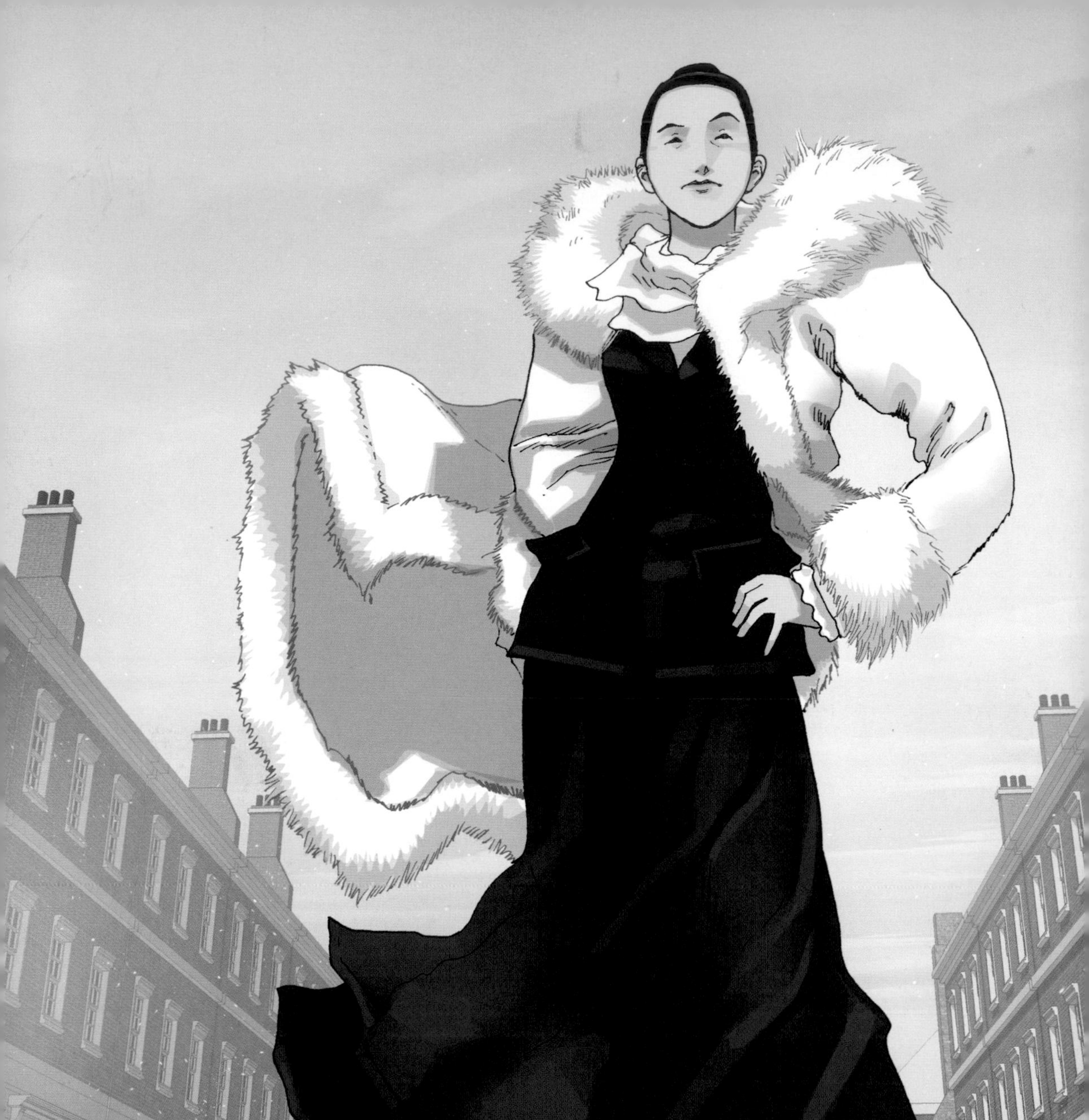

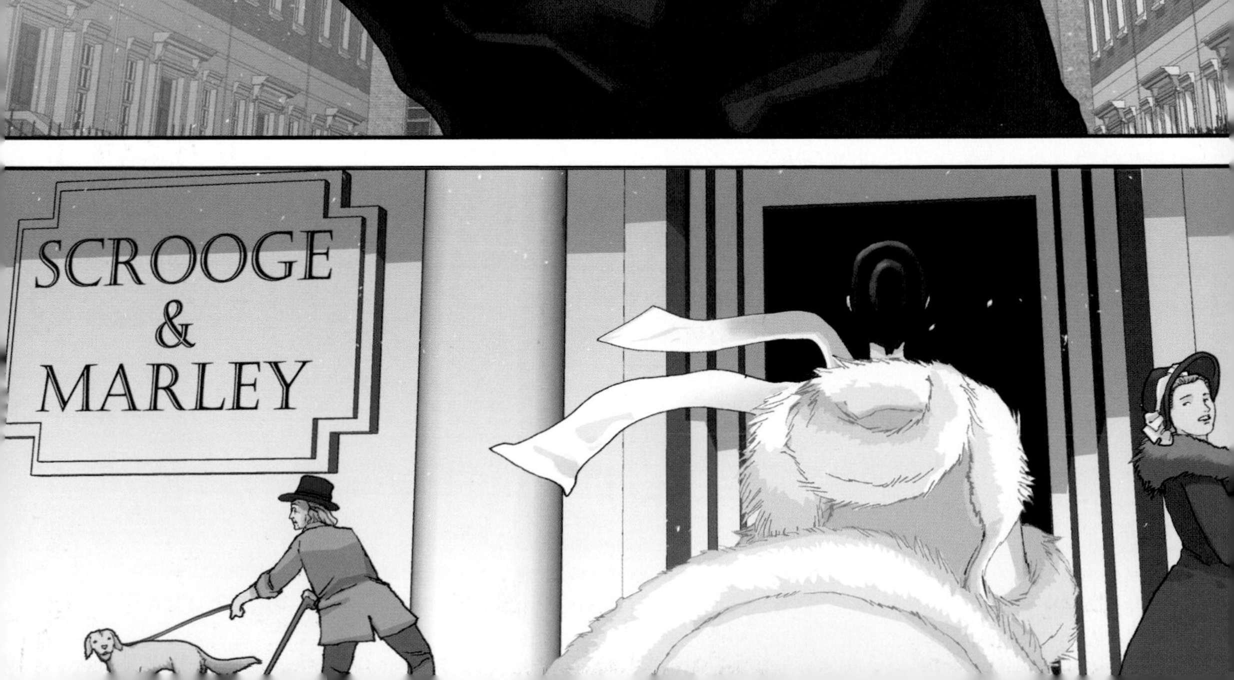
SCROOGE
&
MARLEY

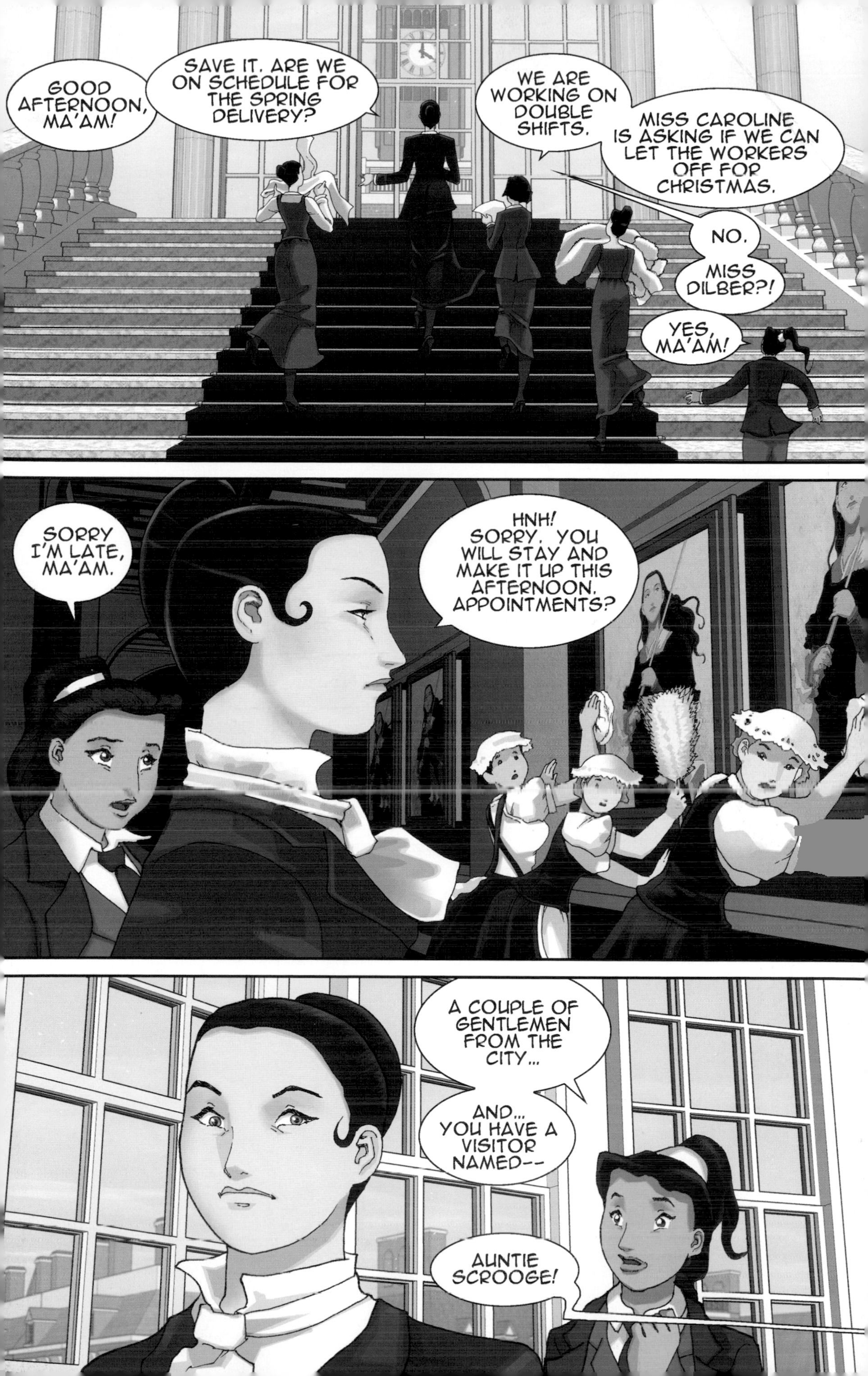
GOOD AFTERNOON, MA'AM!
SAVE IT. ARE WE ON SCHEDULE FOR THE SPRING DELIVERY?
WE ARE WORKING ON DOUBLE SHIFTS.
MISS CAROLINE IS ASKING IF WE CAN LET THE WORKERS OFF FOR CHRISTMAS.
NO.
MISS DILBER?!
YES, MA'AM!
SORRY I'M LATE, MA'AM.
HNH! SORRY. YOU WILL STAY AND MAKE IT UP THIS AFTERNOON. APPOINTMENTS?
A COUPLE OF GENTLEMEN FROM THE CITY...
AND... YOU HAVE A VISITOR NAMED--
AUNTIE SCROOGE!

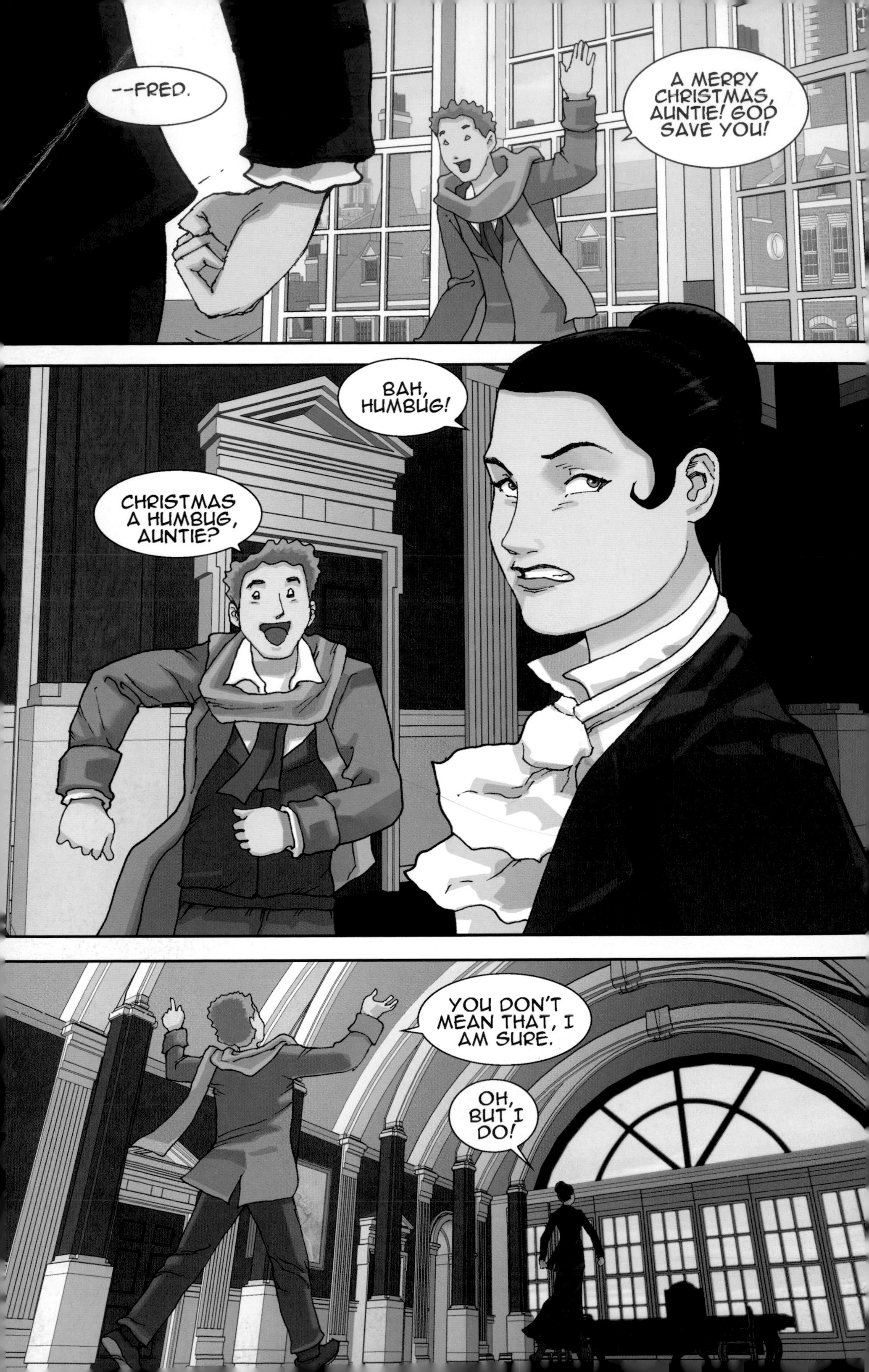
--FRED.
A MERRY CHRISTMAS, AUNTIE! GOD SAVE YOU!
BAH, HUMBUG!
CHRISTMAS A HUMBUG, AUNTIE?
YOU DON'T MEAN THAT, I AM SURE.
OH, BUT I DO!

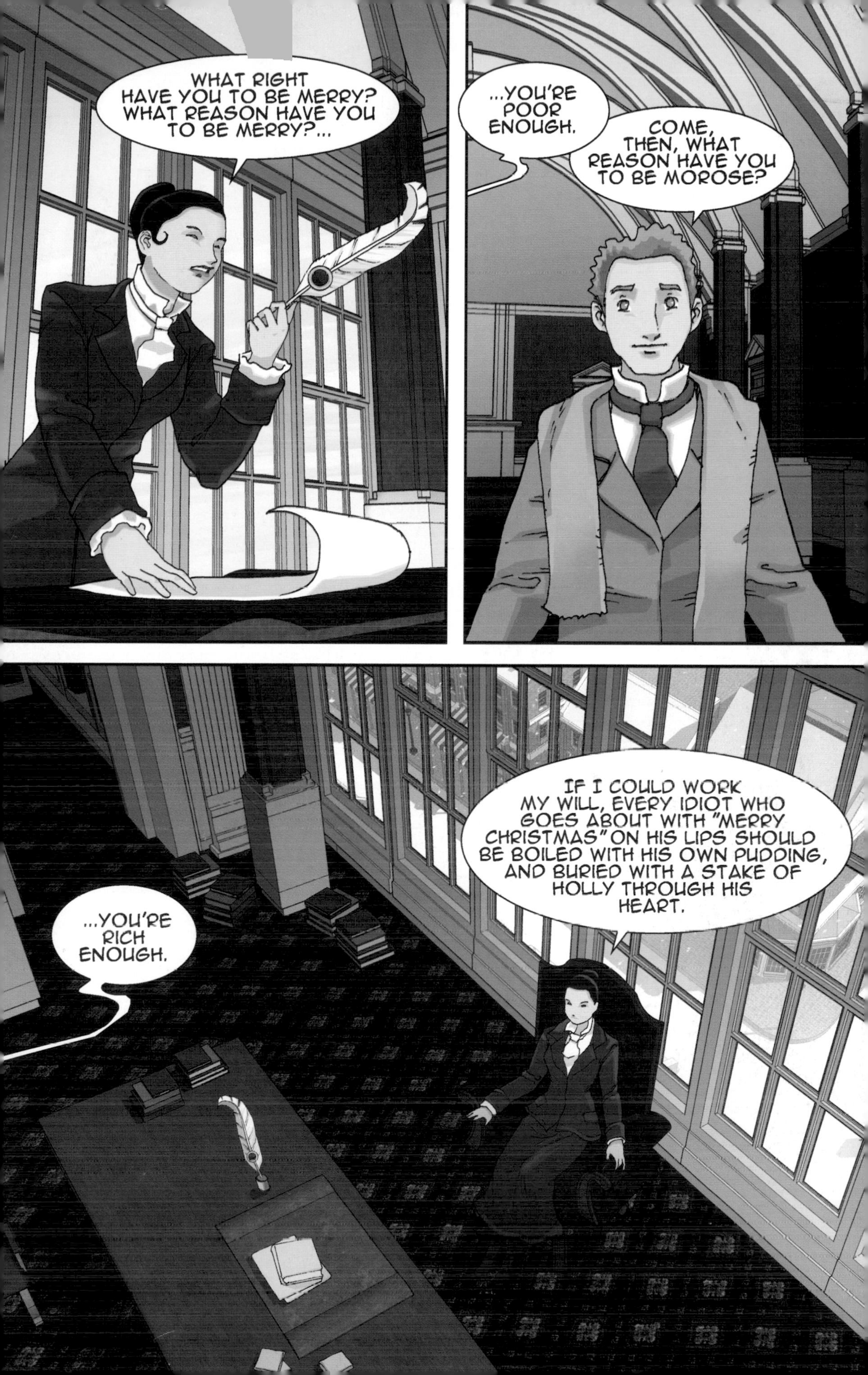
WHAT RIGHT HAVE YOU TO BE MERRY? WHAT REASON HAVE YOU TO BE MERRY?...
...YOU'RE POOR ENOUGH.
COME, THEN, WHAT REASON HAVE YOU TO BE MOROSE?
...YOU'RE RICH ENOUGH.
IF I COULD WORK MY WILL, EVERY IDIOT WHO GOES ABOUT WITH "MERRY CHRISTMAS" ON HIS LIPS SHOULD BE BOILED WITH HIS OWN PUDDING, AND BURIED WITH A STAKE OF HOLLY THROUGH HIS HEART.

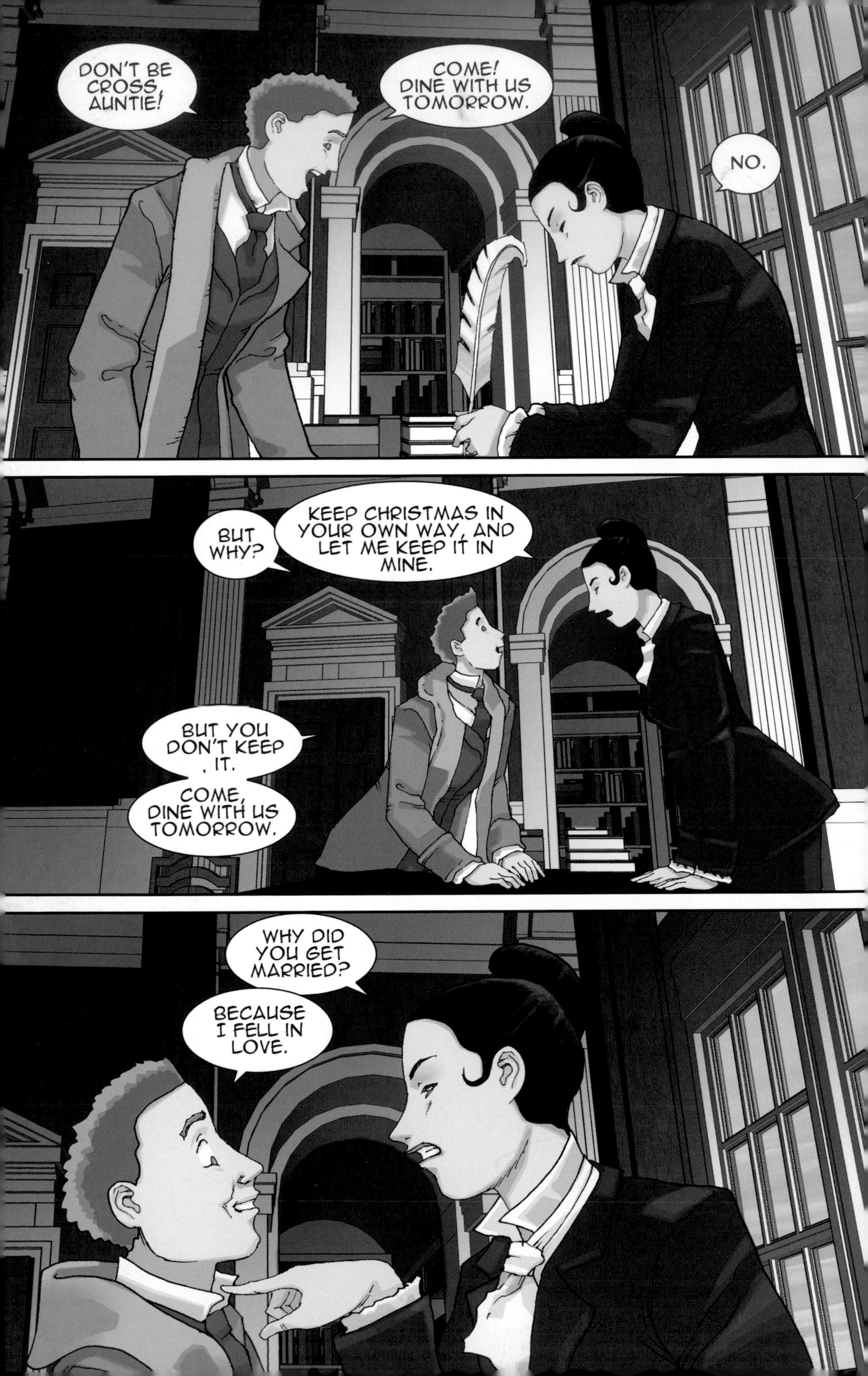
DON'T BE CROSS, AUNTIE!
COME! DINE WITH US TOMORROW.
NO.
BUT WHY?
KEEP CHRISTMAS IN YOUR OWN WAY, AND LET ME KEEP IT IN MINE.
BUT YOU DON'T KEEP IT.
COME, DINE WITH US TOMORROW.
WHY DID YOU GET MARRIED?
BECAUSE I FELL IN LOVE.

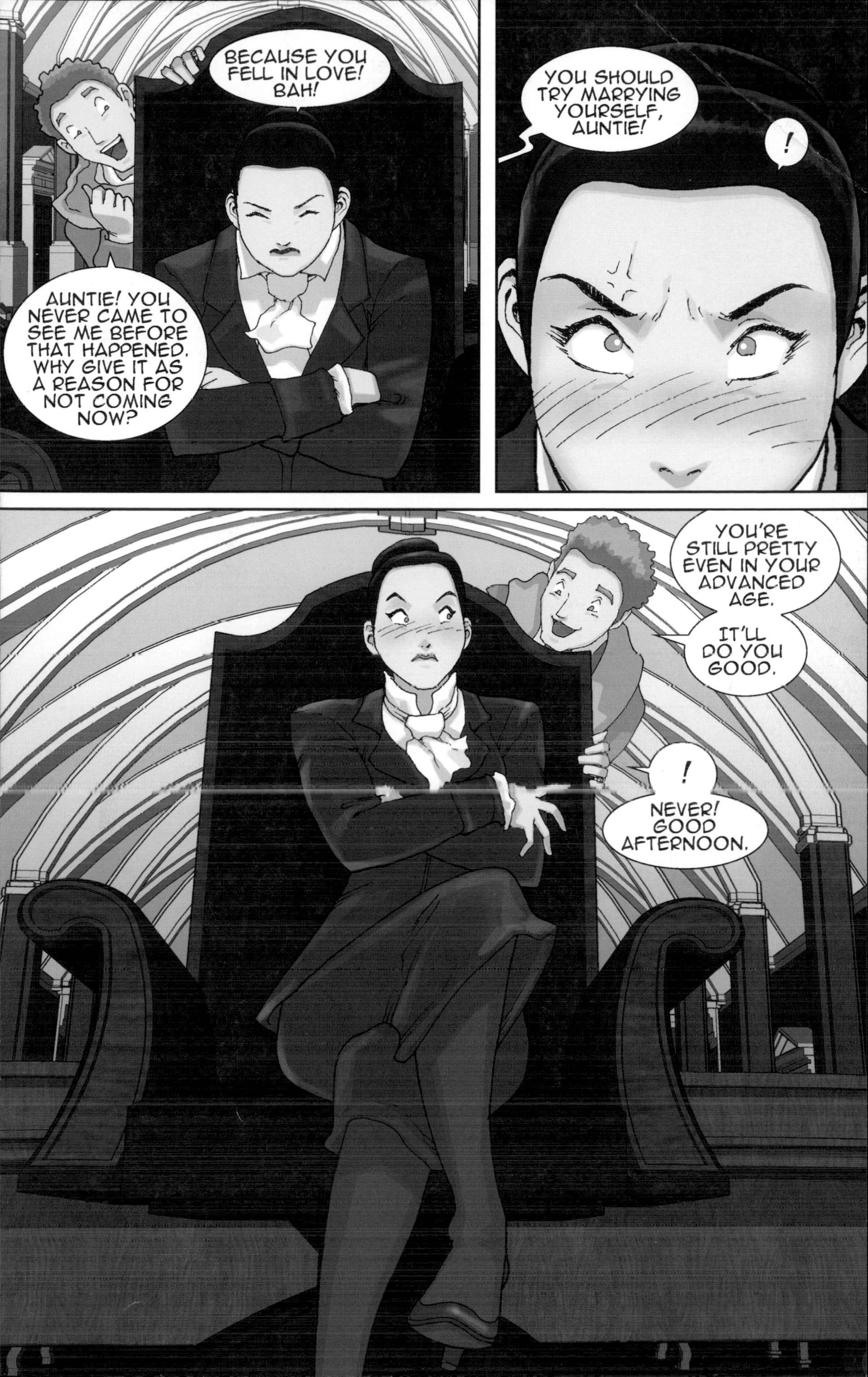
BECAUSE YOU FELL IN LOVE! BAH!
AUNTIE! YOU NEVER CAME TO SEE ME BEFORE THAT HAPPENED. WHY GIVE IT AS A REASON FOR NOT COMING NOW?
YOU SHOULD TRY MARRYING YOURSELF, AUNTIE!
!
YOU'RE STILL PRETTY EVEN IN YOUR ADVANCED AGE.
IT'LL DO YOU GOOD.
!
NEVER! GOOD AFTERNOON.

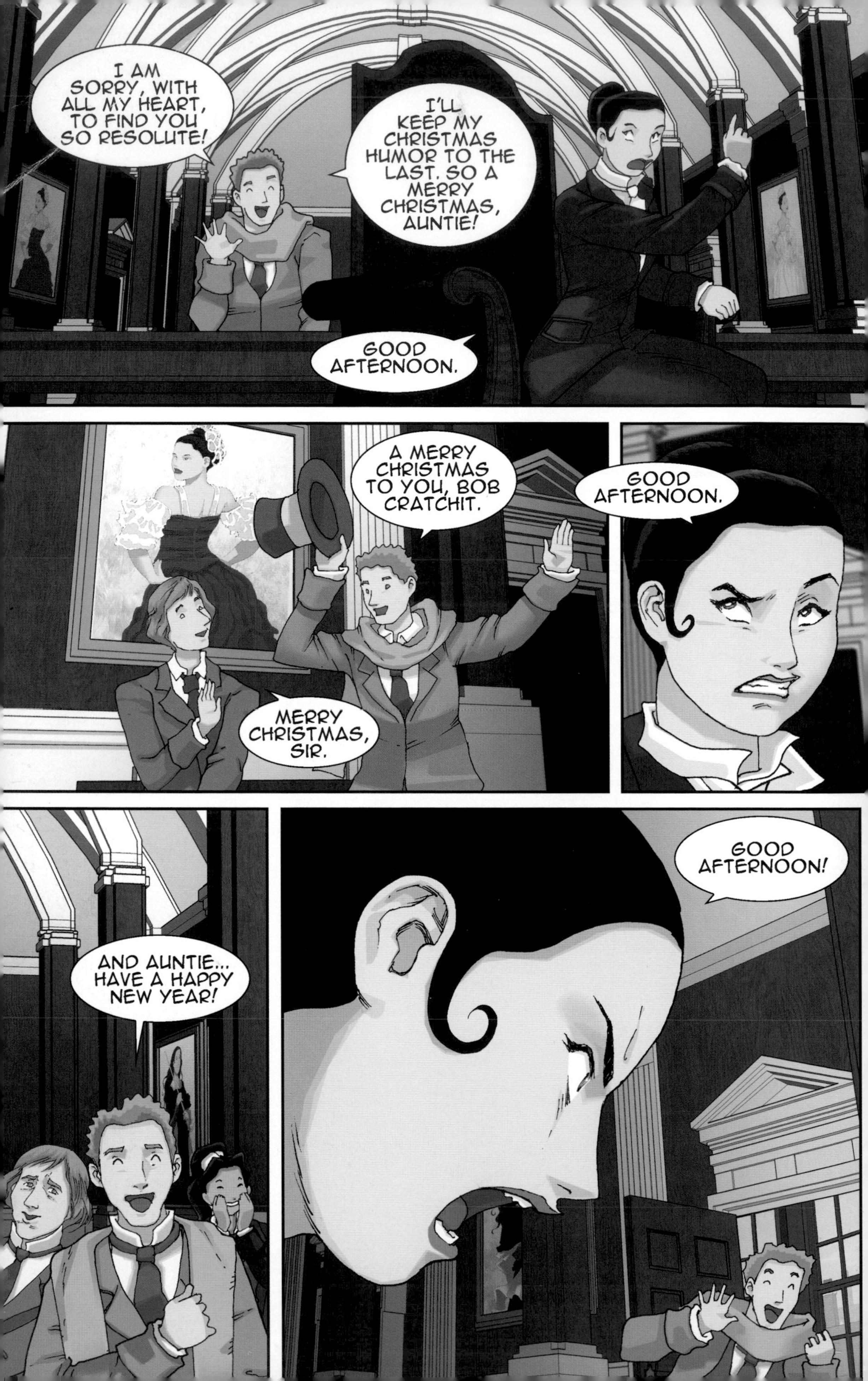

I AM SORRY, WITH ALL MY HEART, TO FIND YOU SO RESOLUTE!
I'LL KEEP MY CHRISTMAS HUMOR TO THE LAST. SO A MERRY CHRISTMAS, AUNTIE!
GOOD AFTERNOON.
A MERRY CHRISTMAS TO YOU, BOB CRATCHIT.
MERRY CHRISTMAS, SIR.
GOOD AFTERNOON.
AND AUNTIE... HAVE A HAPPY NEW YEAR!
GOOD AFTERNOON!

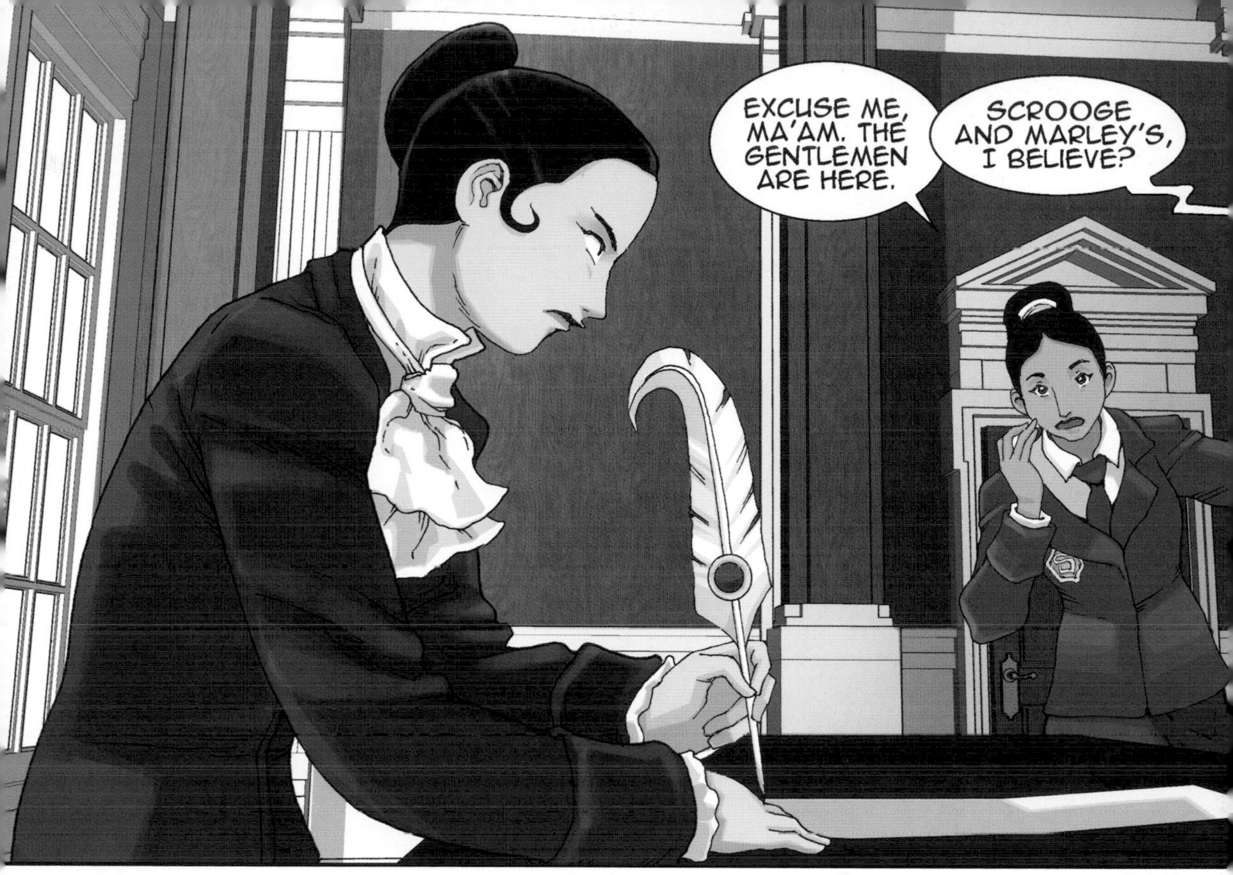
EXCUSE ME, MA'AM. THE GENTLEMEN ARE HERE.
SCROOGE AND MARLEY'S, I BELIEVE?

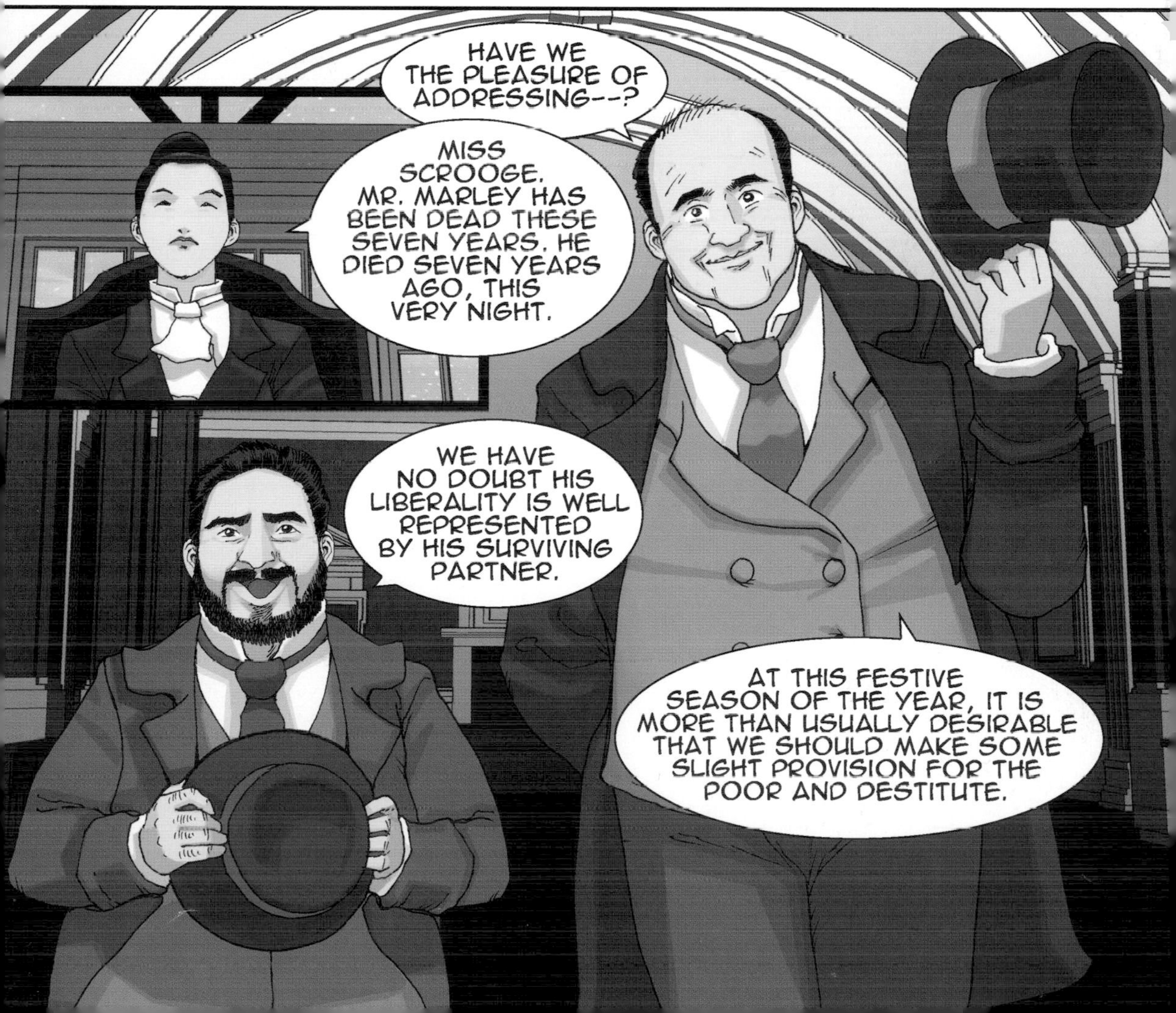
HAVE WE THE PLEASURE OF ADDRESSING--?
MISS SCROOGE. MR. MARLEY HAS BEEN DEAD THESE SEVEN YEARS. HE DIED SEVEN YEARS AGO, THIS VERY NIGHT.
WE HAVE NO DOUBT HIS LIBERALITY IS WELL REPRESENTED BY HIS SURVIVING PARTNER.
AT THIS FESTIVE SEASON OF THE YEAR, IT IS MORE THAN USUALLY DESIRABLE THAT WE SHOULD MAKE SOME SLIGHT PROVISION FOR THE POOR AND DESTITUTE.

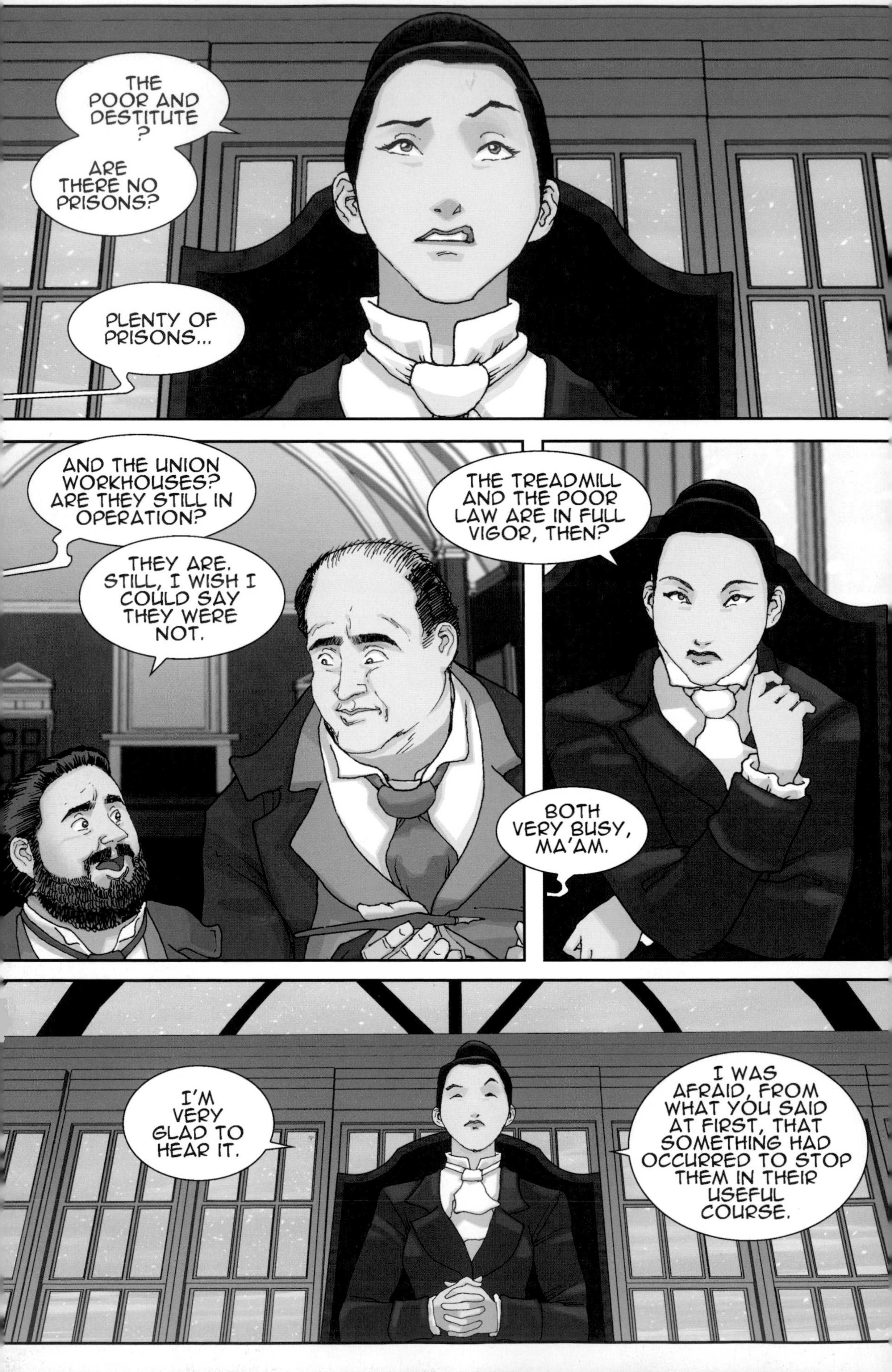
THE POOR AND DESTITUTE?
ARE THERE NO PRISONS?
PLENTY OF PRISONS...
AND THE UNION WORKHOUSES? ARE THEY STILL IN OPERATION?
THEY ARE. STILL, I WISH I COULD SAY THEY WERE NOT.
THE TREADMILL AND THE POOR LAW ARE IN FULL VIGOR, THEN?
BOTH VERY BUSY, MA'AM.
I'M VERY GLAD TO HEAR IT.
I WAS AFRAID, FROM WHAT YOU SAID AT FIRST, THAT SOMETHING HAD OCCURRED TO STOP THEM IN THEIR USEFUL COURSE.

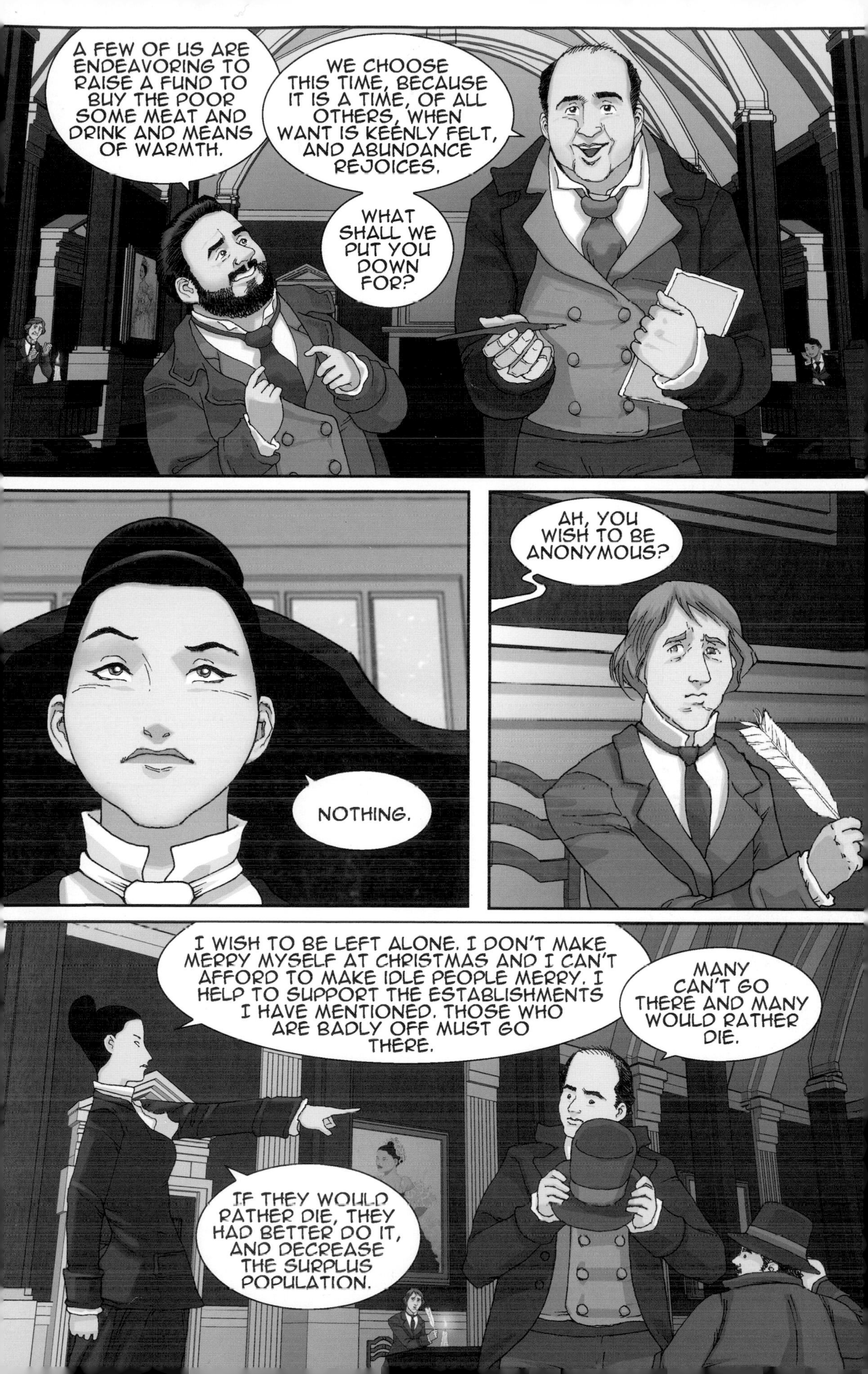
A FEW OF US ARE ENDEAVORING TO RAISE A FUND TO BUY THE POOR SOME MEAT AND DRINK AND MEANS OF WARMTH.
WE CHOOSE THIS TIME, BECAUSE IT IS A TIME, OF ALL OTHERS, WHEN WANT IS KEENLY FELT, AND ABUNDANCE REJOICES.
WHAT SHALL WE PUT YOU DOWN FOR?
NOTHING.
AH, YOU WISH TO BE ANONYMOUS?
I WISH TO BE LEFT ALONE. I DON'T MAKE MERRY MYSELF AT CHRISTMAS AND I CAN'T AFFORD TO MAKE IDLE PEOPLE MERRY. I HELP TO SUPPORT THE ESTABLISHMENTS I HAVE MENTIONED. THOSE WHO ARE BADLY OFF MUST GO THERE.
MANY CAN'T GO THERE AND MANY WOULD RATHER DIE.
IF THEY WOULD RATHER DIE, THEY HAD BETTER DO IT, AND DECREASE THE SURPLUS POPULATION.

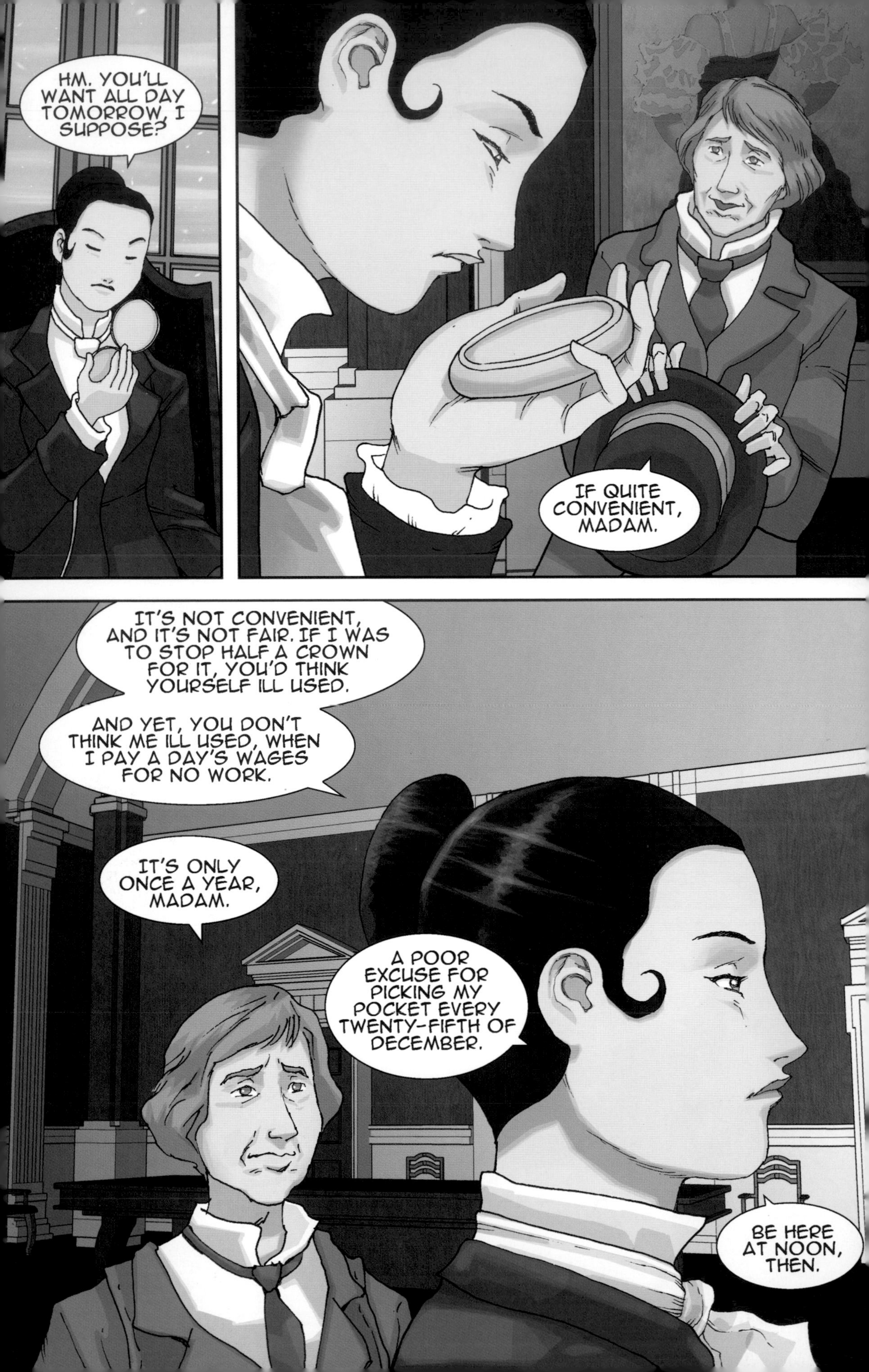
HM. YOU'LL WANT ALL DAY TOMORROW, I SUPPOSE?
IF QUITE CONVENIENT, MADAM.
IT'S NOT CONVENIENT, AND IT'S NOT FAIR. IF I WAS TO STOP HALF A CROWN FOR IT, YOU'D THINK YOURSELF ILL USED.
AND YET, YOU DON'T THINK ME ILL USED, WHEN I PAY A DAY'S WAGES FOR NO WORK.
IT'S ONLY ONCE A YEAR, MADAM.
A POOR EXCUSE FOR PICKING MY POCKET EVERY TWENTY-FIFTH OF DECEMBER.
BE HERE AT NOON, THEN.

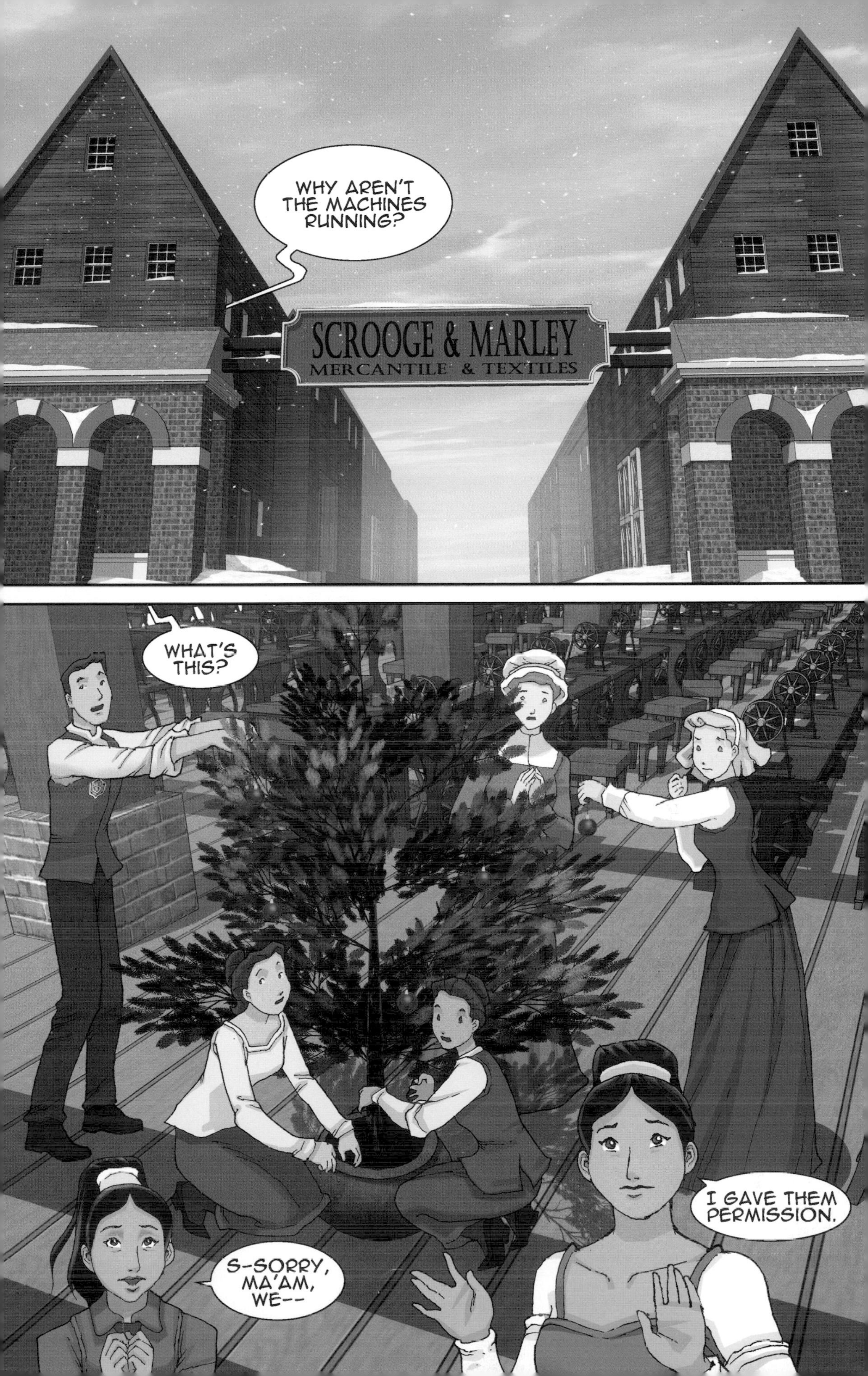
WHY AREN'T THE MACHINES RUNNING?
SCROOGE & MARLEY
MERCANTILE & TEXTILES
WHAT'S THIS?
I GAVE THEM PERMISSION.
S-SORRY, MA'AM, WE--

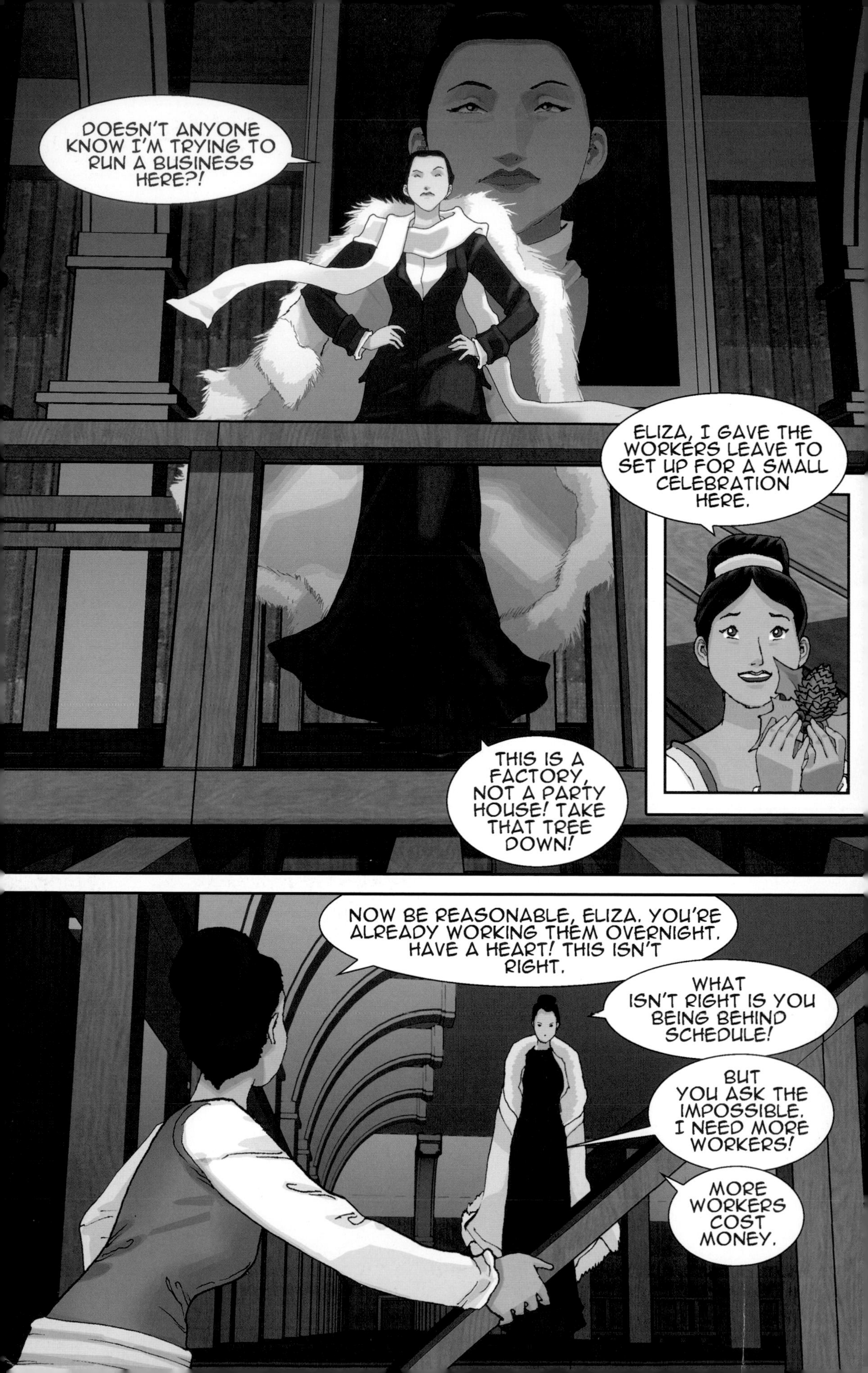
DOESN'T ANYONE KNOW I'M TRYING TO RUN A BUSINESS HERE?!
ELIZA, I GAVE THE WORKERS LEAVE TO SET UP FOR A SMALL CELEBRATION HERE.
THIS IS A FACTORY, NOT A PARTY HOUSE! TAKE THAT TREE DOWN!
NOW BE REASONABLE, ELIZA. YOU'RE ALREADY WORKING THEM OVERNIGHT. HAVE A HEART! THIS ISN'T RIGHT.
WHAT ISN'T RIGHT IS YOU BEING BEHIND SCHEDULE!
BUT YOU ASK THE IMPOSSIBLE. I NEED MORE WORKERS!
MORE WORKERS COST MONEY.

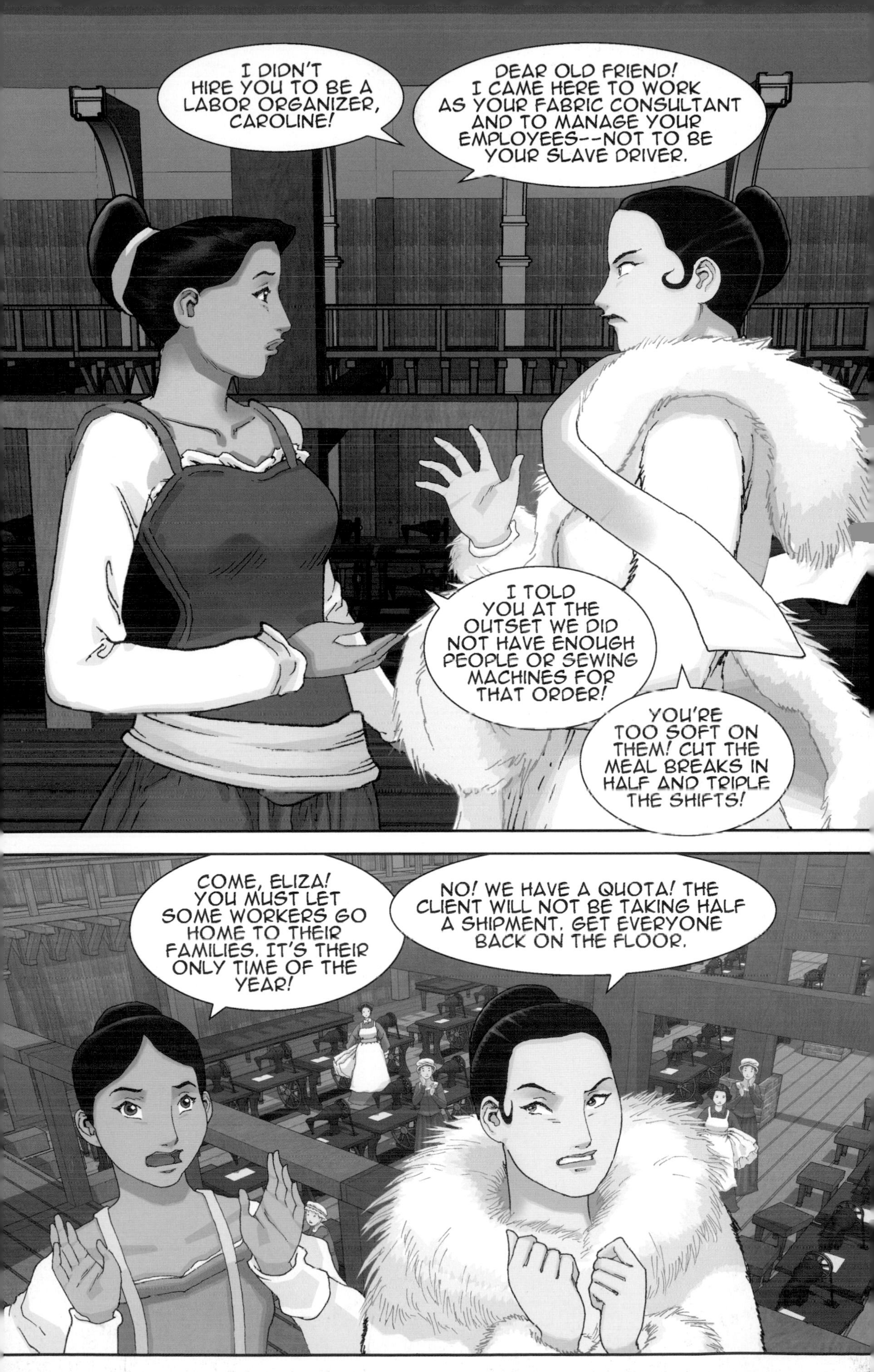
I DIDN'T HIRE YOU TO BE A LABOR ORGANIZER, CAROLINE!
DEAR OLD FRIEND! I CAME HERE TO WORK AS YOUR FABRIC CONSULTANT AND TO MANAGE YOUR EMPLOYEES--NOT TO BE YOUR SLAVE DRIVER.
I TOLD YOU AT THE OUTSET WE DID NOT HAVE ENOUGH PEOPLE OR SEWING MACHINES FOR THAT ORDER!
YOU'RE TOO SOFT ON THEM! CUT THE MEAL BREAKS IN HALF AND TRIPLE THE SHIFTS!
COME, ELIZA! YOU MUST LET SOME WORKERS GO HOME TO THEIR FAMILIES. IT'S THEIR ONLY TIME OF THE YEAR!
NO! WE HAVE A QUOTA! THE CLIENT WILL NOT BE TAKING HALF A SHIPMENT. GET EVERYONE BACK ON THE FLOOR.

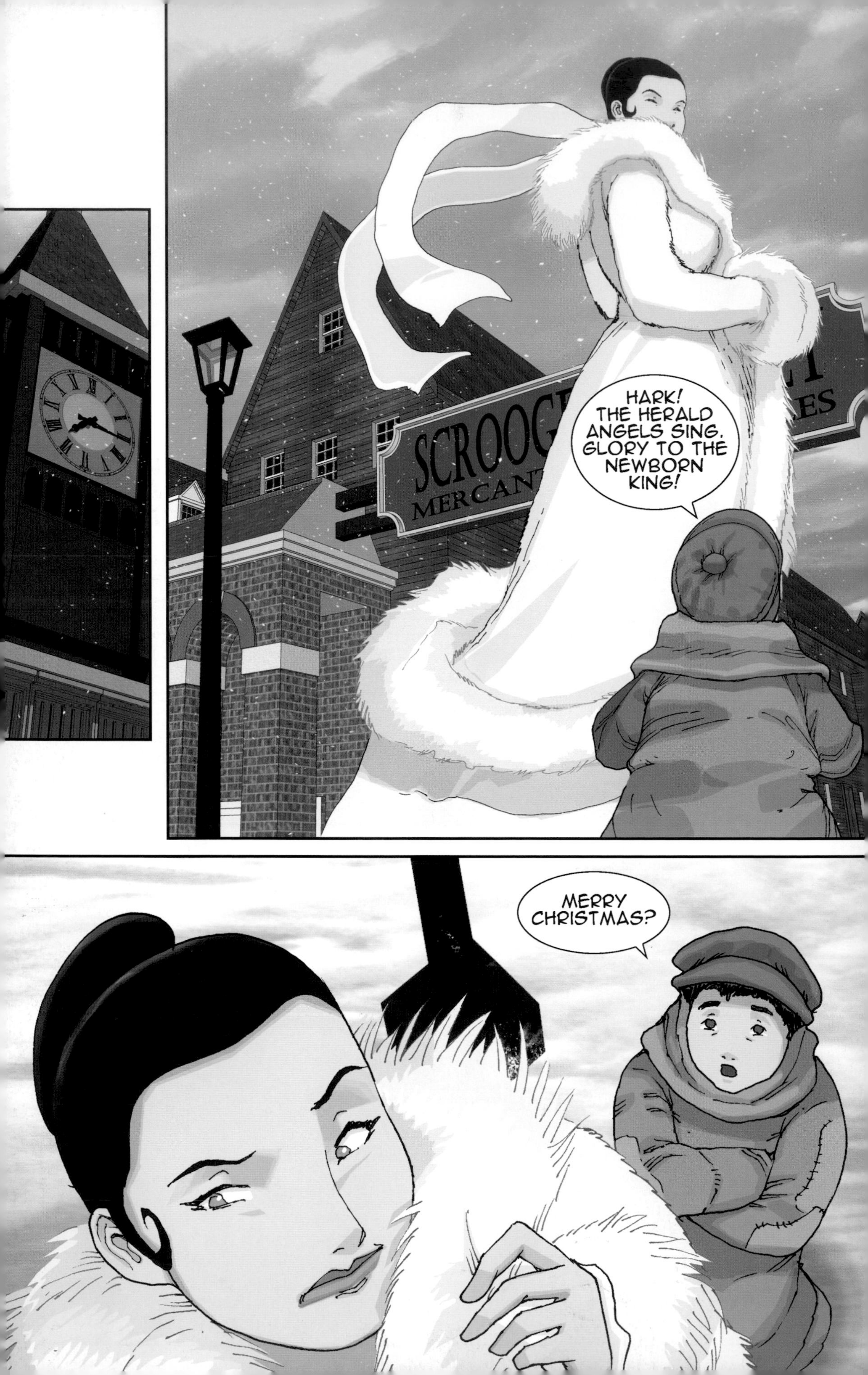
HARK! THE HERALD ANGELS SING. GLORY TO THE NEWBORN KING!
MERRY CHRISTMAS?

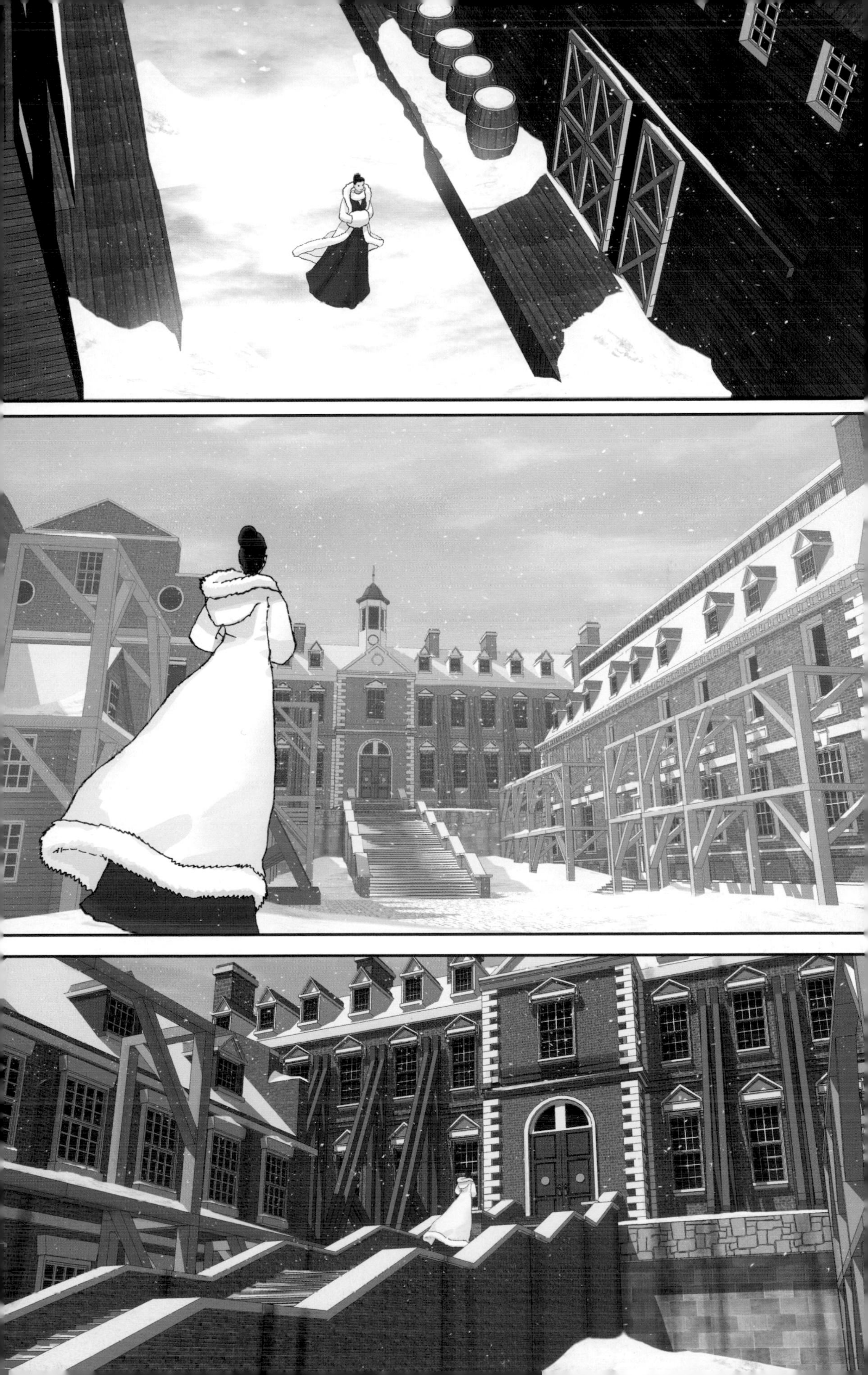

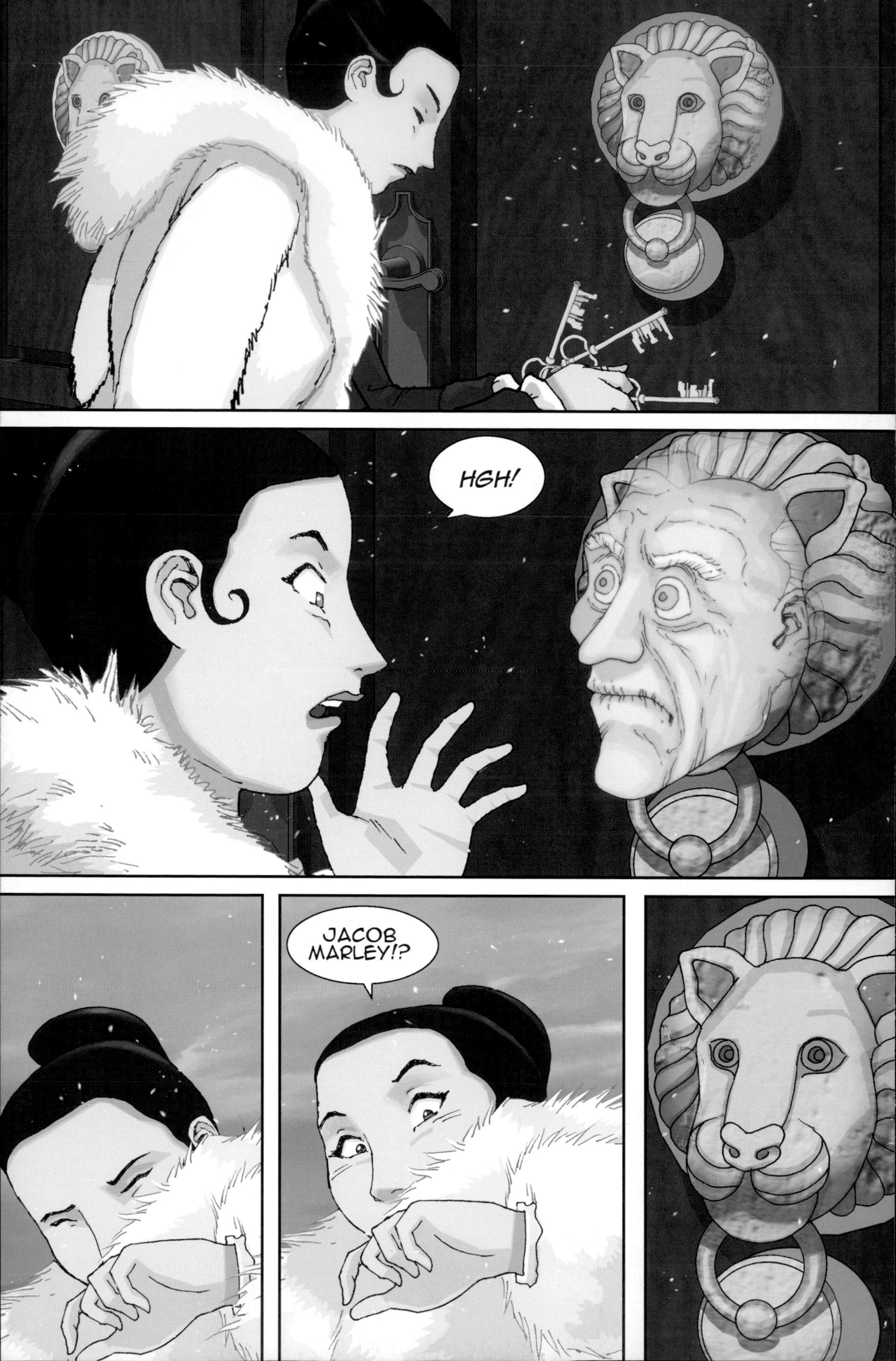
HGH!
JACOB MARLEY!?

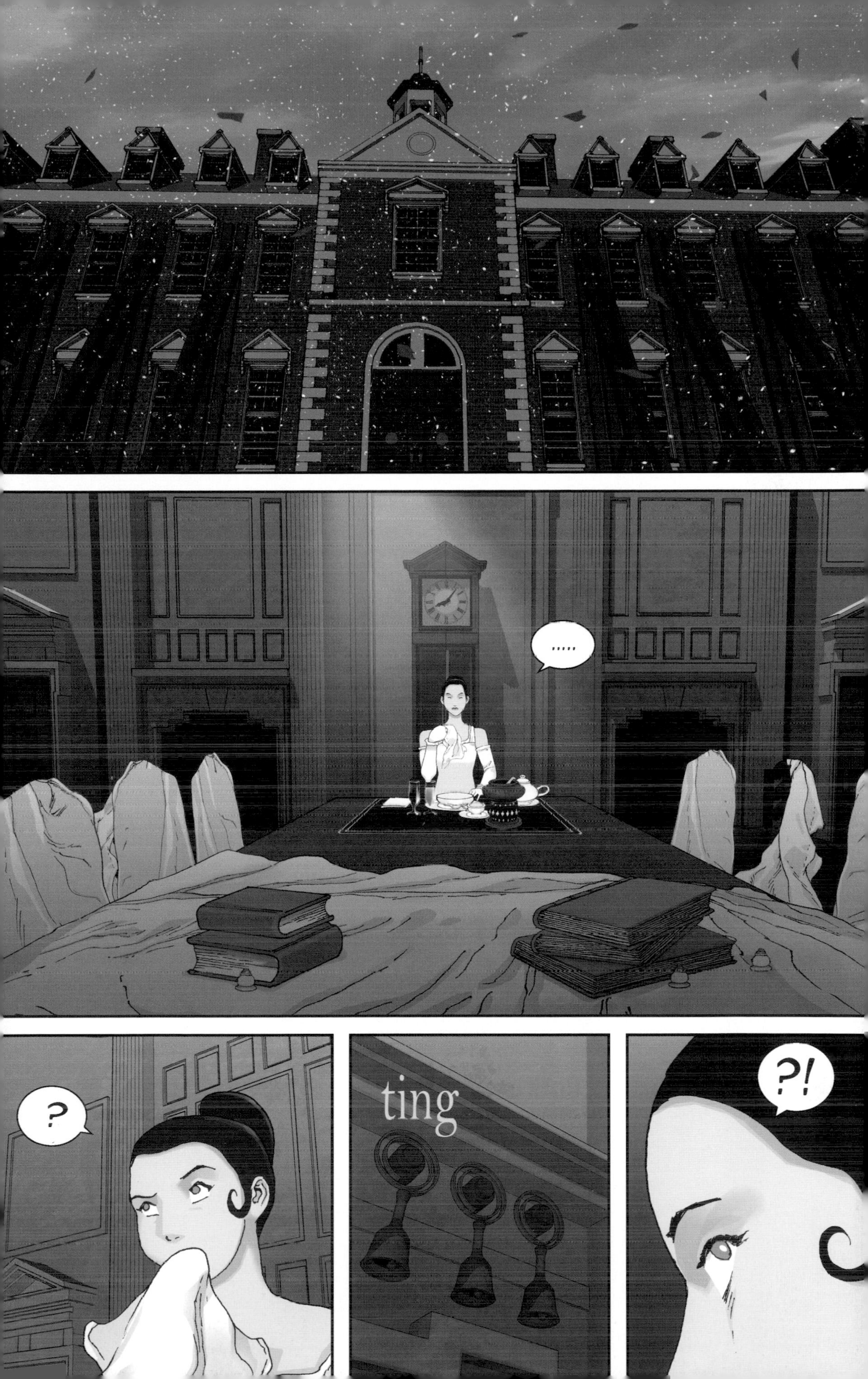
.....
?
ting
?!

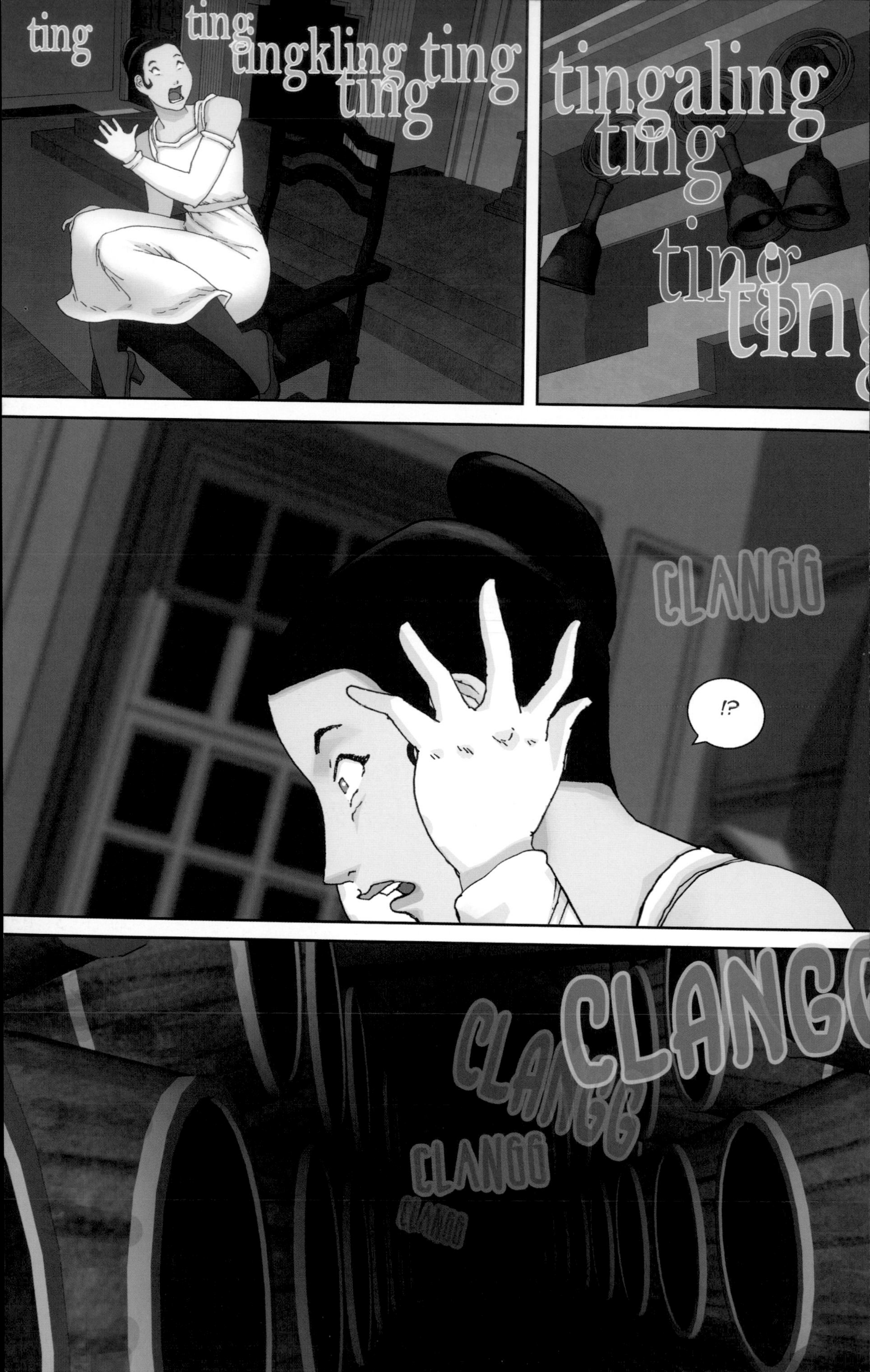
ting
ting
tingkling ting
ting
tingaling
ting
ting
ting
CLANGG
!?
CLANGG
CLANGG
CLANGG
CLANGG

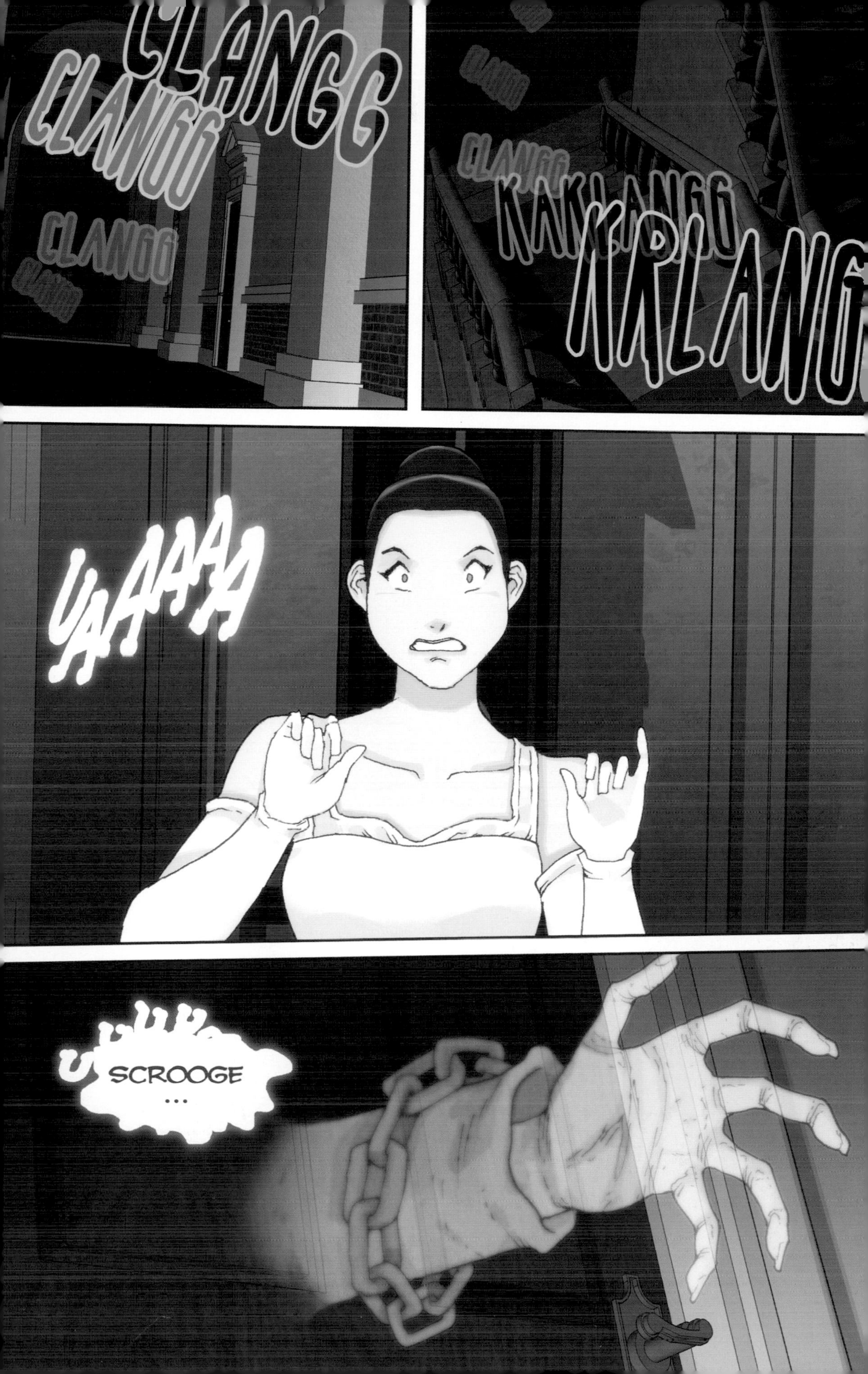
CLANGG
CLANGG
CLANGG
CLANGG
KAKLANGG
KRLANG
YAAAAA
SCROOGE
...

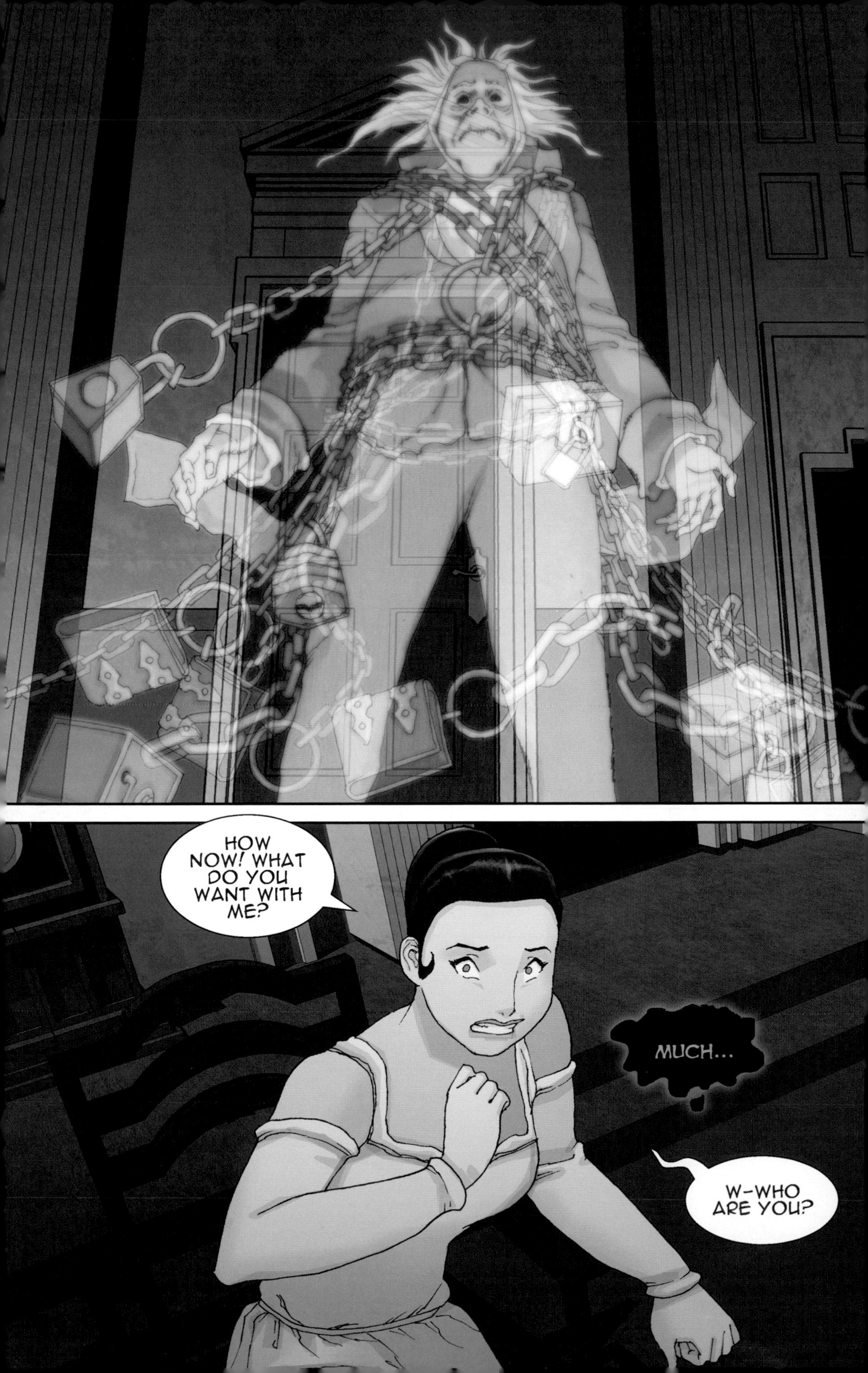
HOW NOW! WHAT DO YOU WANT WITH ME?
MUCH...
W-WHO ARE YOU?

UUUUUUUU UUU A A A A

IN LIFE I WAS YOUR PARTNER, JACOB MARLEY.

YOU DON'T BELIEVE IN ME, DO YOU?

N-NO, I DON'T. Y-YOU COULD BE A HALLUCINATION... A FIGMENT OF MY IMAGINA--

UUAAAAAAA A

YOU OF THE WORLDLY MIND! DO YOU BELIEVE IN ME OR NOT?

MERCY! I DO! I DO! I MUST. BUT WHY DO YOU WALK THE EARTH, AND WHY DO YOU HAUNT ME?

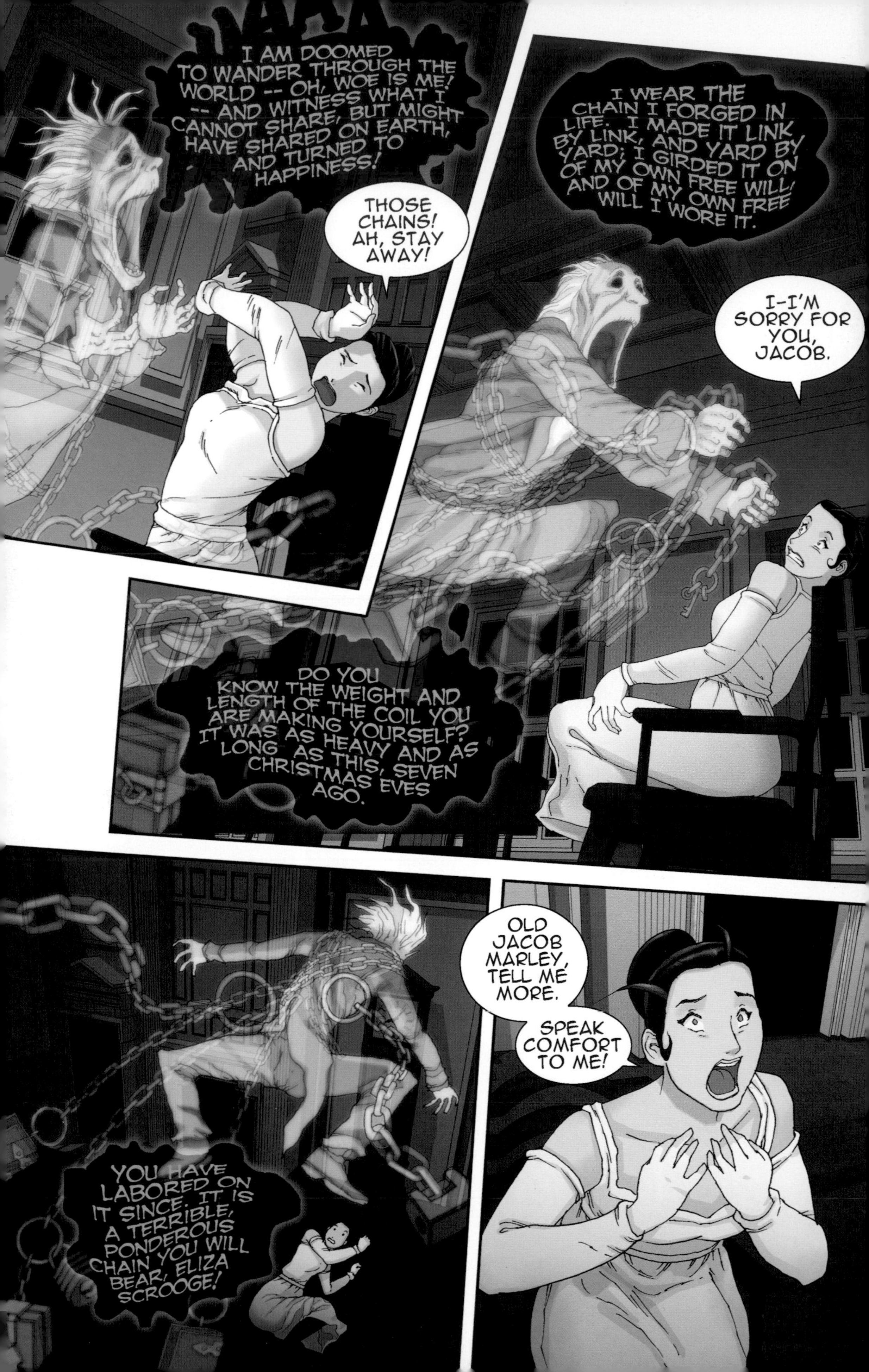
I AM DOOMED TO WANDER THROUGH THE WORLD -- OH, WOE IS ME! -- AND WITNESS WHAT I CANNOT SHARE, BUT MIGHT HAVE SHARED ON EARTH, AND TURNED TO HAPPINESS!
THOSE CHAINS! AH, STAY AWAY!
I WEAR THE CHAIN I FORGED IN LIFE. I MADE IT LINK BY LINK, AND YARD BY YARD; I GIRDED IT ON OF MY OWN FREE WILL, AND OF MY OWN FREE WILL I WORE IT.
I-I'M SORRY FOR YOU, JACOB.
DO YOU KNOW THE WEIGHT AND LENGTH OF THE COIL YOU ARE MAKING YOURSELF? IT WAS AS HEAVY AND AS LONG AS THIS, SEVEN CHRISTMAS EVES AGO.
YOU HAVE LABORED ON IT SINCE. IT IS A TERRIBLE, PONDEROUS CHAIN YOU WILL BEAR, ELIZA SCROOGE!
OLD JACOB MARLEY, TELL ME MORE.
SPEAK COMFORT TO ME!

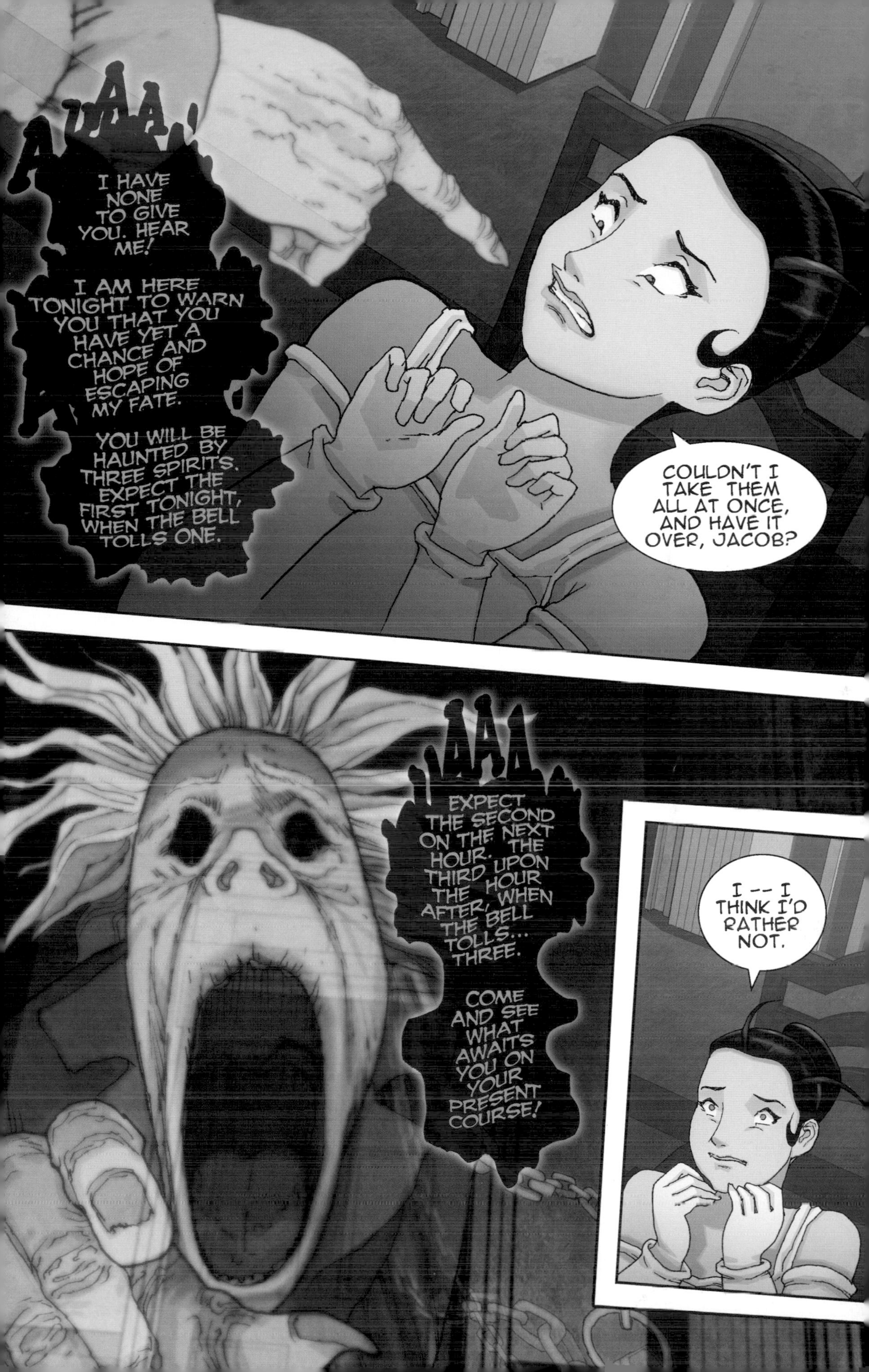
AAAAA!
I HAVE NONE TO GIVE YOU. HEAR ME!
I AM HERE TONIGHT TO WARN YOU THAT YOU HAVE YET A CHANCE AND HOPE OF ESCAPING MY FATE.
YOU WILL BE HAUNTED BY THREE SPIRITS. EXPECT THE FIRST TONIGHT, WHEN THE BELL TOLLS ONE.
COULDN'T I TAKE THEM ALL AT ONCE, AND HAVE IT OVER, JACOB?
AAA
EXPECT THE SECOND ON THE NEXT HOUR. THE THIRD UPON THE HOUR AFTER, WHEN THE BELL TOLLS... THREE.
COME AND SEE WHAT AWAITS YOU ON YOUR PRESENT COURSE!
I -- I THINK I'D RATHER NOT.

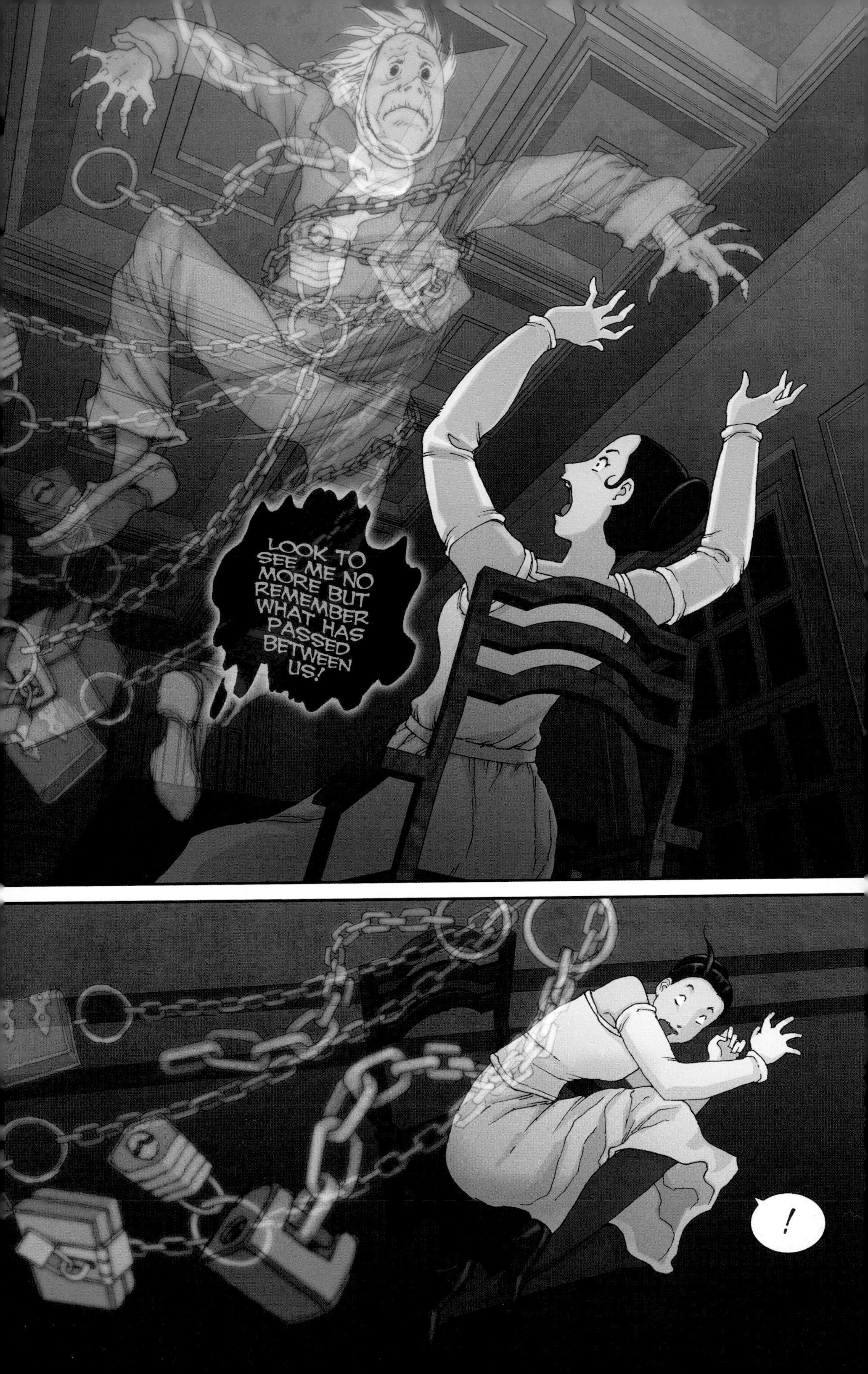
LOOK TO SEE ME NO MORE BUT REMEMBER WHAT HAS PASSED BETWEEN US!
!

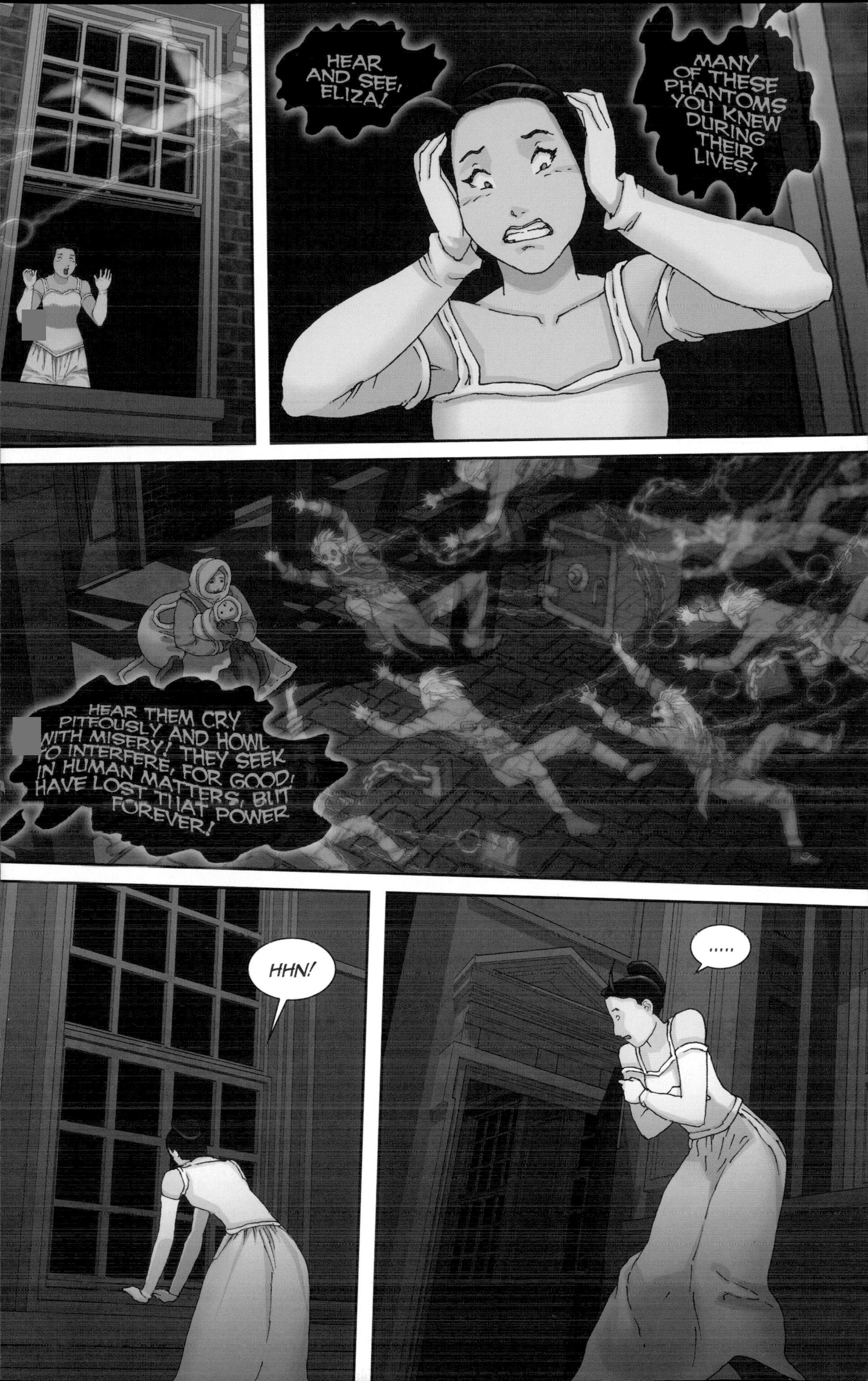
HEAR AND SEE, ELIZA!
MANY OF THESE PHANTOMS YOU KNEW DURING THEIR LIVES!
HEAR THEM CRY PITEOUSLY WITH MISERY! AND HOWL TO INTERFERE, FOR GOOD IN HUMAN MATTERS, BUT HAVE LOST THAT POWER FOREVER! THEY SEEK
HHN!
.....

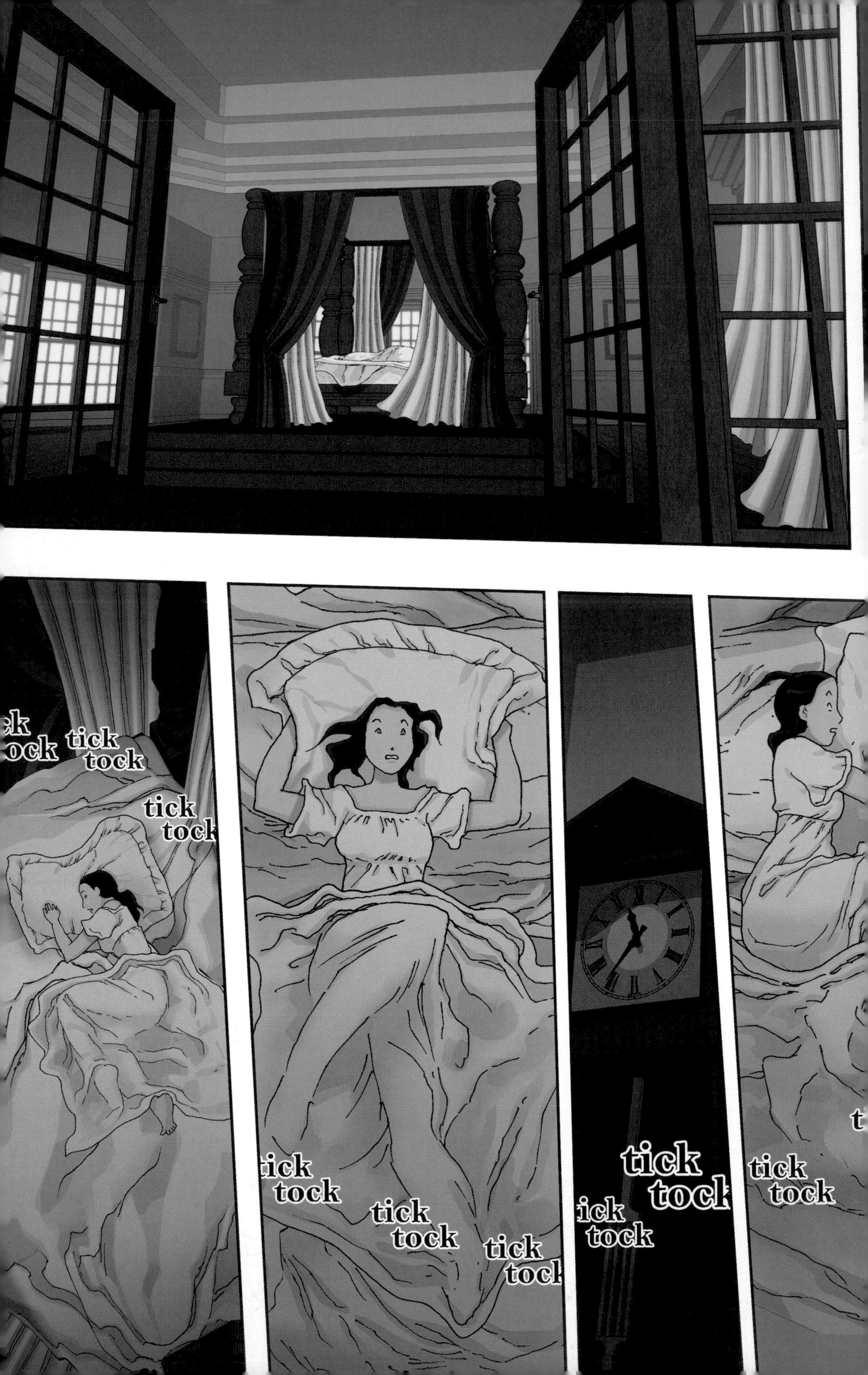
ck ock
tick tock
tick tock
tick tock
tick tock
tick tock
tick tock
ick tock
tick tock

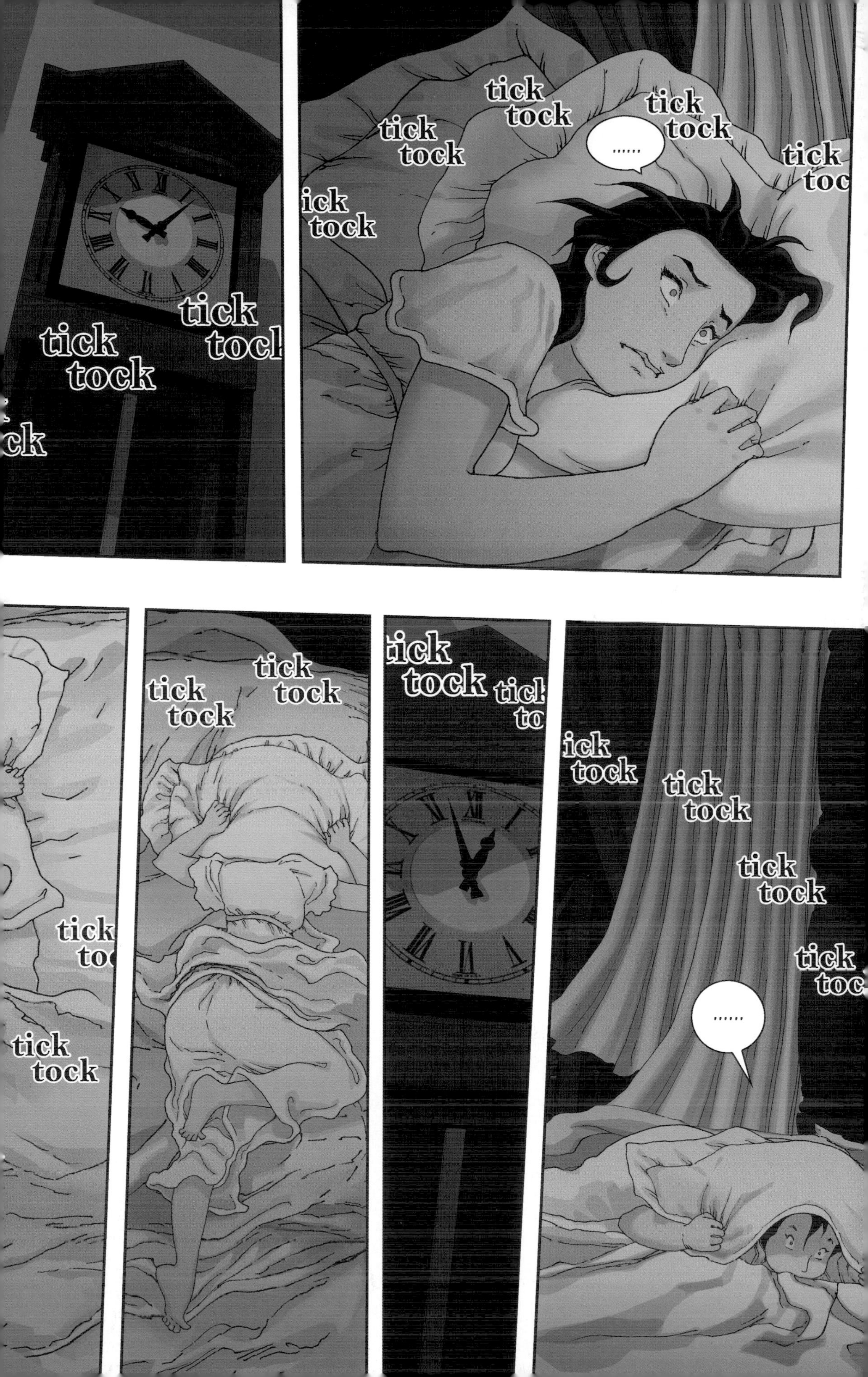

tick tock
tick tock
ck
ick tock
tick tock
tick tock
tick tock
......
tick toc
tick tock
tick tock
tick toc
tick tock
tick tock
ick tock
tick tock
tick tock
tick toc
......

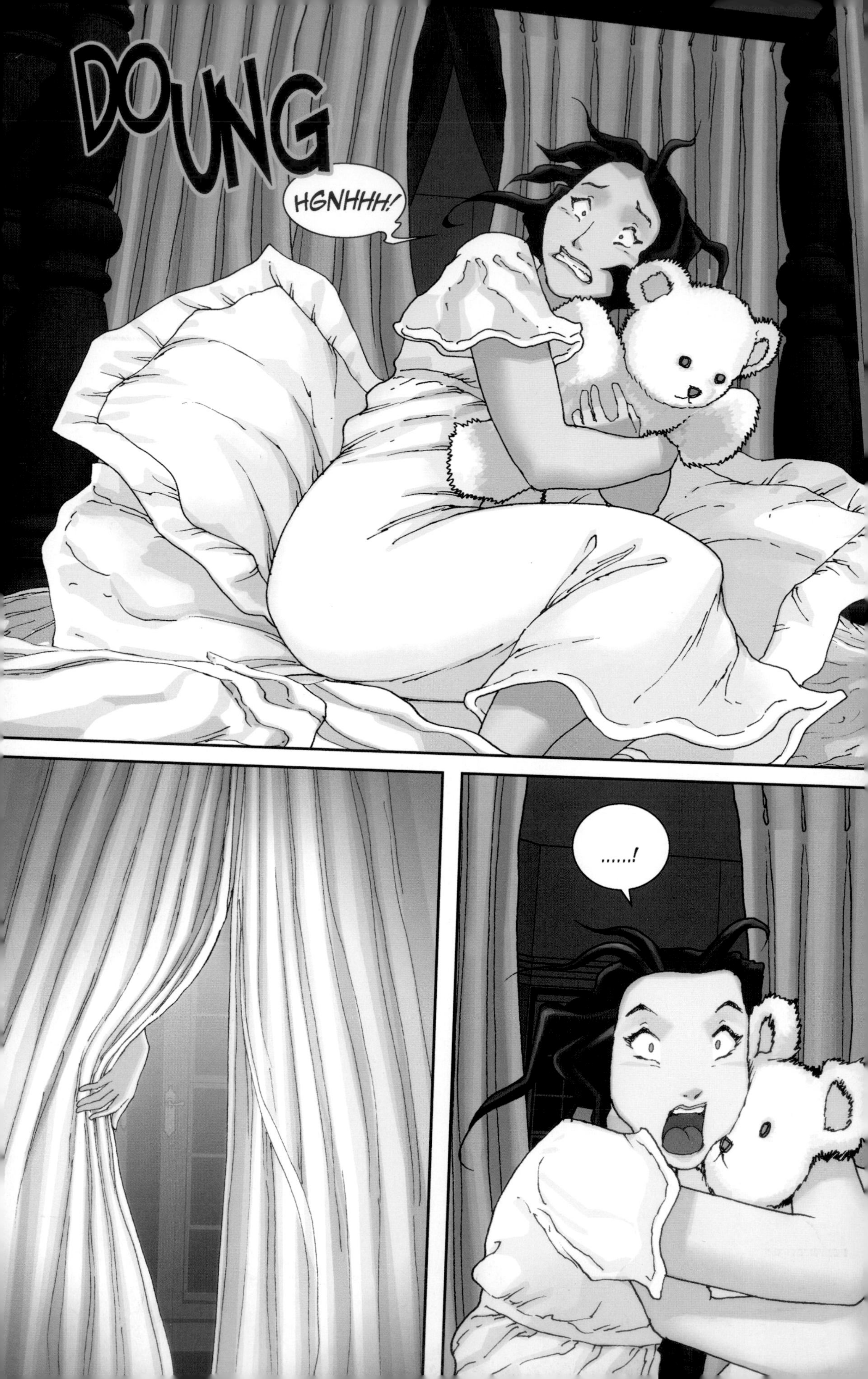
DOUNG
HGNHHH!
......!

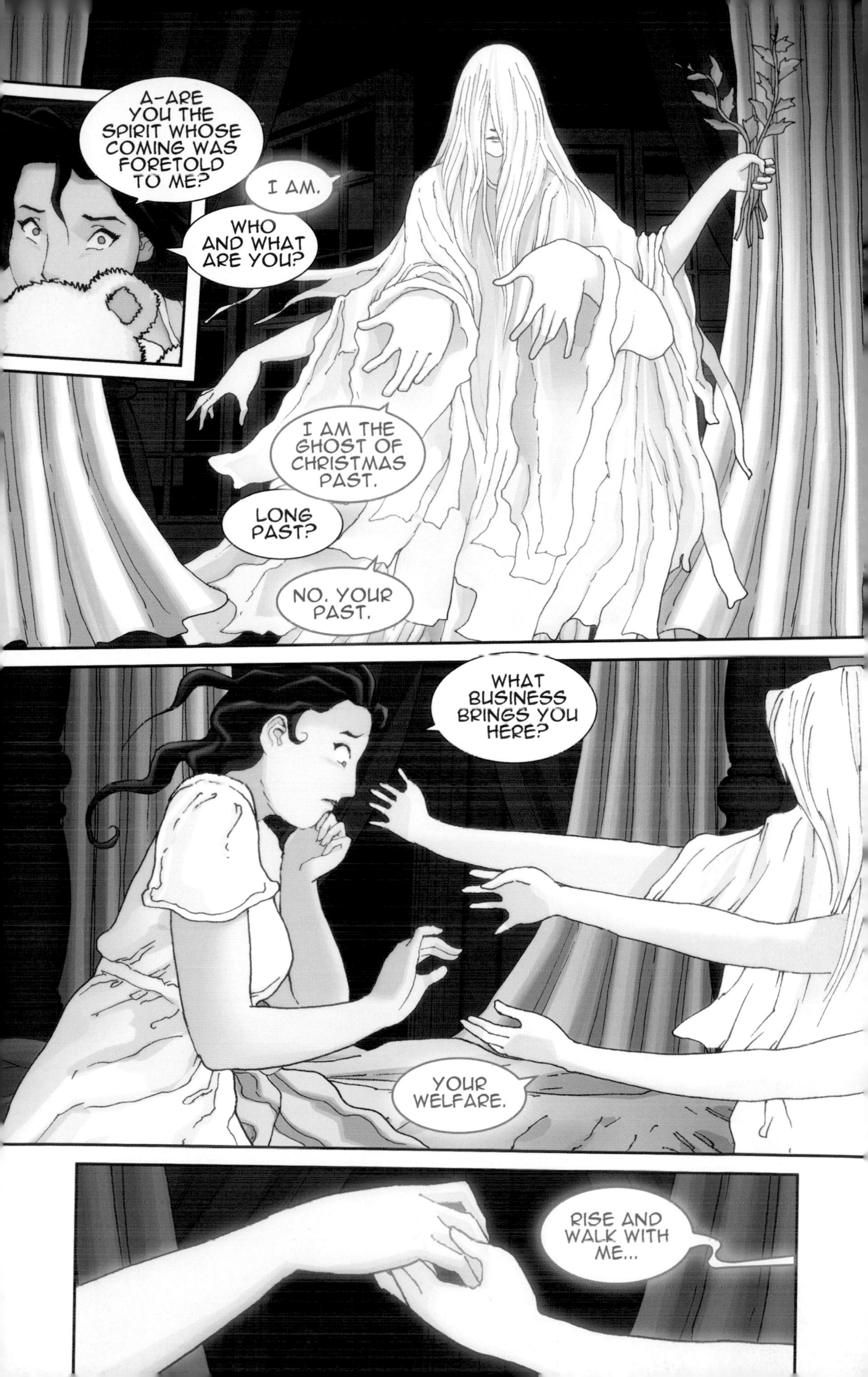
A-ARE YOU THE SPIRIT WHOSE COMING WAS FORETOLD TO ME?
I AM.
WHO AND WHAT ARE YOU?
I AM THE GHOST OF CHRISTMAS PAST.
LONG PAST?
NO. YOUR PAST.
WHAT BUSINESS BRINGS YOU HERE?
YOUR WELFARE.
RISE AND WALK WITH ME...

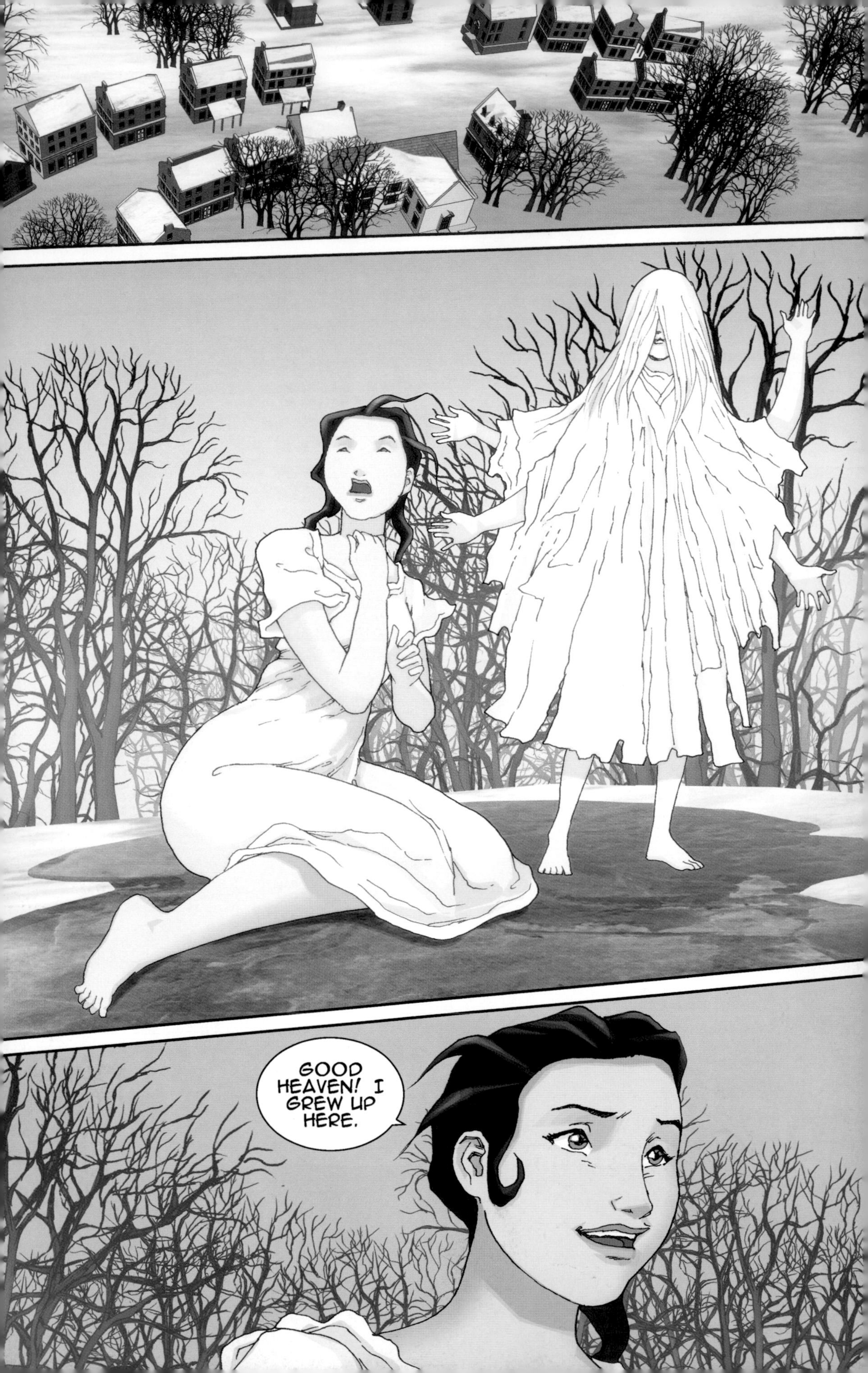
GOOD HEAVEN! I GREW UP HERE.

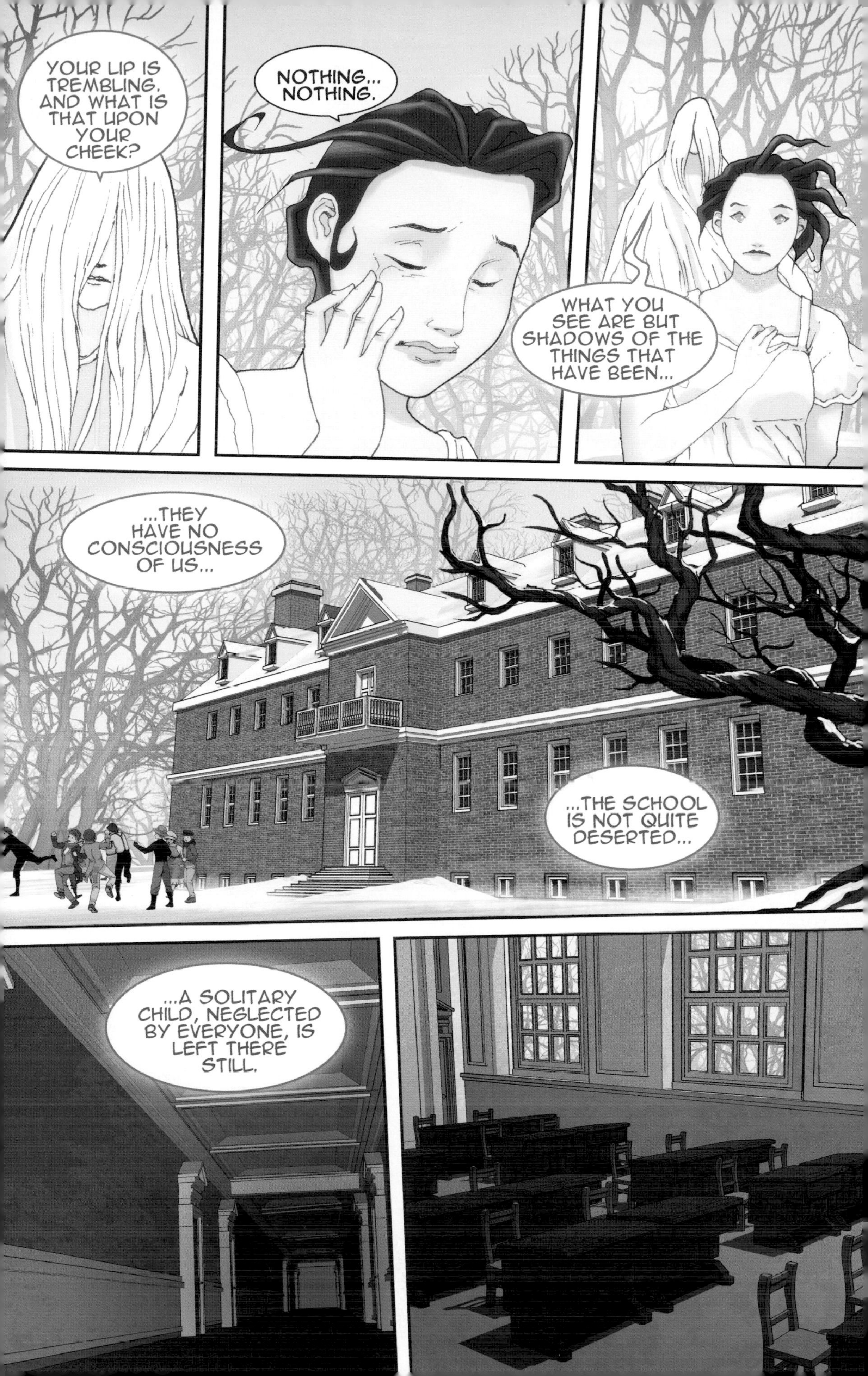
YOUR LIP IS TREMBLING. AND WHAT IS THAT UPON YOUR CHEEK?
NOTHING... NOTHING.
WHAT YOU SEE ARE BUT SHADOWS OF THE THINGS THAT HAVE BEEN...
...THEY HAVE NO CONSCIOUSNESS OF US...
...THE SCHOOL IS NOT QUITE DESERTED...
...A SOLITARY CHILD, NEGLECTED BY EVERYONE, IS LEFT THERE STILL.

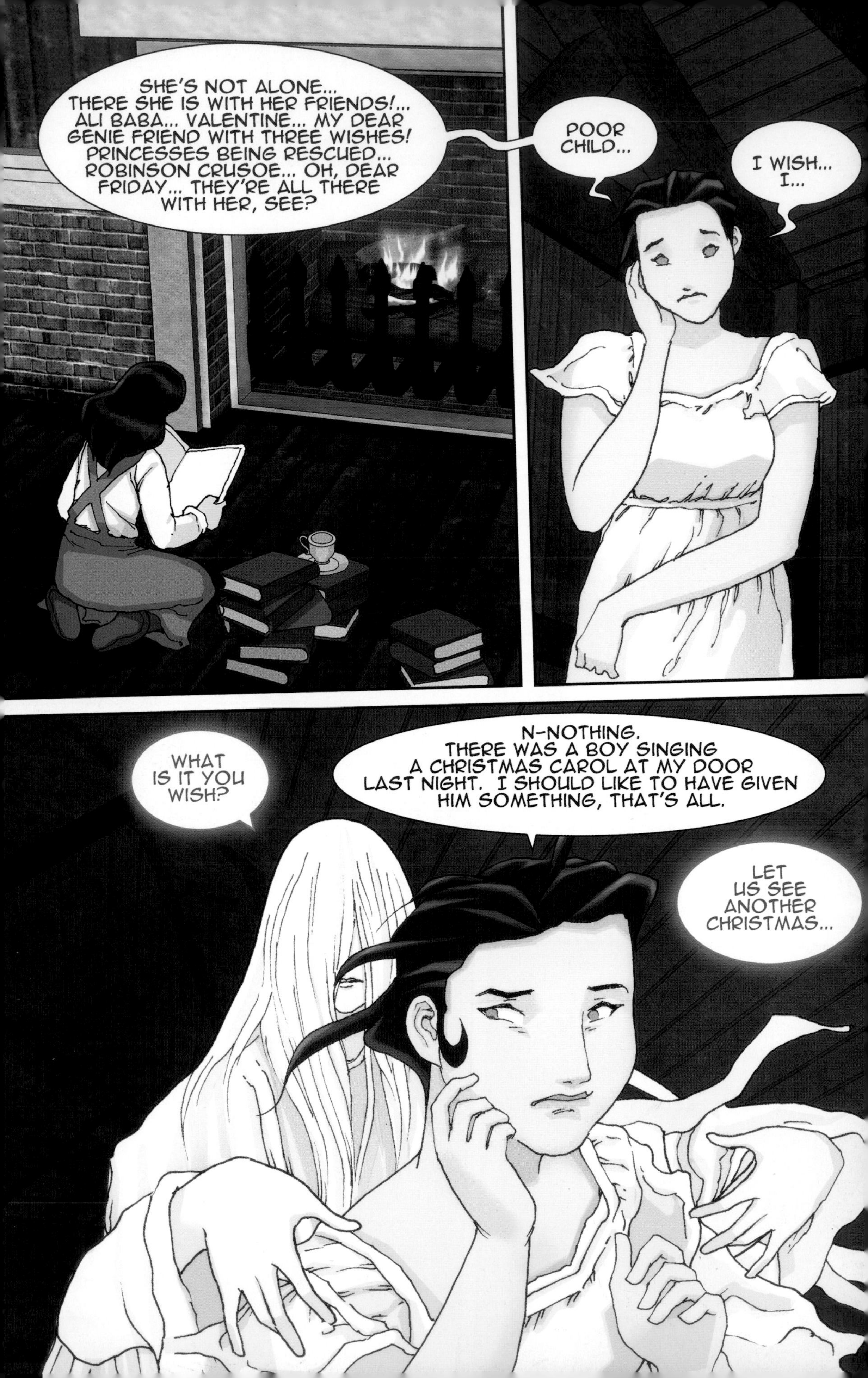
SHE'S NOT ALONE... THERE SHE IS WITH HER FRIENDS!... ALI BABA... VALENTINE... MY DEAR GENIE FRIEND WITH THREE WISHES! PRINCESSES BEING RESCUED... ROBINSON CRUSOE... OH, DEAR FRIDAY... THEY'RE ALL THERE WITH HER, SEE?
POOR CHILD...
I WISH... I...
WHAT IS IT YOU WISH?
N-NOTHING. THERE WAS A BOY SINGING A CHRISTMAS CAROL AT MY DOOR LAST NIGHT. I SHOULD LIKE TO HAVE GIVEN HIM SOMETHING, THAT'S ALL.
LET US SEE ANOTHER CHRISTMAS...

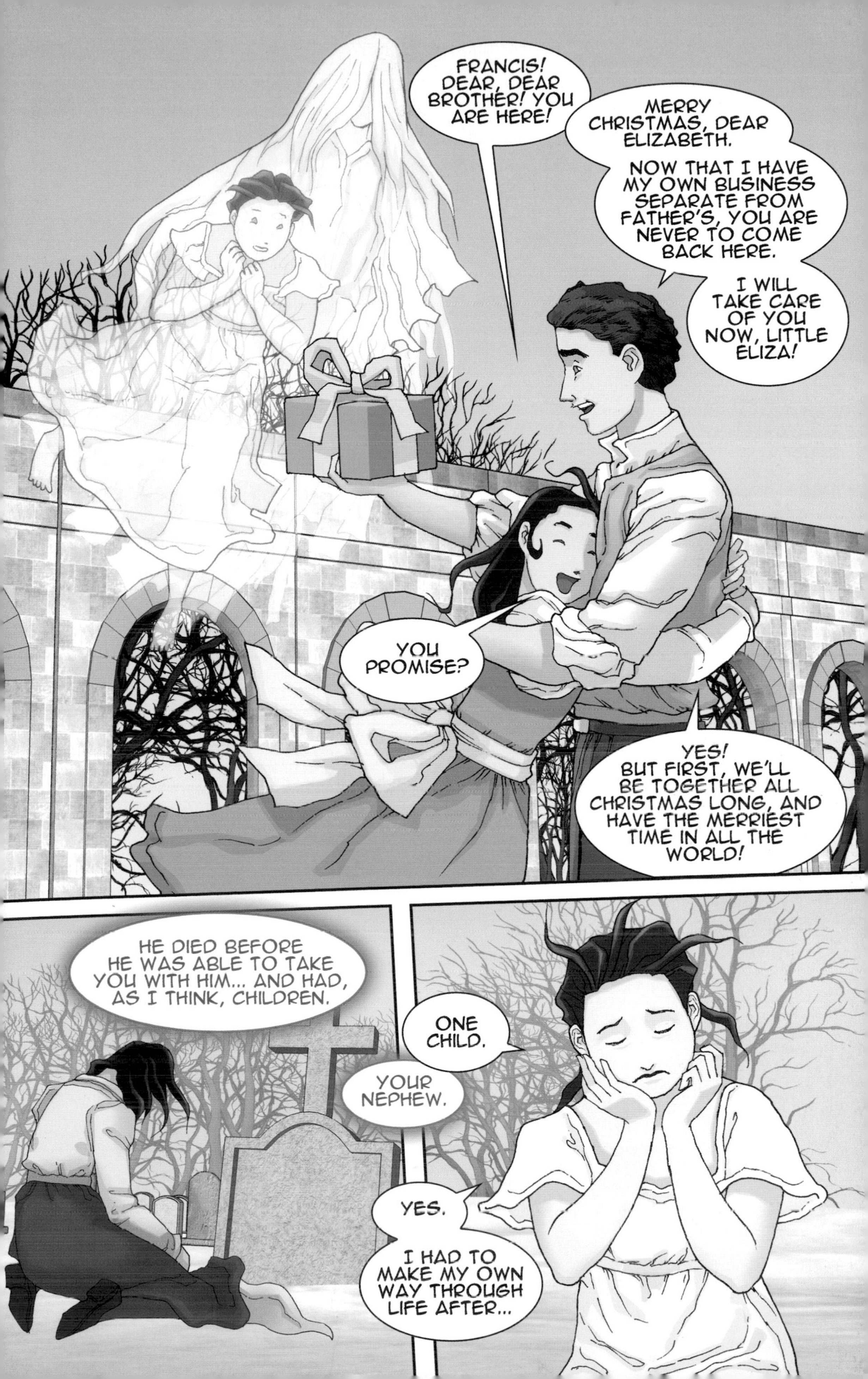
FRANCIS! DEAR, DEAR BROTHER! YOU ARE HERE!
MERRY CHRISTMAS, DEAR ELIZABETH.
NOW THAT I HAVE MY OWN BUSINESS SEPARATE FROM FATHER'S, YOU ARE NEVER TO COME BACK HERE.
I WILL TAKE CARE OF YOU NOW, LITTLE ELIZA!
YOU PROMISE?
YES! BUT FIRST, WE'LL BE TOGETHER ALL CHRISTMAS LONG, AND HAVE THE MERRIEST TIME IN ALL THE WORLD!
HE DIED BEFORE HE WAS ABLE TO TAKE YOU WITH HIM... AND HAD, AS I THINK, CHILDREN.
ONE CHILD.
YOUR NEPHEW.
YES.
I HAD TO MAKE MY OWN WAY THROUGH LIFE AFTER...

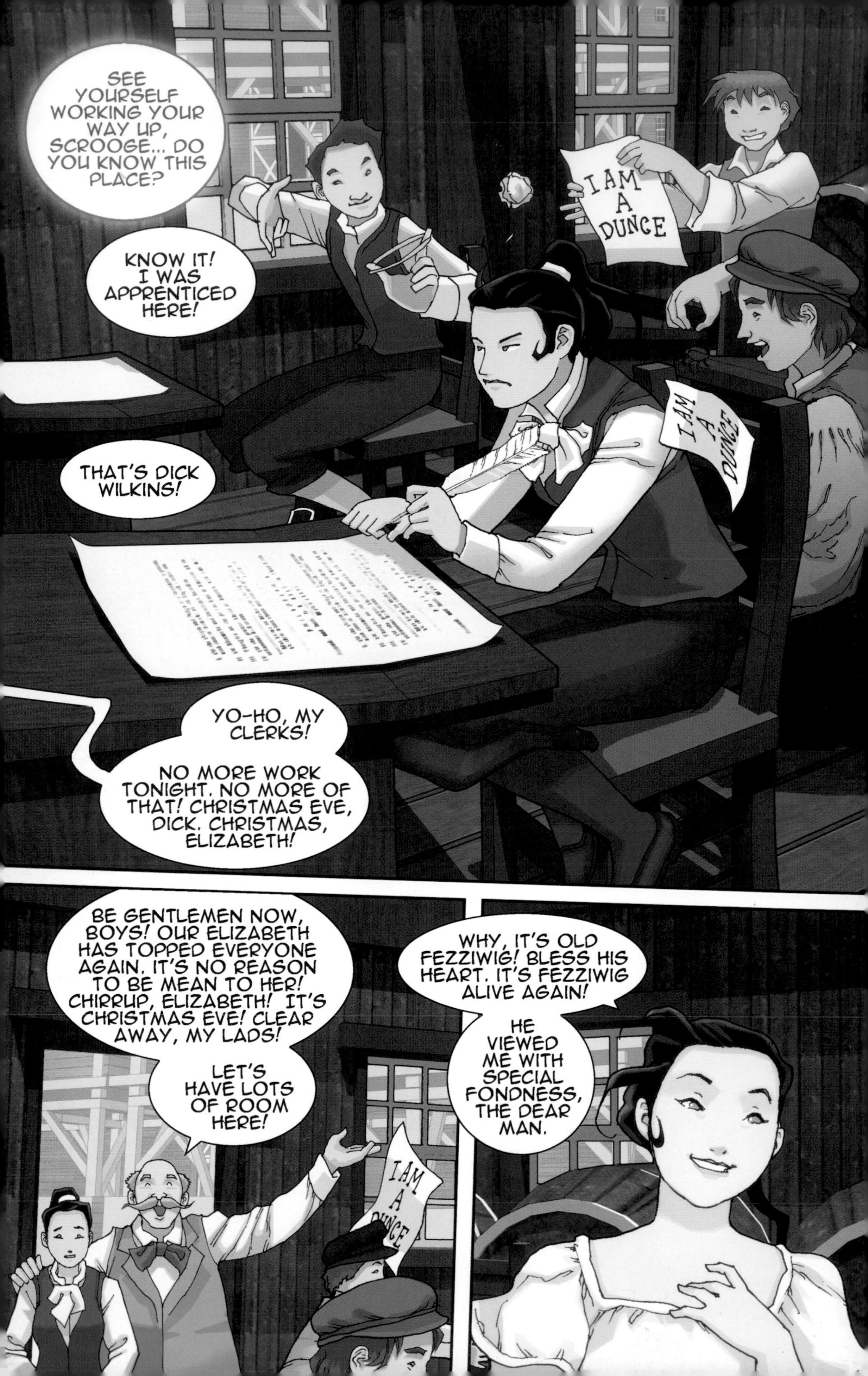

SEE YOURSELF WORKING YOUR WAY UP, SCROOGE... DO YOU KNOW THIS PLACE?
I AM A DUNCE
KNOW IT! I WAS APPRENTICED HERE!
I AM A DUNCE
THAT'S DICK WILKINS!
YO-HO, MY CLERKS!
NO MORE WORK TONIGHT. NO MORE OF THAT! CHRISTMAS EVE, DICK. CHRISTMAS, ELIZABETH!
BE GENTLEMEN NOW, BOYS! OUR ELIZABETH HAS TOPPED EVERYONE AGAIN. IT'S NO REASON TO BE MEAN TO HER! CHIRRUP, ELIZABETH! IT'S CHRISTMAS EVE! CLEAR AWAY, MY LADS!
LET'S HAVE LOTS OF ROOM HERE!
WHY, IT'S OLD FEZZIWIG! BLESS HIS HEART. IT'S FEZZIWIG ALIVE AGAIN!
HE VIEWED ME WITH SPECIAL FONDNESS, THE DEAR MAN.

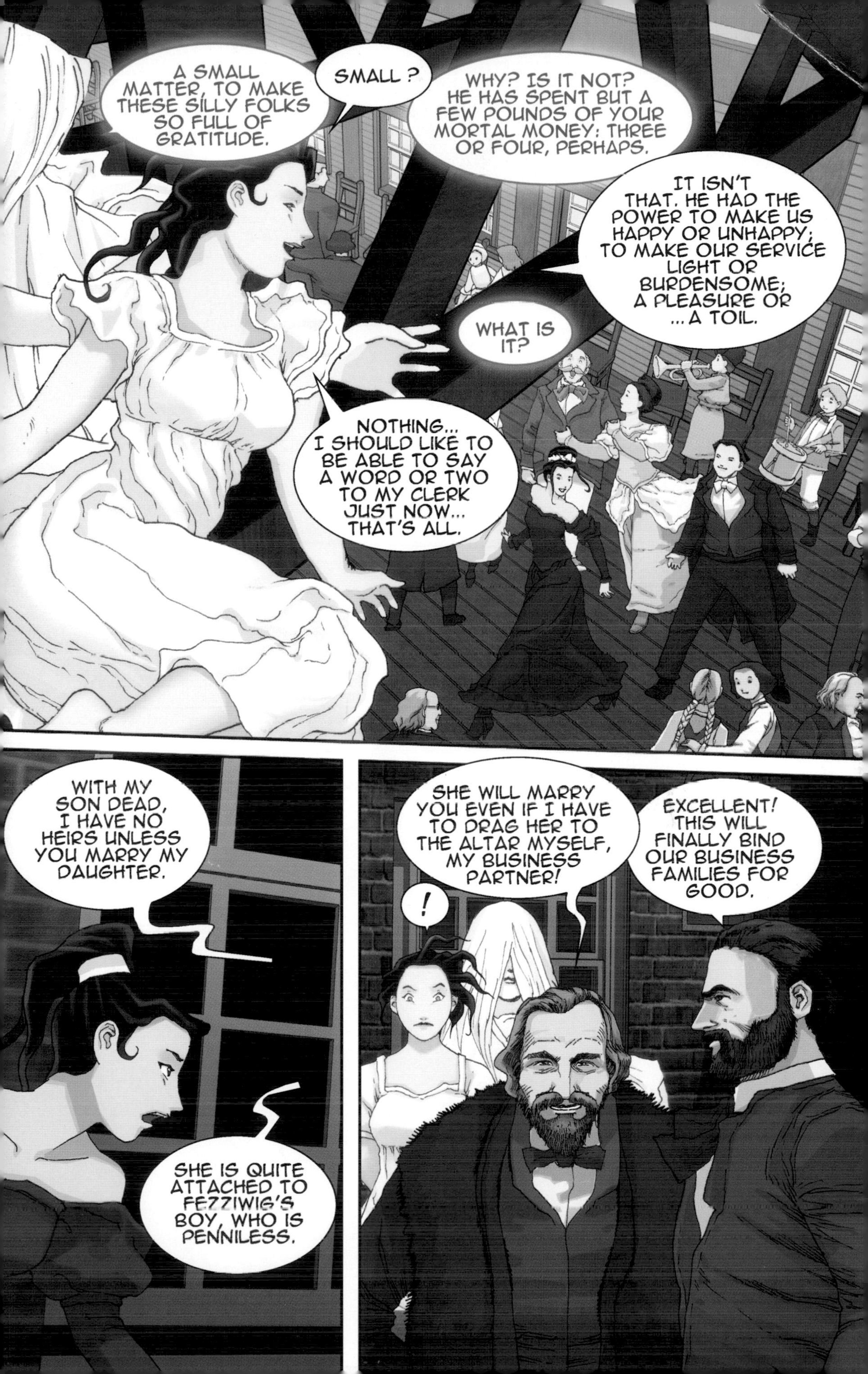
A SMALL MATTER, TO MAKE THESE SILLY FOLKS SO FULL OF GRATITUDE.
SMALL ?
WHY? IS IT NOT? HE HAS SPENT BUT A FEW POUNDS OF YOUR MORTAL MONEY: THREE OR FOUR, PERHAPS.
IT ISN'T THAT. HE HAD THE POWER TO MAKE US HAPPY OR UNHAPPY; TO MAKE OUR SERVICE LIGHT OR BURDENSOME; A PLEASURE OR ... A TOIL.
WHAT IS IT?
NOTHING... I SHOULD LIKE TO BE ABLE TO SAY A WORD OR TWO TO MY CLERK JUST NOW... THAT'S ALL.
WITH MY SON DEAD, I HAVE NO HEIRS UNLESS YOU MARRY MY DAUGHTER.
SHE IS QUITE ATTACHED TO FEZZIWIG'S BOY, WHO IS PENNILESS.
SHE WILL MARRY YOU EVEN IF I HAVE TO DRAG HER TO THE ALTAR MYSELF, MY BUSINESS PARTNER!
EXCELLENT! THIS WILL FINALLY BIND OUR BUSINESS FAMILIES FOR GOOD.
!

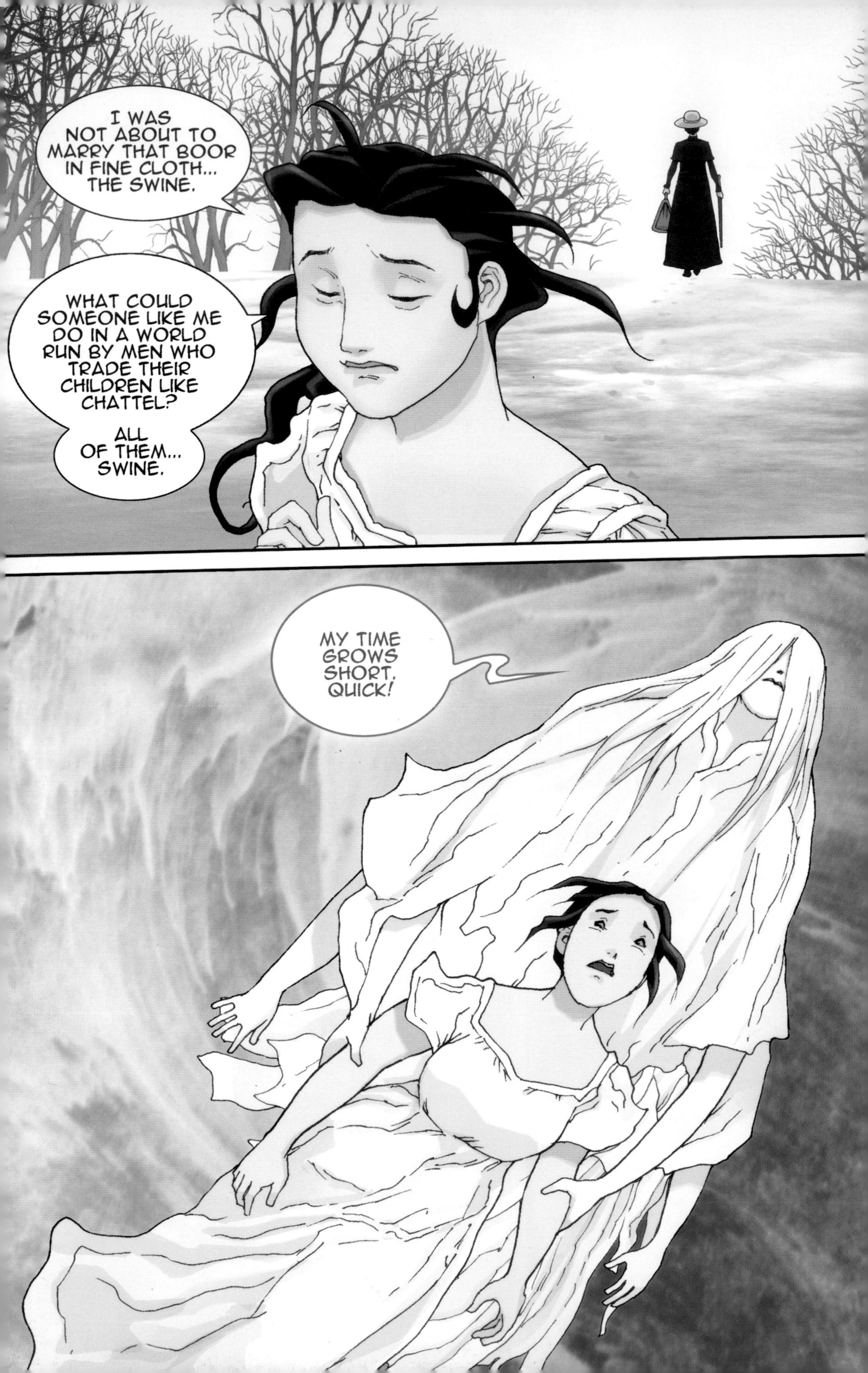
I WAS NOT ABOUT TO MARRY THAT BOOR IN FINE CLOTH... THE SWINE.
WHAT COULD SOMEONE LIKE ME DO IN A WORLD RUN BY MEN WHO TRADE THEIR CHILDREN LIKE CHATTEL?
ALL OF THEM... SWINE.
MY TIME GROWS SHORT. QUICK!

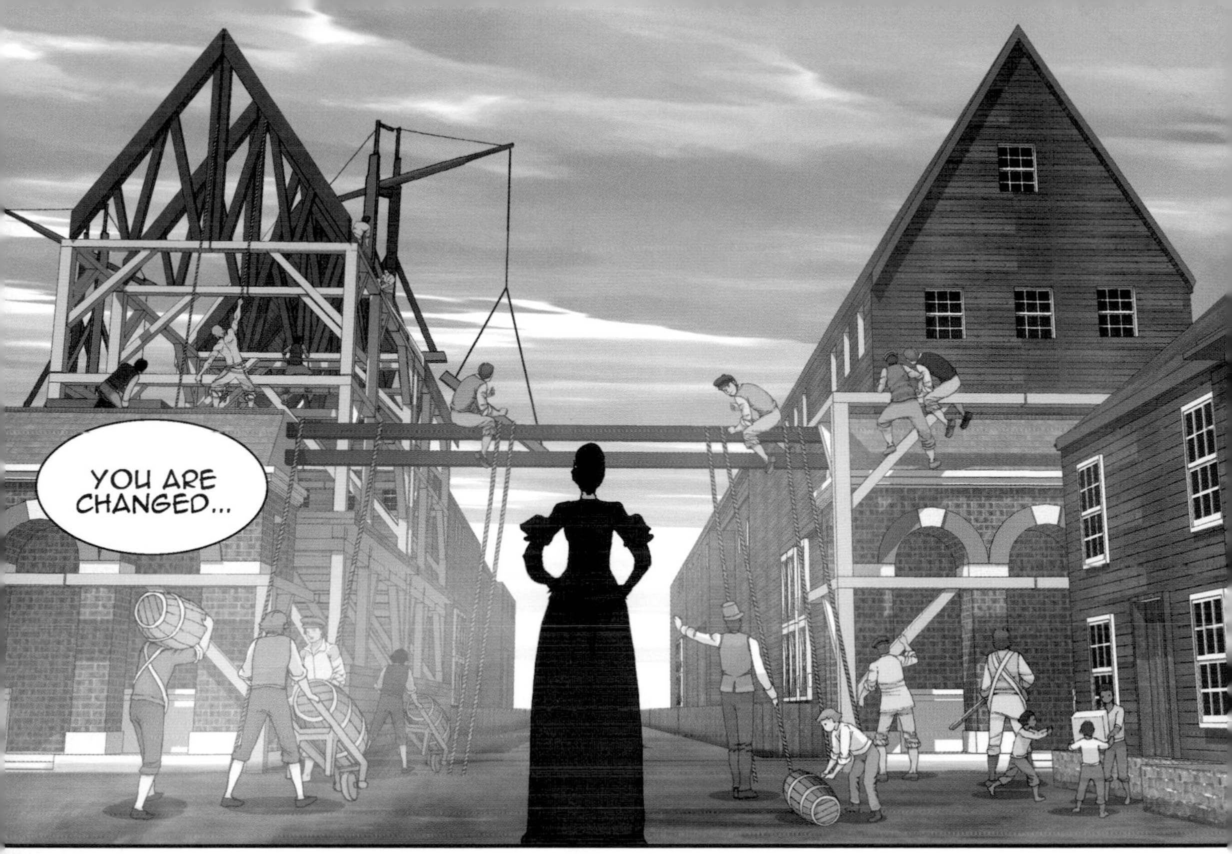
YOU ARE CHANGED...

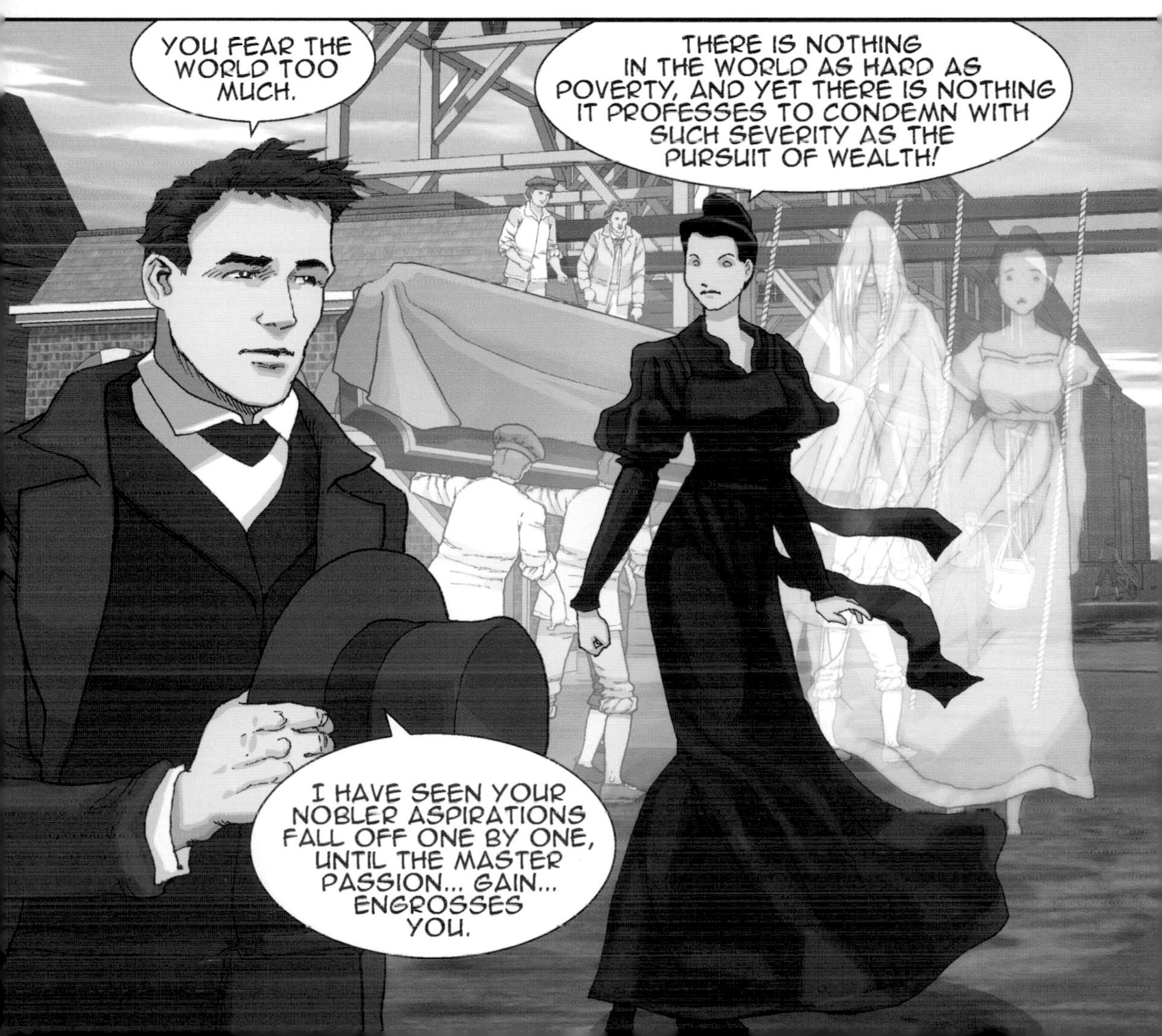
YOU FEAR THE WORLD TOO MUCH.
THERE IS NOTHING IN THE WORLD AS HARD AS POVERTY, AND YET THERE IS NOTHING IT PROFESSES TO CONDEMN WITH SUCH SEVERITY AS THE PURSUIT OF WEALTH!
I HAVE SEEN YOUR NOBLER ASPIRATIONS FALL OFF ONE BY ONE, UNTIL THE MASTER PASSION... GAIN... ENGROSSES YOU.

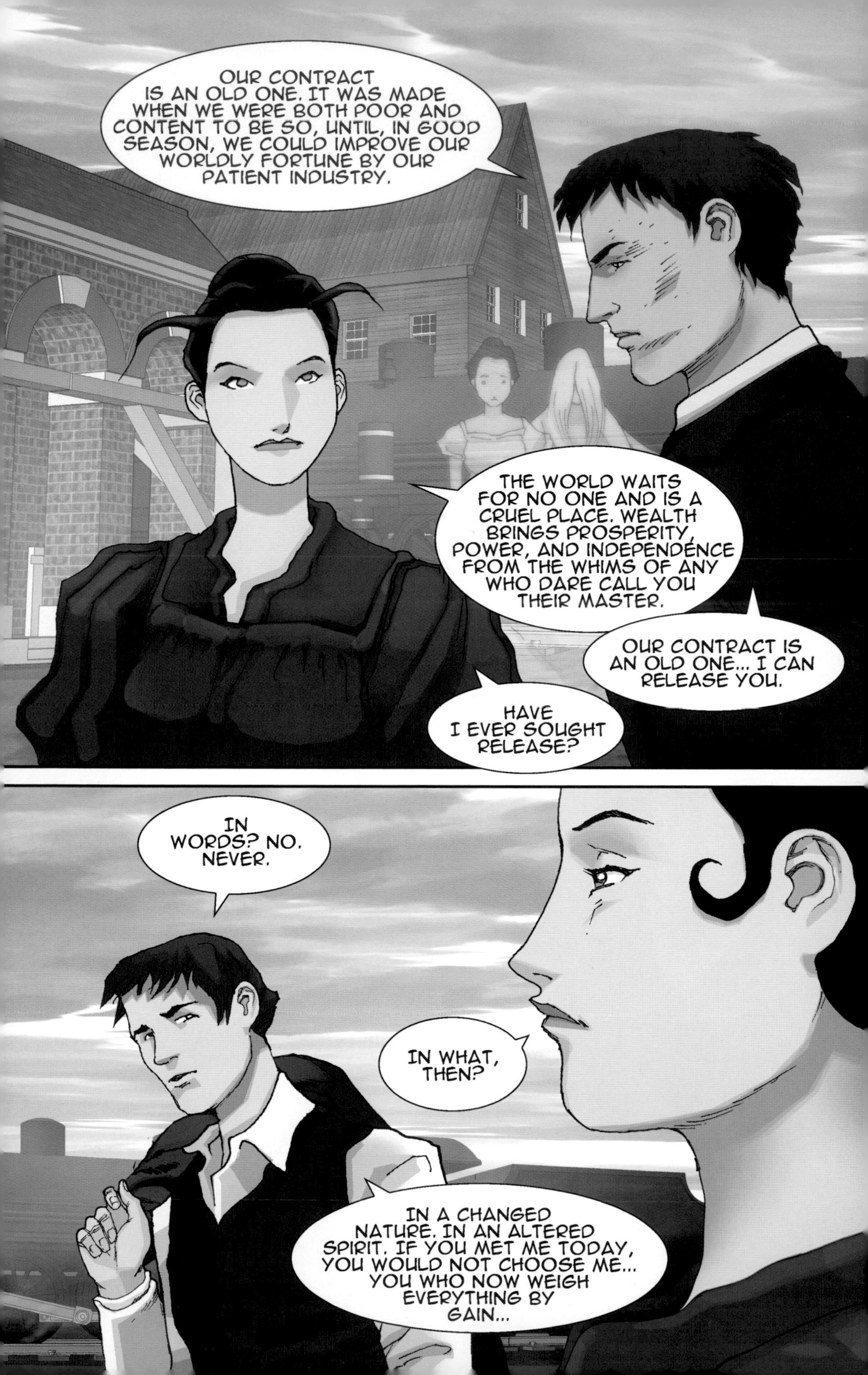
OUR CONTRACT IS AN OLD ONE. IT WAS MADE WHEN WE WERE BOTH POOR AND CONTENT TO BE SO, UNTIL, IN GOOD SEASON, WE COULD IMPROVE OUR WORLDLY FORTUNE BY OUR PATIENT INDUSTRY.
THE WORLD WAITS FOR NO ONE AND IS A CRUEL PLACE. WEALTH BRINGS PROSPERITY, POWER, AND INDEPENDENCE FROM THE WHIMS OF ANY WHO DARE CALL YOU THEIR MASTER.
OUR CONTRACT IS AN OLD ONE... I CAN RELEASE YOU.
HAVE I EVER SOUGHT RELEASE?
IN WORDS? NO. NEVER.
IN WHAT, THEN?
IN A CHANGED NATURE. IN AN ALTERED SPIRIT. IF YOU MET ME TODAY, YOU WOULD NOT CHOOSE ME... YOU WHO NOW WEIGH EVERYTHING BY GAIN...

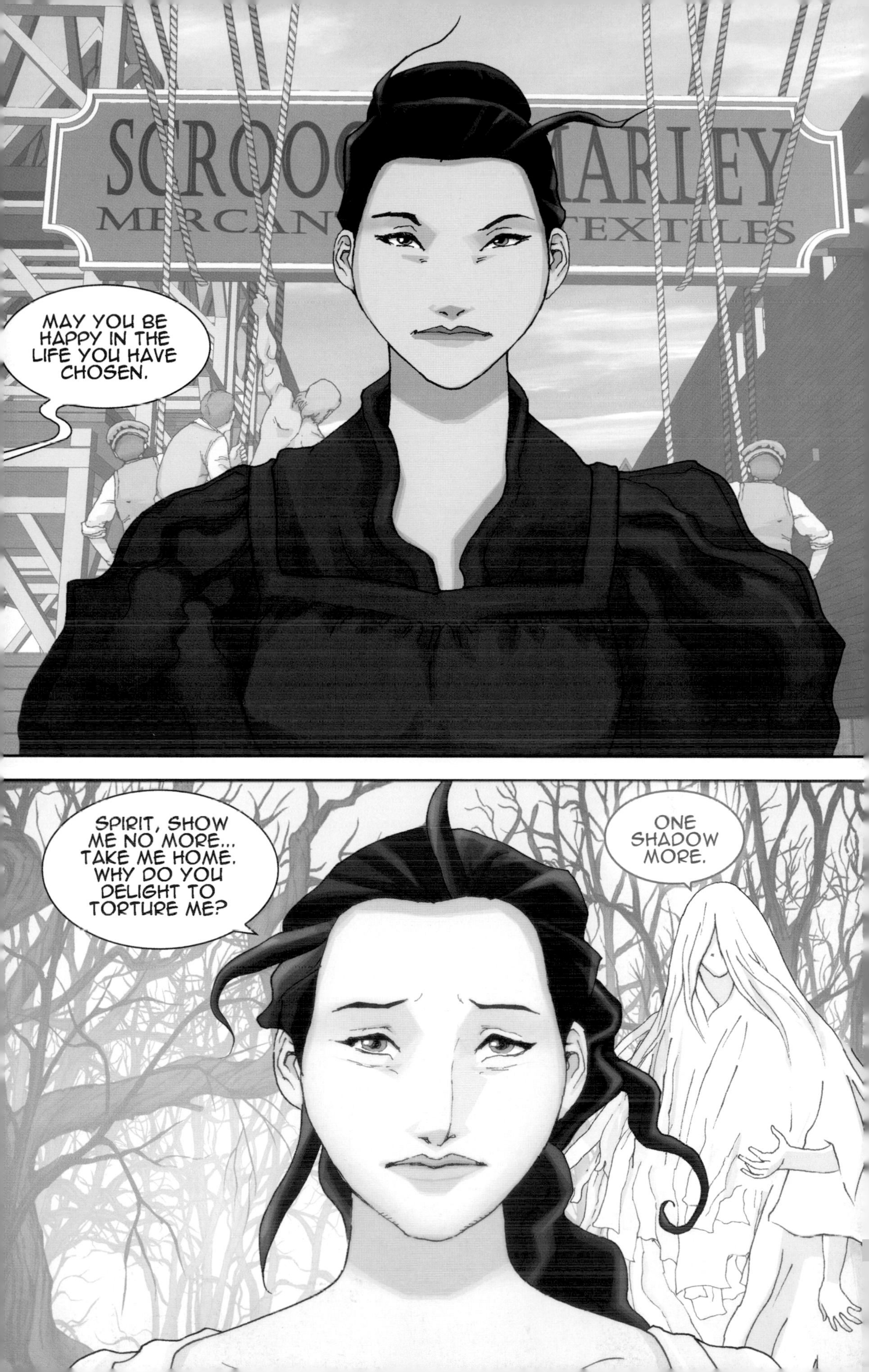
TEXTILES
MAY YOU BE HAPPY IN THE LIFE YOU HAVE CHOSEN.
SPIRIT, SHOW ME NO MORE... TAKE ME HOME. WHY DO YOU DELIGHT TO TORTURE ME?
ONE SHADOW MORE.

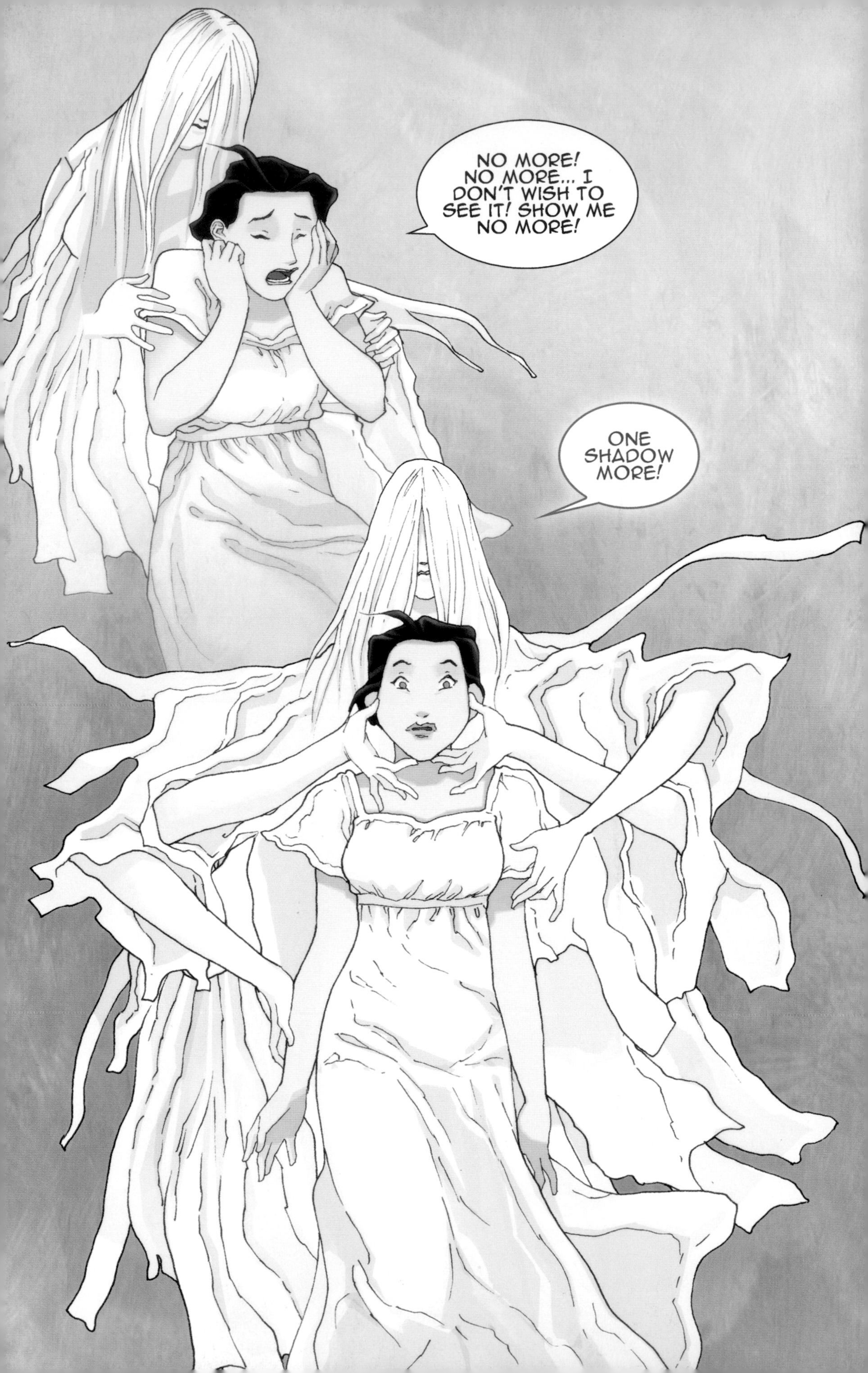
NO MORE! NO MORE... I DON'T WISH TO SEE IT! SHOW ME NO MORE!
ONE SHADOW MORE!

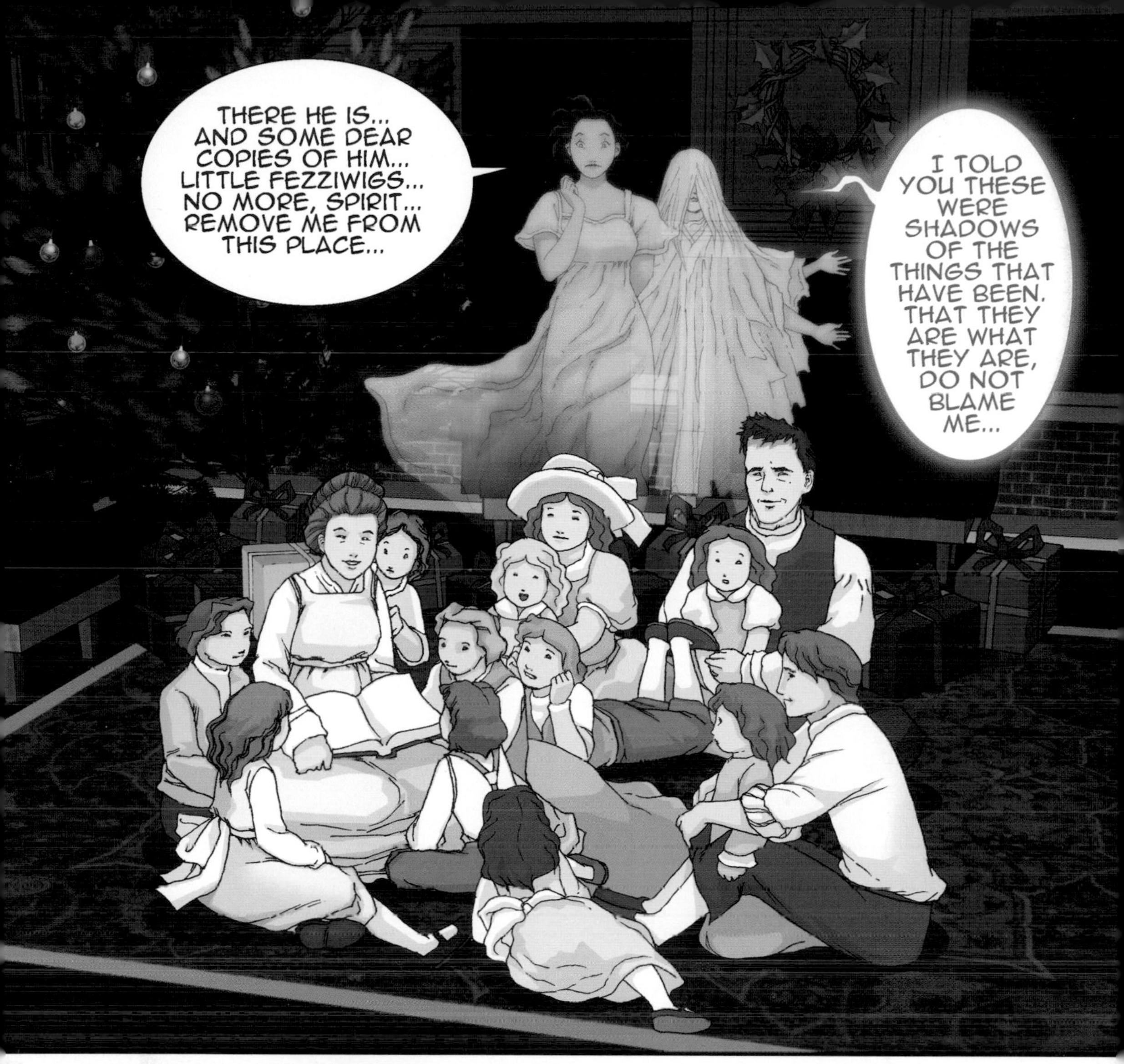
THERE HE IS... AND SOME DEAR COPIES OF HIM... LITTLE FEZZIWIGS... NO MORE, SPIRIT... REMOVE ME FROM THIS PLACE...
I TOLD YOU THESE WERE SHADOWS OF THE THINGS THAT HAVE BEEN. THAT THEY ARE WHAT THEY ARE, DO NOT BLAME ME...

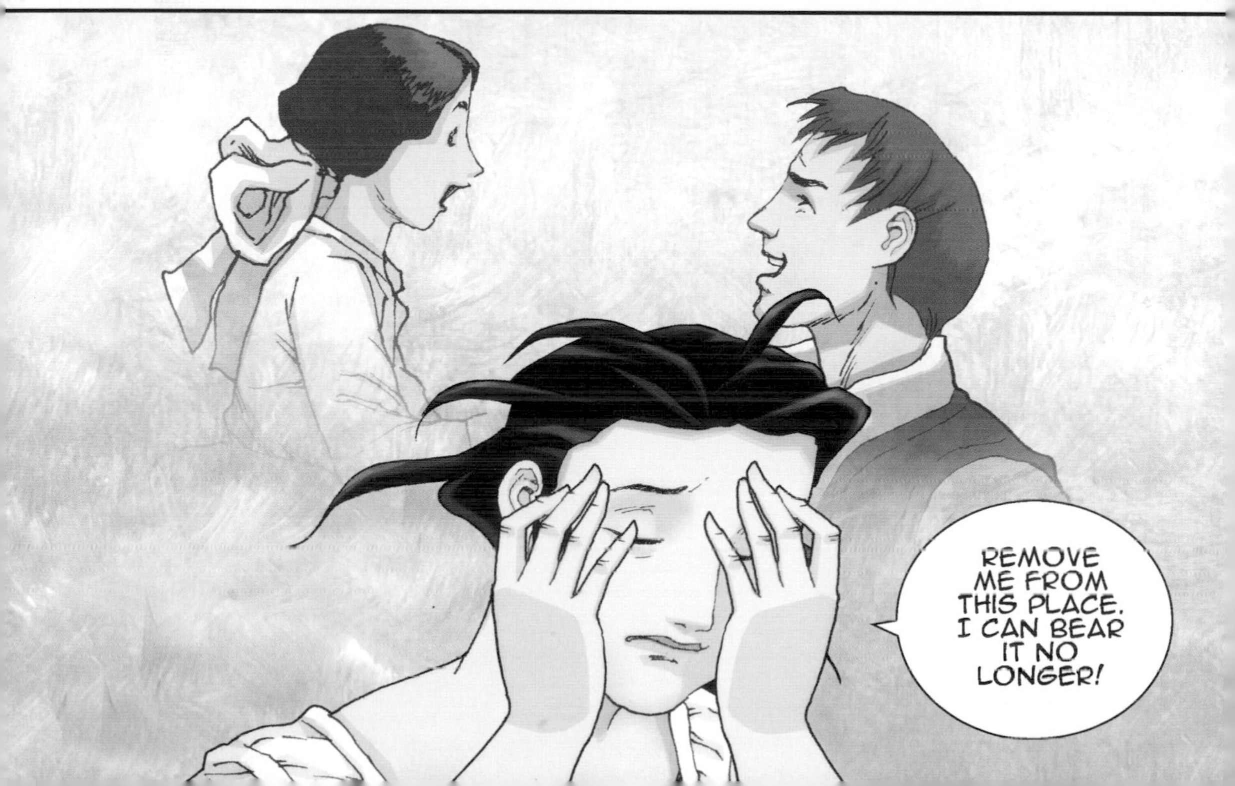
REMOVE ME FROM THIS PLACE. I CAN BEAR IT NO LONGER!

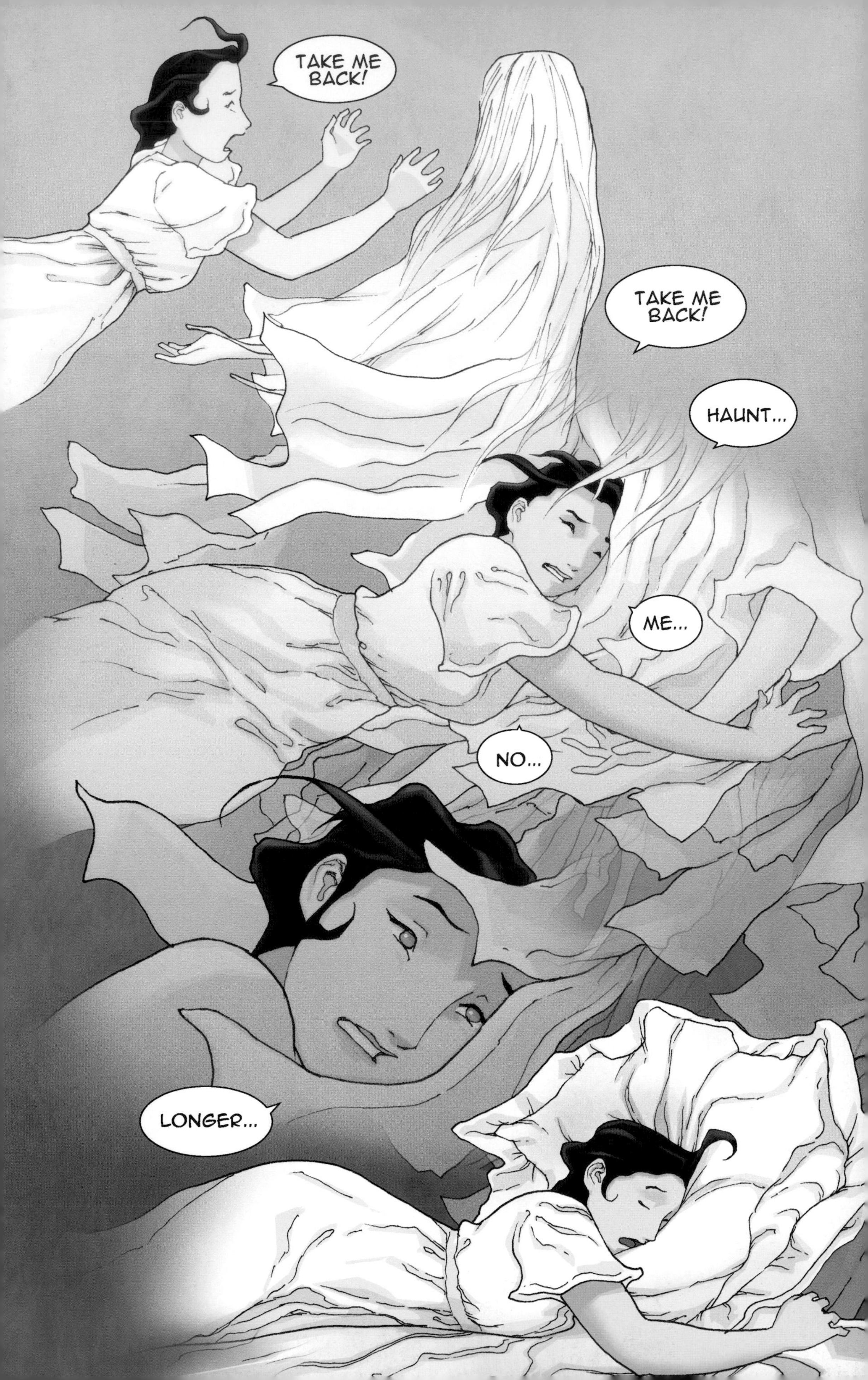
TAKE ME BACK!
TAKE ME BACK!
HAUNT...
ME...
NO...
LONGER...

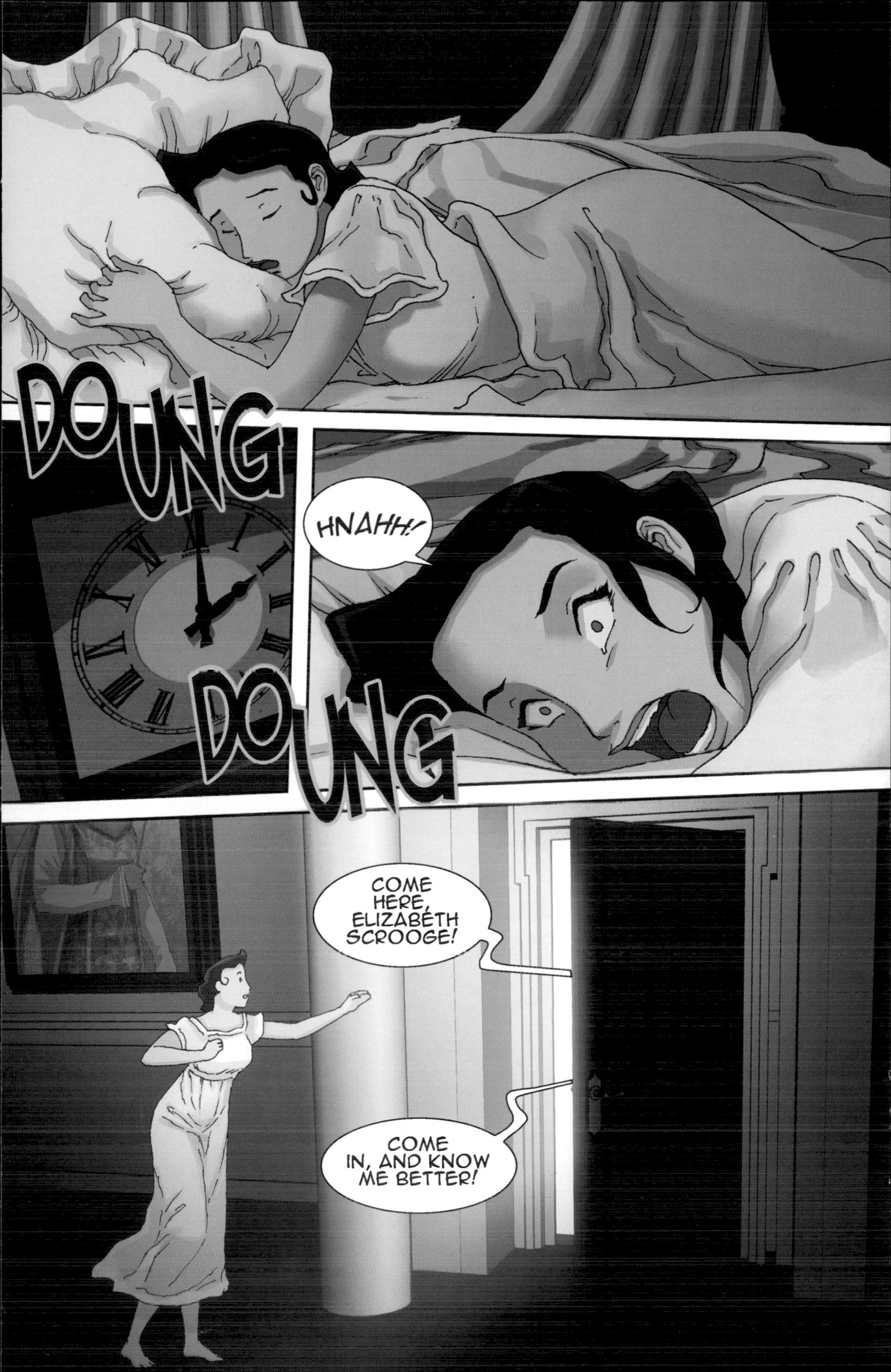
DOUNG
HNAHH!
DOUNG
COME HERE, ELIZABETH SCROOGE!
COME IN, AND KNOW ME BETTER!

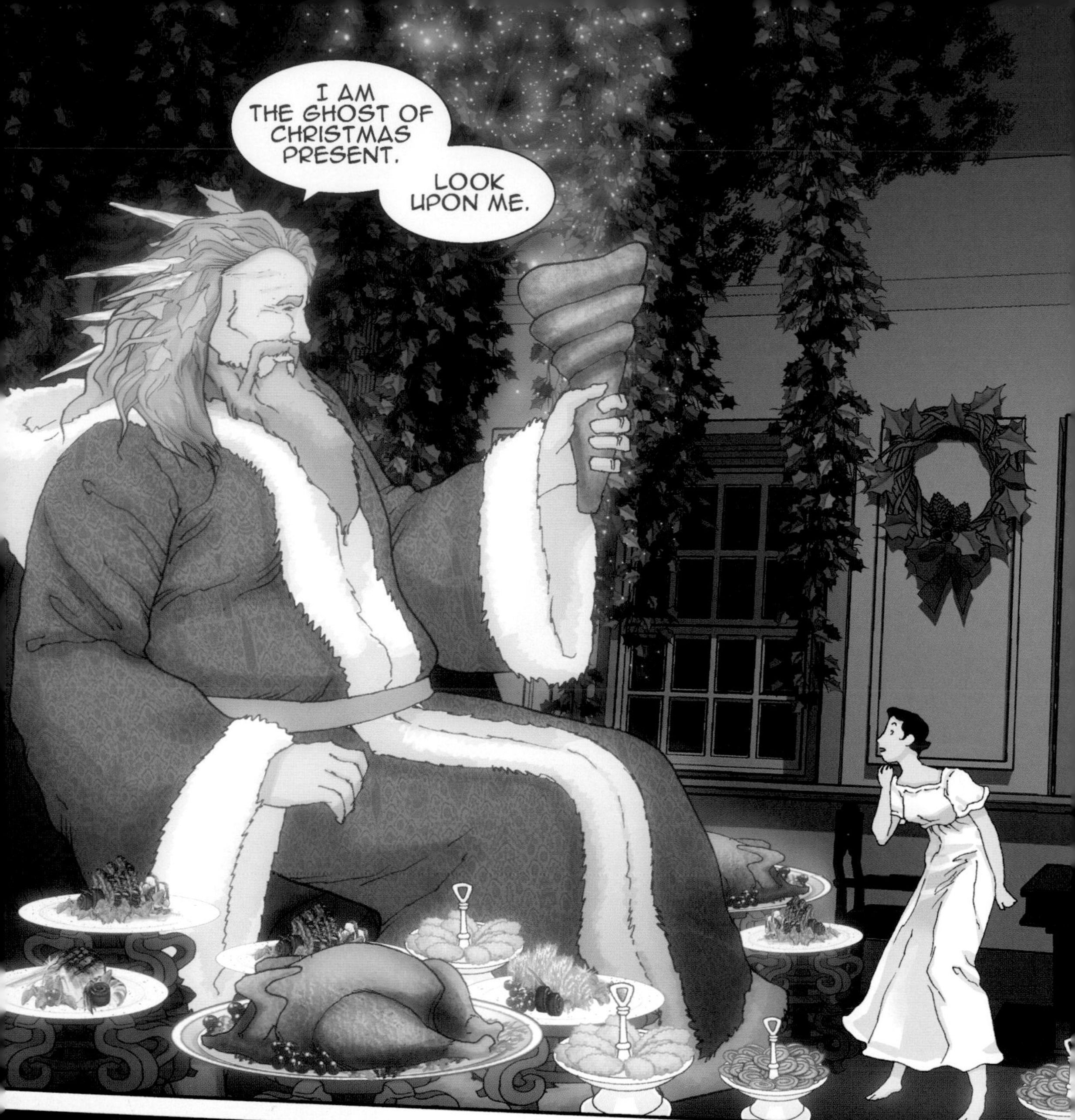
I AM THE GHOST OF CHRISTMAS PRESENT.
LOOK UPON ME.
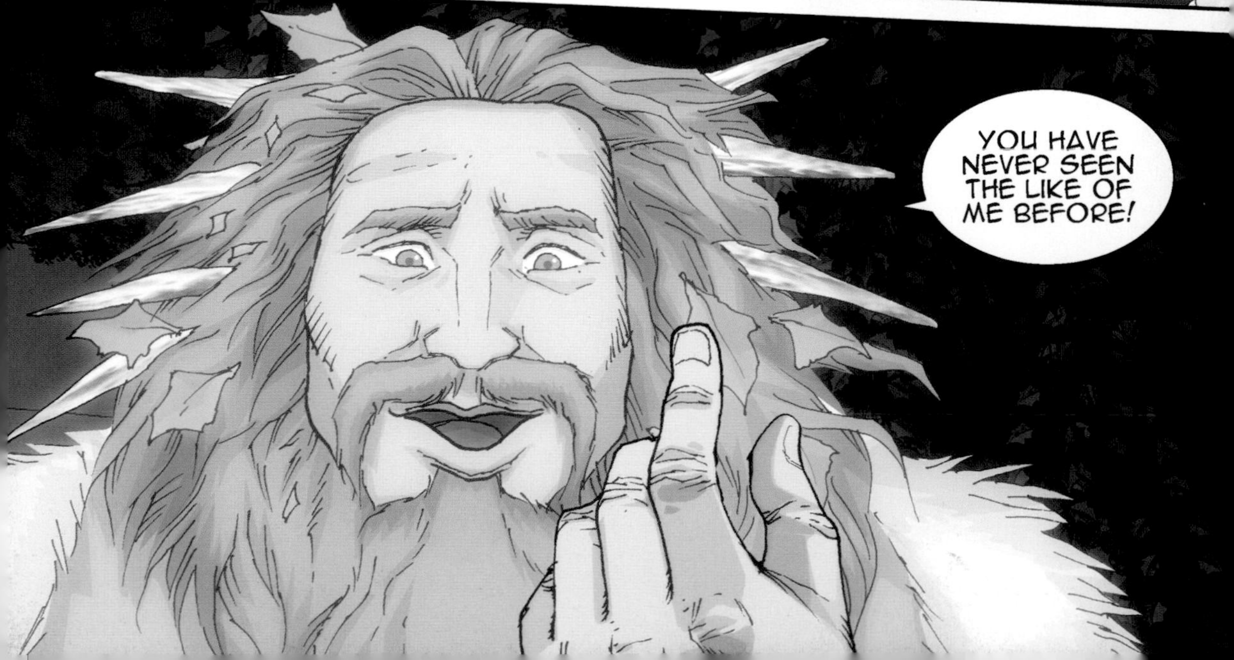
YOU HAVE NEVER SEEN THE LIKE OF ME BEFORE!

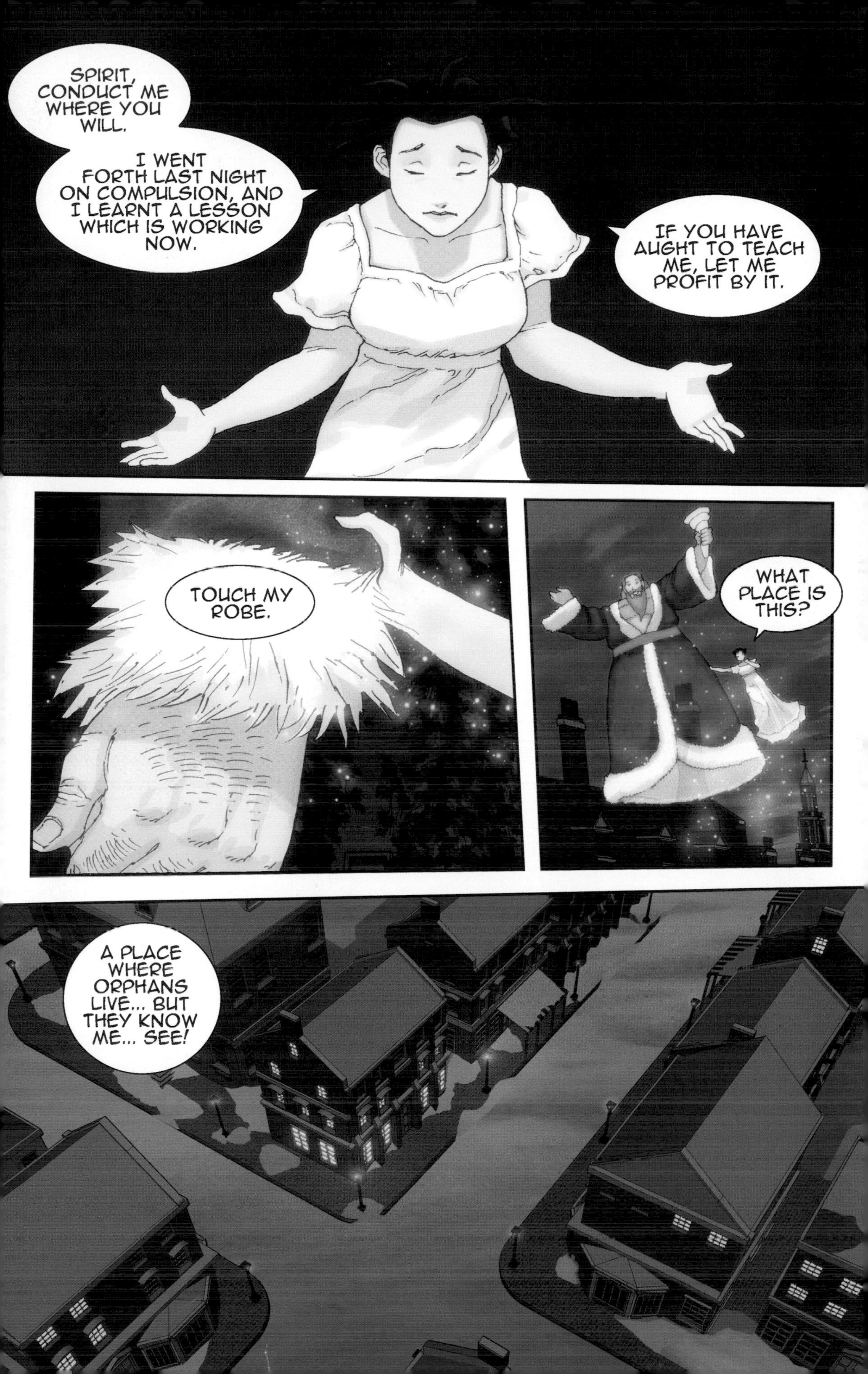
SPIRIT, CONDUCT ME WHERE YOU WILL.
I WENT FORTH LAST NIGHT ON COMPULSION, AND I LEARNT A LESSON WHICH IS WORKING NOW.
IF YOU HAVE AUGHT TO TEACH ME, LET ME PROFIT BY IT.
TOUCH MY ROBE.
WHAT PLACE IS THIS?
A PLACE WHERE ORPHANS LIVE... BUT THEY KNOW ME... SEE!

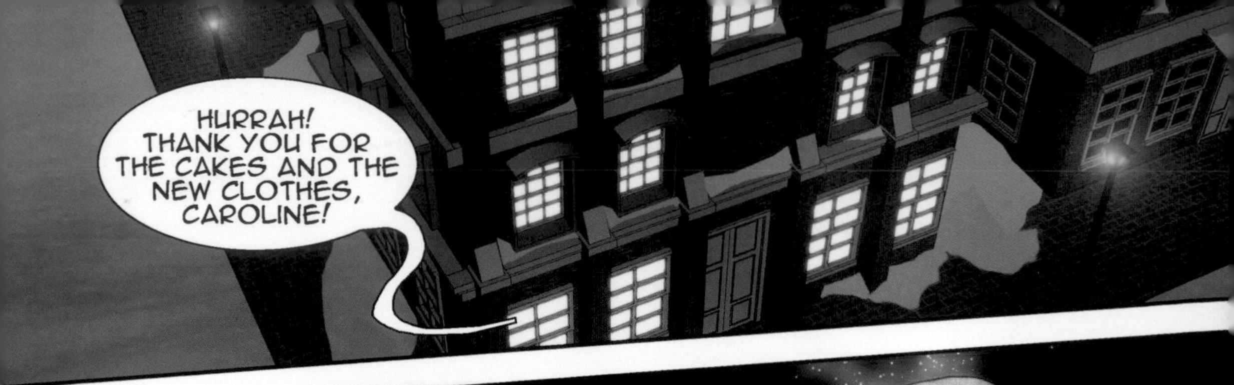
HURRAH! THANK YOU FOR THE CAKES AND THE NEW CLOTHES, CAROLINE!

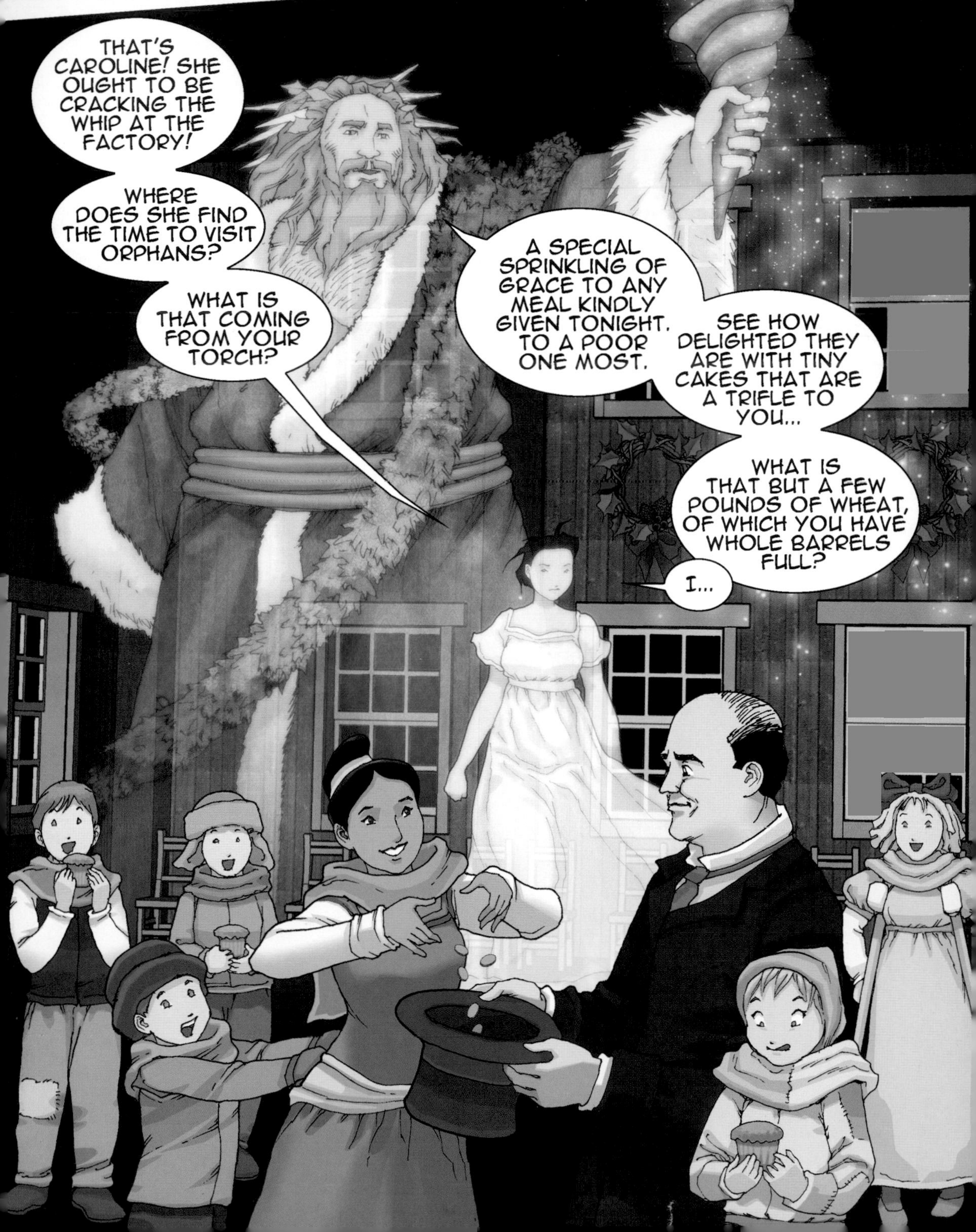
THAT'S CAROLINE! SHE OUGHT TO BE CRACKING THE WHIP AT THE FACTORY!
WHERE DOES SHE FIND THE TIME TO VISIT ORPHANS?
WHAT IS THAT COMING FROM YOUR TORCH?
A SPECIAL SPRINKLING OF GRACE TO ANY MEAL KINDLY GIVEN TONIGHT. TO A POOR ONE MOST.
SEE HOW DELIGHTED THEY ARE WITH TINY CAKES THAT ARE A TRIFLE TO YOU...
WHAT IS THAT BUT A FEW POUNDS OF WHEAT, OF WHICH YOU HAVE WHOLE BARRELS FULL?
I...

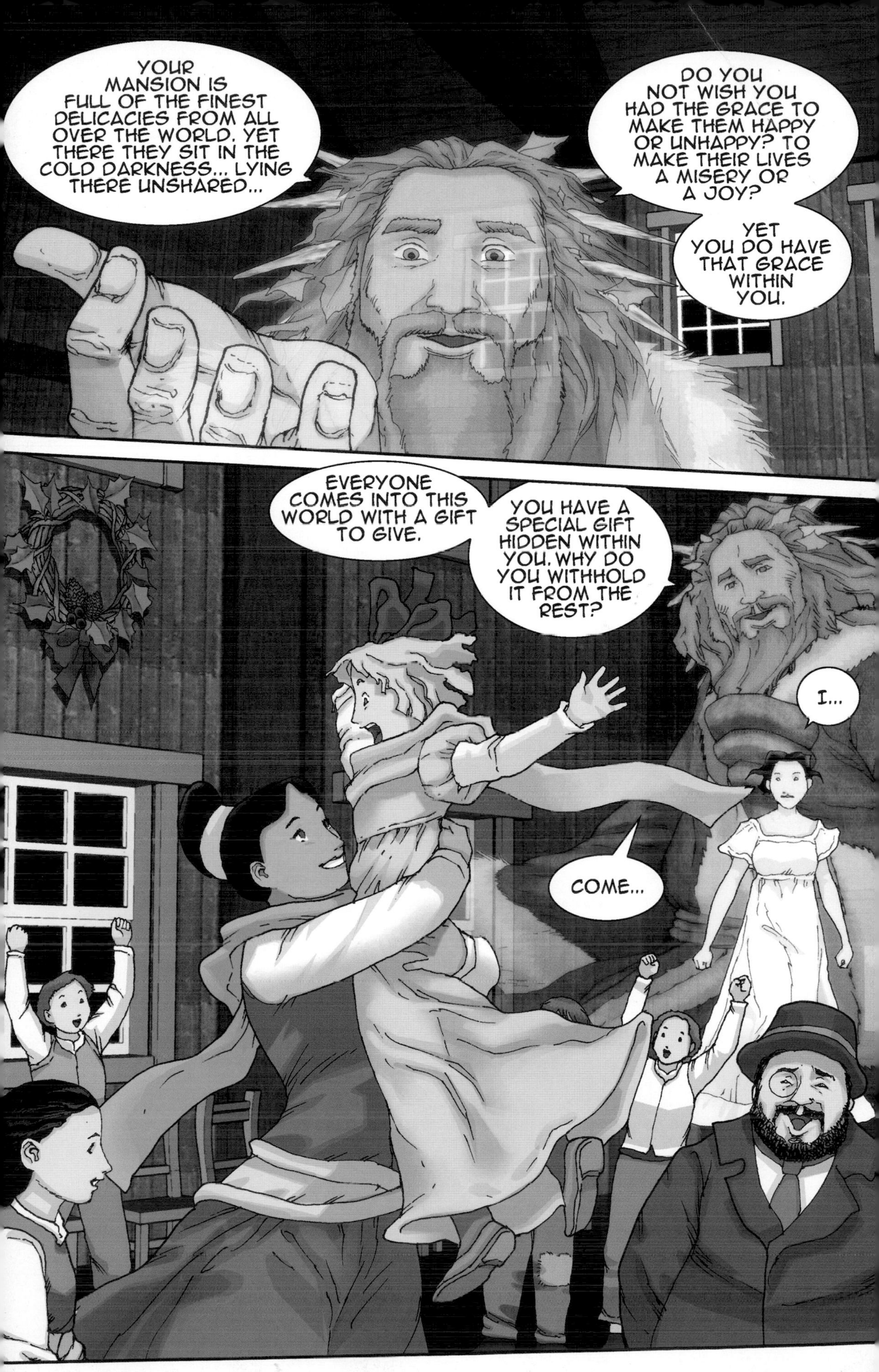
YOUR MANSION IS FULL OF THE FINEST DELICACIES FROM ALL OVER THE WORLD. YET THERE THEY SIT IN THE COLD DARKNESS... LYING THERE UNSHARED...
DO YOU NOT WISH YOU HAD THE GRACE TO MAKE THEM HAPPY OR UNHAPPY? TO MAKE THEIR LIVES A MISERY OR A JOY?
YET YOU DO HAVE THAT GRACE WITHIN YOU.
EVERYONE COMES INTO THIS WORLD WITH A GIFT TO GIVE.
YOU HAVE A SPECIAL GIFT HIDDEN WITHIN YOU. WHY DO YOU WITHHOLD IT FROM THE REST?
I...
COME...

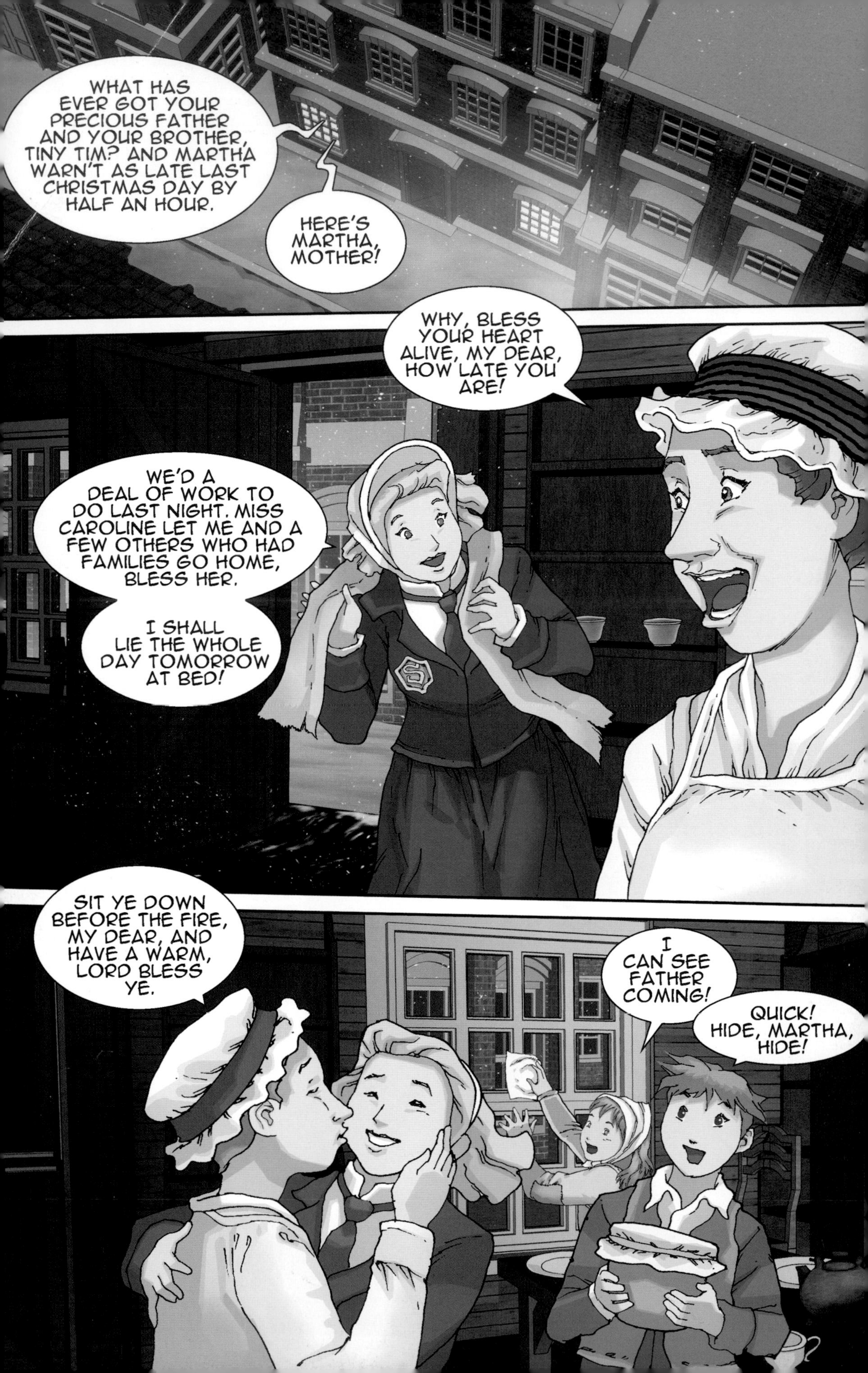
WHAT HAS EVER GOT YOUR PRECIOUS FATHER AND YOUR BROTHER, TINY TIM? AND MARTHA WARN'T AS LATE LAST CHRISTMAS DAY BY HALF AN HOUR.
HERE'S MARTHA, MOTHER!
WHY, BLESS YOUR HEART ALIVE, MY DEAR, HOW LATE YOU ARE!
WE'D A DEAL OF WORK TO DO LAST NIGHT. MISS CAROLINE LET ME AND A FEW OTHERS WHO HAD FAMILIES GO HOME, BLESS HER.
I SHALL LIE THE WHOLE DAY TOMORROW AT BED!
SIT YE DOWN BEFORE THE FIRE, MY DEAR, AND HAVE A WARM, LORD BLESS YE.
I CAN SEE FATHER COMING!
QUICK! HIDE, MARTHA, HIDE!

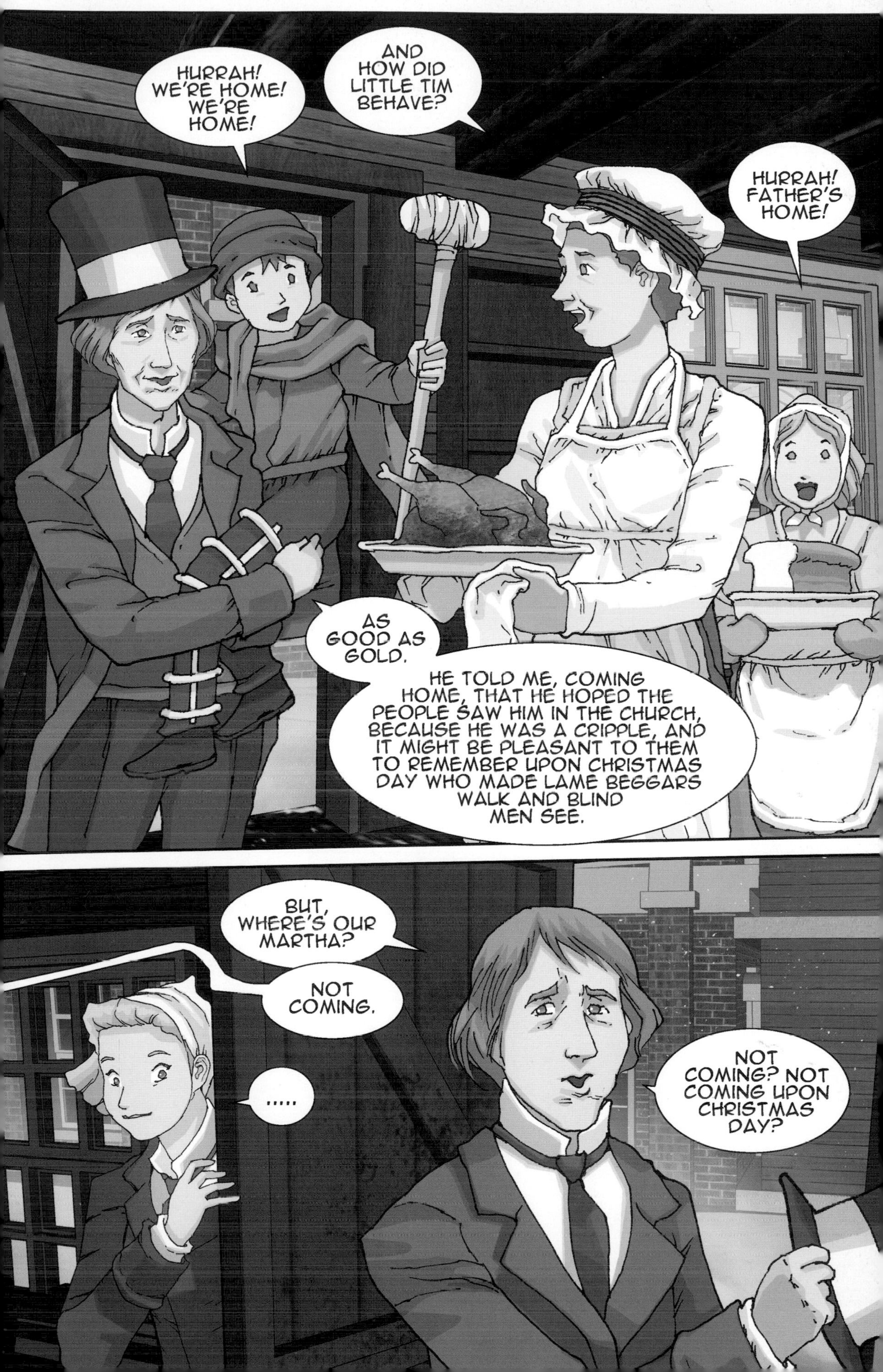
HURRAH! WE'RE HOME! WE'RE HOME!
AND HOW DID LITTLE TIM BEHAVE?
HURRAH! FATHER'S HOME!
AS GOOD AS GOLD.
HE TOLD ME, COMING HOME, THAT HE HOPED THE PEOPLE SAW HIM IN THE CHURCH, BECAUSE HE WAS A CRIPPLE, AND IT MIGHT BE PLEASANT TO THEM TO REMEMBER UPON CHRISTMAS DAY WHO MADE LAME BEGGARS WALK AND BLIND MEN SEE.
BUT, WHERE'S OUR MARTHA?
NOT COMING.
.....
NOT COMING? NOT COMING UPON CHRISTMAS DAY?

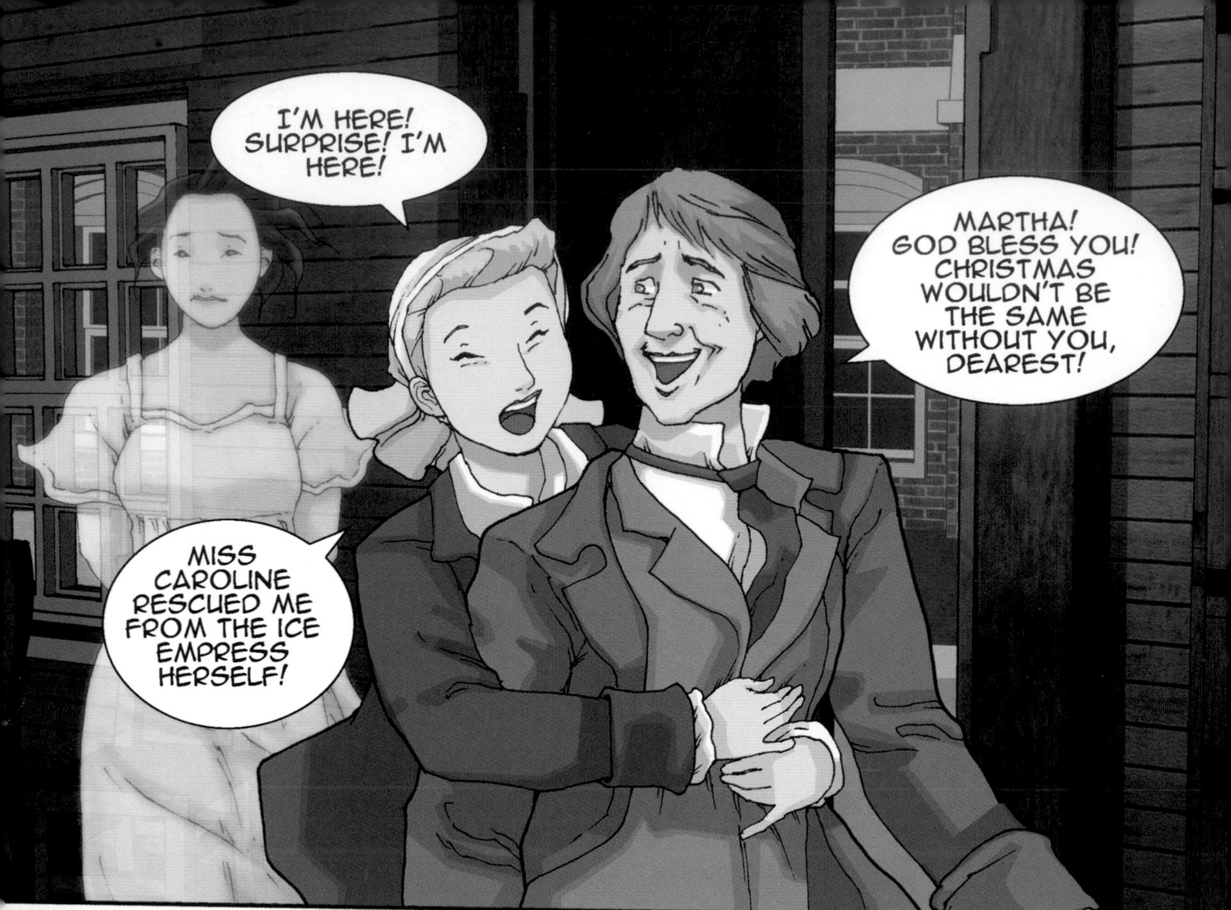
I'M HERE! SURPRISE! I'M HERE!
MARTHA! GOD BLESS YOU! CHRISTMAS WOULDN'T BE THE SAME WITHOUT YOU, DEAREST!
MISS CAROLINE RESCUED ME FROM THE ICE EMPRESS HERSELF!

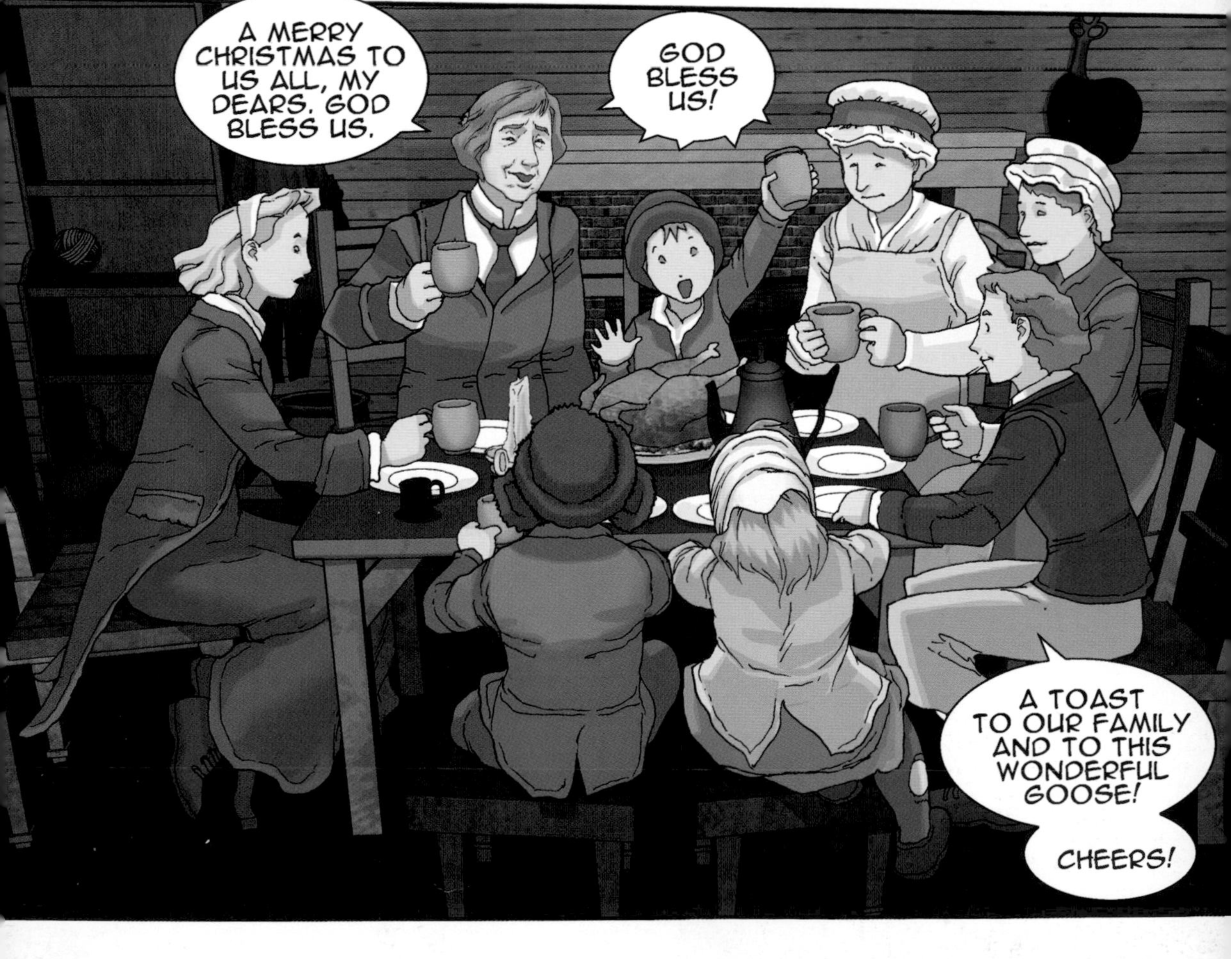
A MERRY CHRISTMAS TO US ALL, MY DEARS. GOD BLESS US.
GOD BLESS US!
A TOAST TO OUR FAMILY AND TO THIS WONDERFUL GOOSE!
CHEERS!

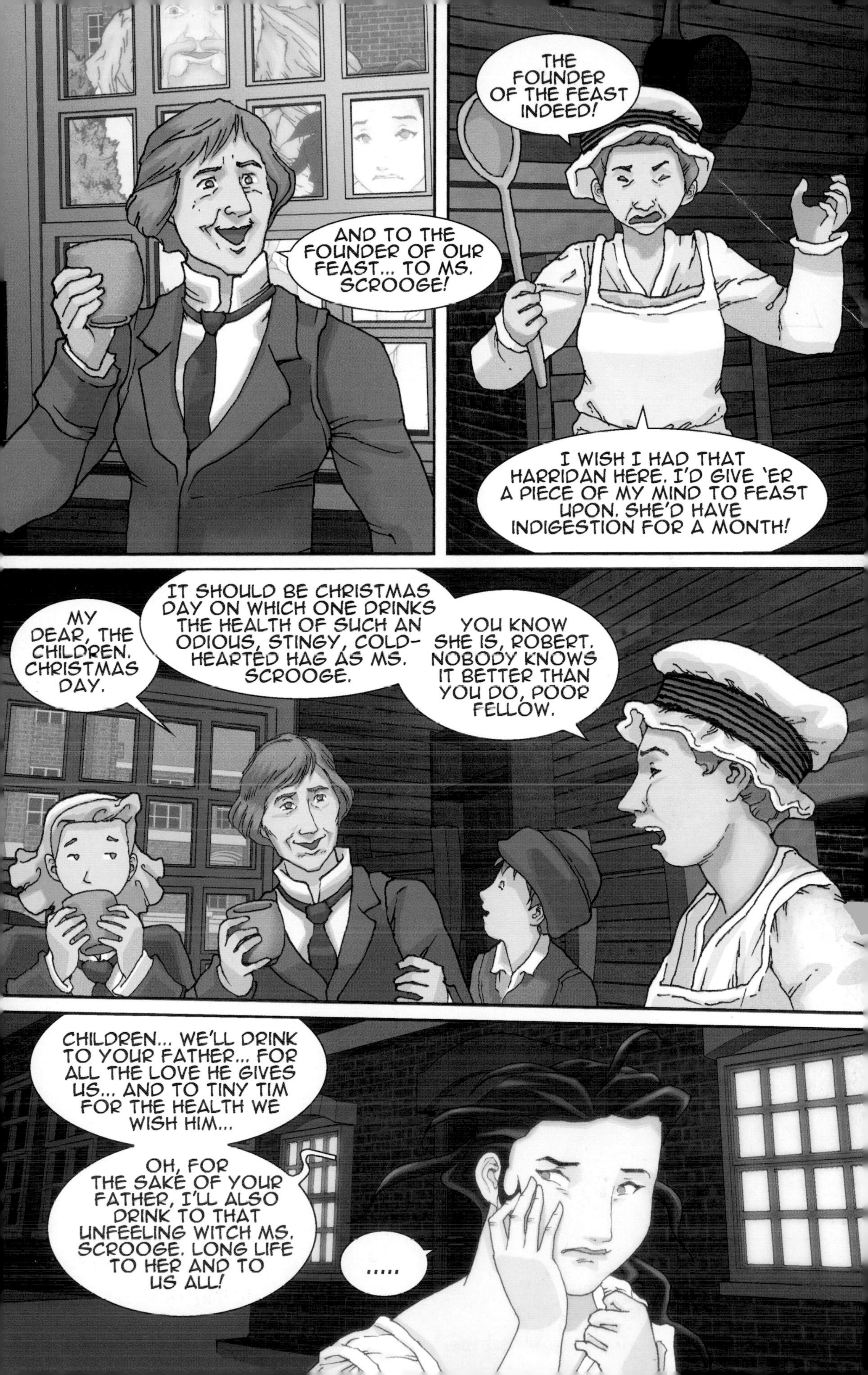
AND TO THE FOUNDER OF OUR FEAST... TO MS. SCROOGE!
THE FOUNDER OF THE FEAST INDEED!
I WISH I HAD THAT HARRIDAN HERE. I'D GIVE 'ER A PIECE OF MY MIND TO FEAST UPON. SHE'D HAVE INDIGESTION FOR A MONTH!
MY DEAR, THE CHILDREN. CHRISTMAS DAY.
IT SHOULD BE CHRISTMAS DAY ON WHICH ONE DRINKS THE HEALTH OF SUCH AN ODIOUS, STINGY, COLD-HEARTED HAG AS MS. SCROOGE.
YOU KNOW SHE IS, ROBERT. NOBODY KNOWS IT BETTER THAN YOU DO, POOR FELLOW.
CHILDREN... WE'LL DRINK TO YOUR FATHER... FOR ALL THE LOVE HE GIVES US... AND TO TINY TIM FOR THE HEALTH WE WISH HIM...
OH, FOR THE SAKE OF YOUR FATHER, I'LL ALSO DRINK TO THAT UNFEELING WITCH MS. SCROOGE. LONG LIFE TO HER AND TO US ALL!
.....

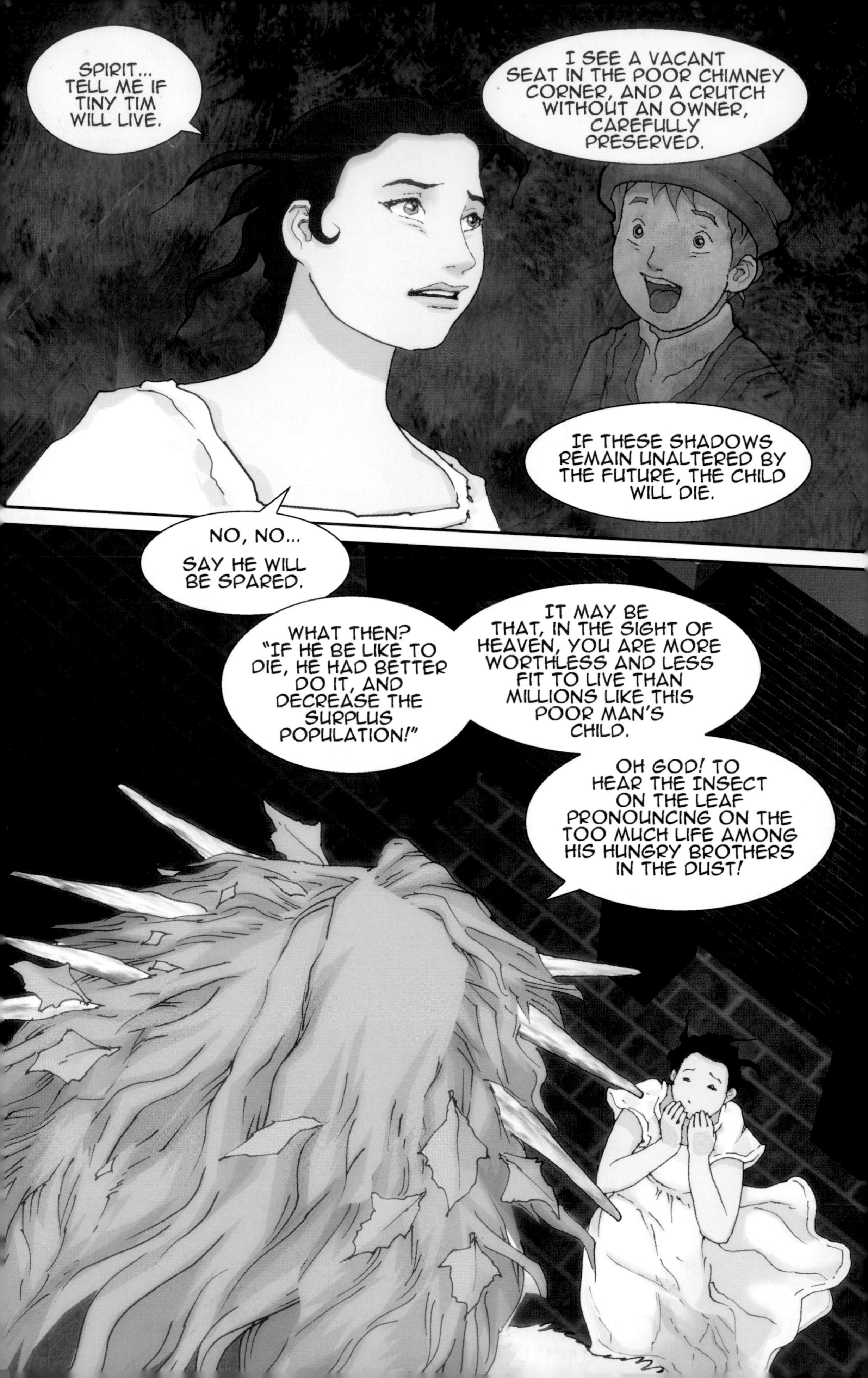
SPIRIT... TELL ME IF TINY TIM WILL LIVE.
I SEE A VACANT SEAT IN THE POOR CHIMNEY CORNER, AND A CRUTCH WITHOUT AN OWNER, CAREFULLY PRESERVED.
IF THESE SHADOWS REMAIN UNALTERED BY THE FUTURE, THE CHILD WILL DIE.
NO, NO...
SAY HE WILL BE SPARED.
WHAT THEN? "IF HE BE LIKE TO DIE, HE HAD BETTER DO IT, AND DECREASE THE SURPLUS POPULATION!"
IT MAY BE THAT, IN THE SIGHT OF HEAVEN, YOU ARE MORE WORTHLESS AND LESS FIT TO LIVE THAN MILLIONS LIKE THIS POOR MAN'S CHILD.
OH GOD! TO HEAR THE INSECT ON THE LEAF PRONOUNCING ON THE TOO MUCH LIFE AMONG HIS HUNGRY BROTHERS IN THE DUST!

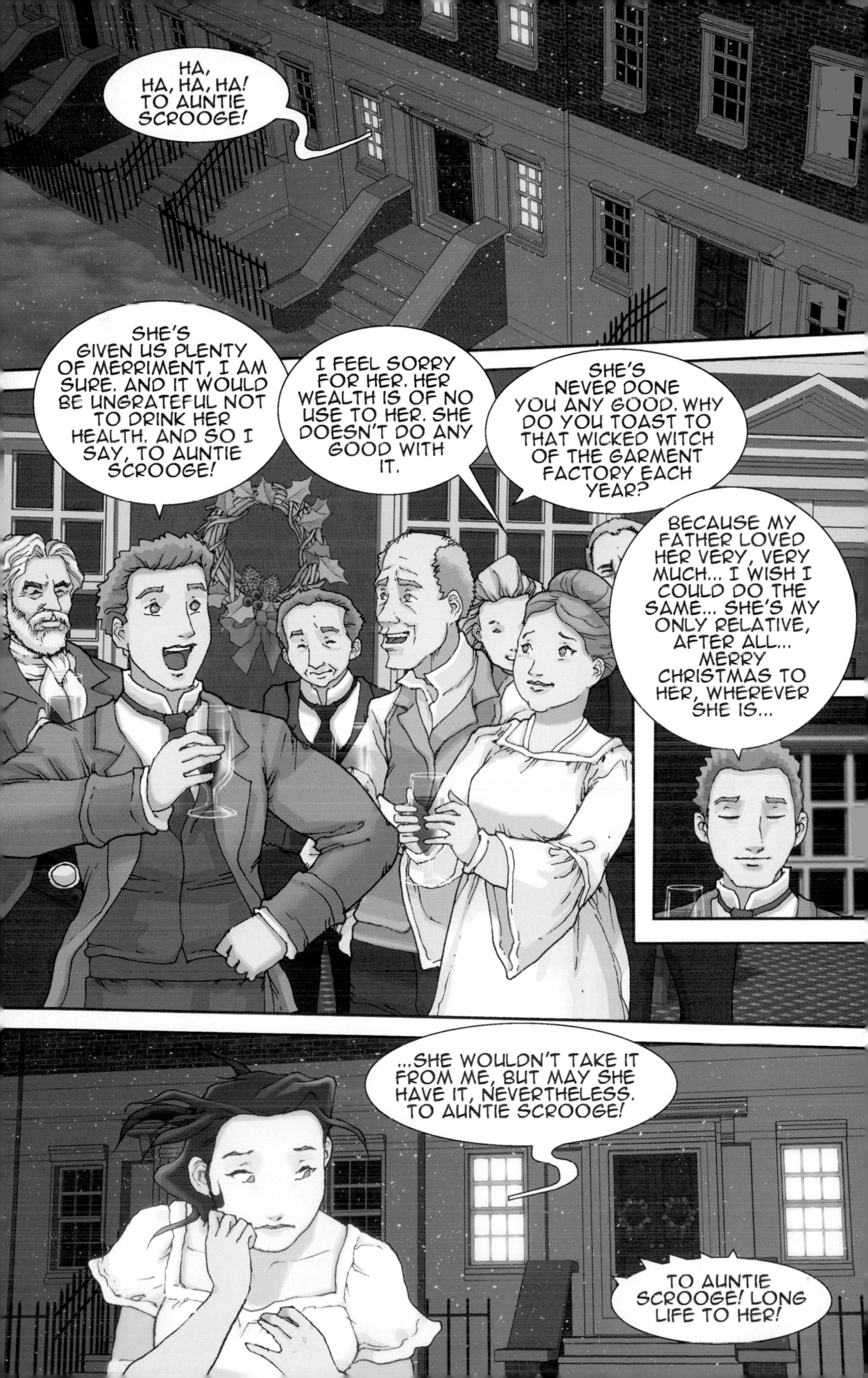
HA, HA, HA, HA! TO AUNTIE SCROOGE!
SHE'S GIVEN US PLENTY OF MERRIMENT, I AM SURE. AND IT WOULD BE UNGRATEFUL NOT TO DRINK HER HEALTH. AND SO I SAY, TO AUNTIE SCROOGE!
I FEEL SORRY FOR HER. HER WEALTH IS OF NO USE TO HER. SHE DOESN'T DO ANY GOOD WITH IT.
SHE'S NEVER DONE YOU ANY GOOD. WHY DO YOU TOAST TO THAT WICKED WITCH OF THE GARMENT FACTORY EACH YEAR?
BECAUSE MY FATHER LOVED HER VERY, VERY MUCH... I WISH I COULD DO THE SAME... SHE'S MY ONLY RELATIVE, AFTER ALL... MERRY CHRISTMAS TO HER, WHEREVER SHE IS...
...SHE WOULDN'T TAKE IT FROM ME, BUT MAY SHE HAVE IT, NEVERTHELESS. TO AUNTIE SCROOGE!
TO AUNTIE SCROOGE! LONG LIFE TO HER!

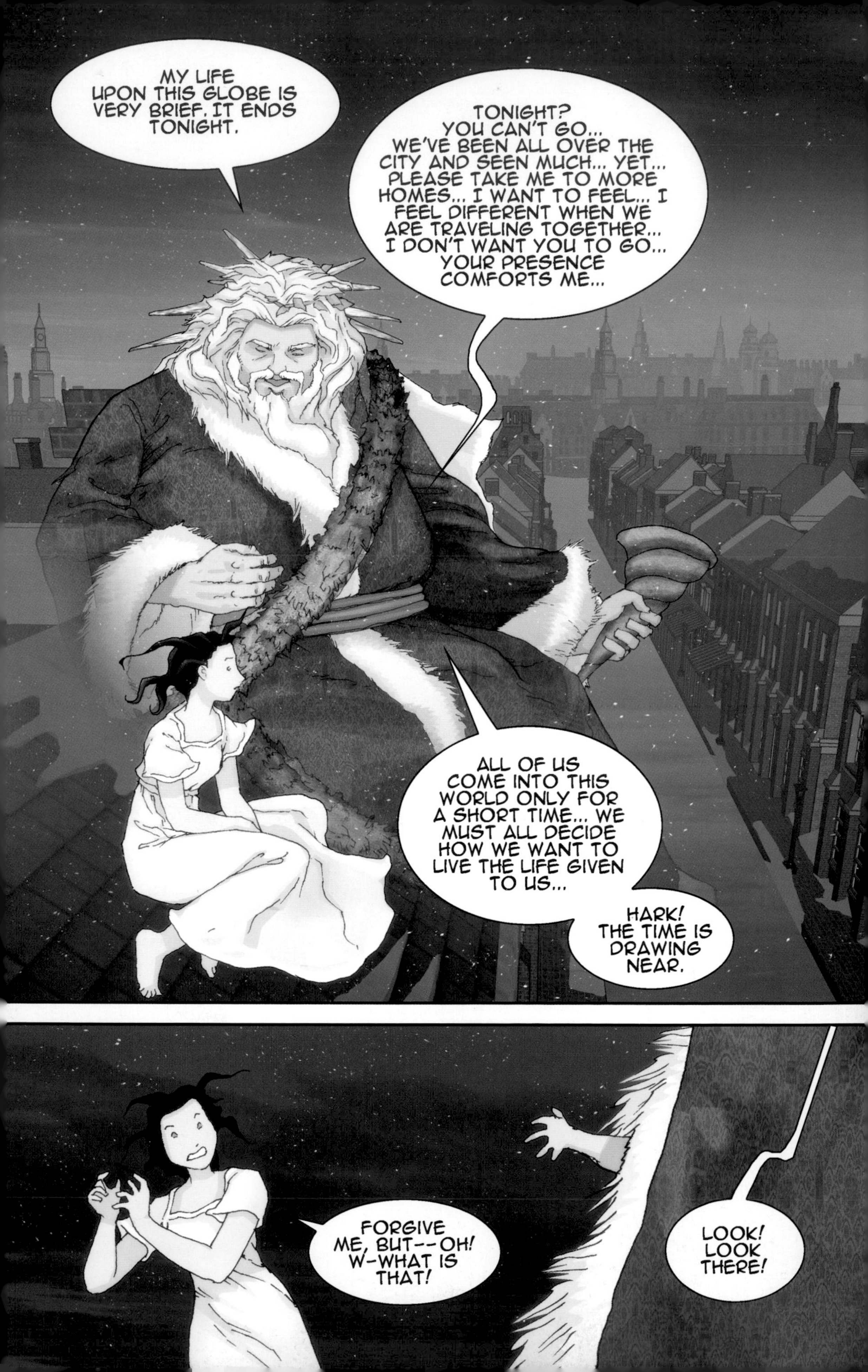
MY LIFE UPON THIS GLOBE IS VERY BRIEF. IT ENDS TONIGHT.
TONIGHT? YOU CAN'T GO... WE'VE BEEN ALL OVER THE CITY AND SEEN MUCH... YET... PLEASE TAKE ME TO MORE HOMES... I WANT TO FEEL... I FEEL DIFFERENT WHEN WE ARE TRAVELING TOGETHER... I DON'T WANT YOU TO GO... YOUR PRESENCE COMFORTS ME...
ALL OF US COME INTO THIS WORLD ONLY FOR A SHORT TIME... WE MUST ALL DECIDE HOW WE WANT TO LIVE THE LIFE GIVEN TO US...
HARK! THE TIME IS DRAWING NEAR.
FORGIVE ME, BUT--OH! W-WHAT IS THAT!
LOOK! LOOK THERE!

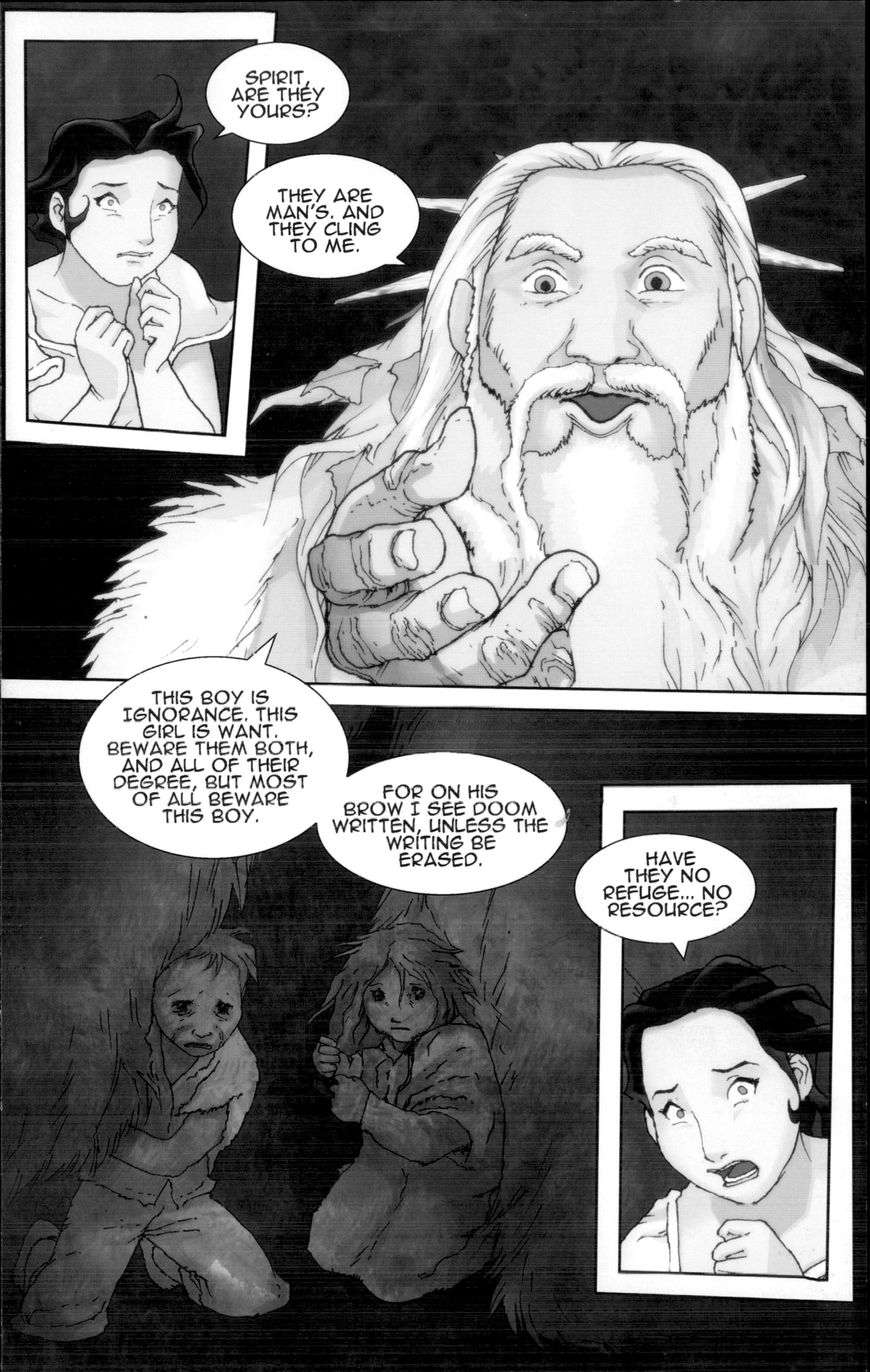
SPIRIT, ARE THEY YOURS?
THEY ARE MAN'S. AND THEY CLING TO ME.
THIS BOY IS IGNORANCE. THIS GIRL IS WANT. BEWARE THEM BOTH, AND ALL OF THEIR DEGREE, BUT MOST OF ALL BEWARE THIS BOY.
FOR ON HIS BROW I SEE DOOM WRITTEN, UNLESS THE WRITING BE ERASED.
HAVE THEY NO REFUGE... NO RESOURCE?

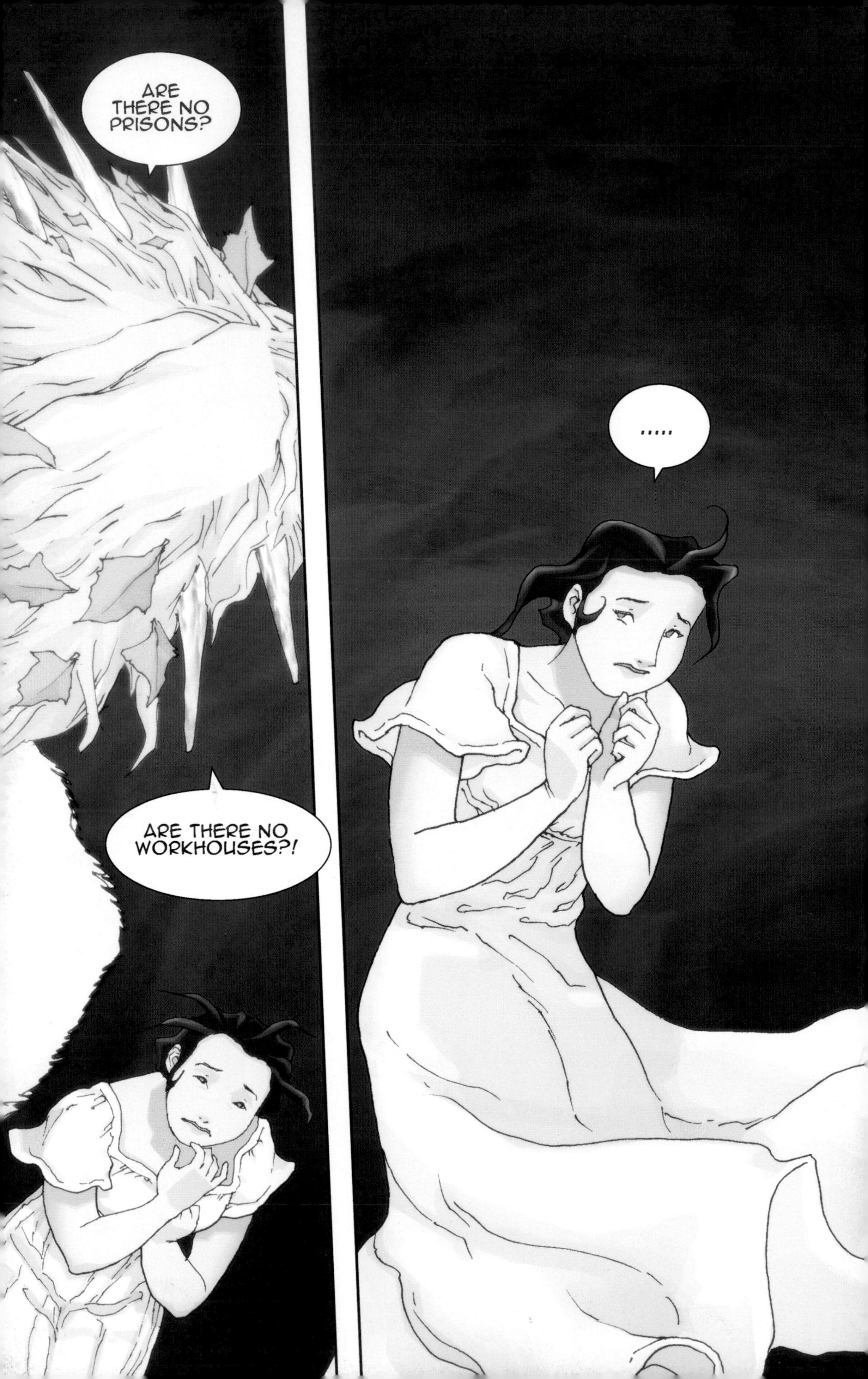
ARE THERE NO PRISONS?
ARE THERE NO WORKHOUSES?!
.....

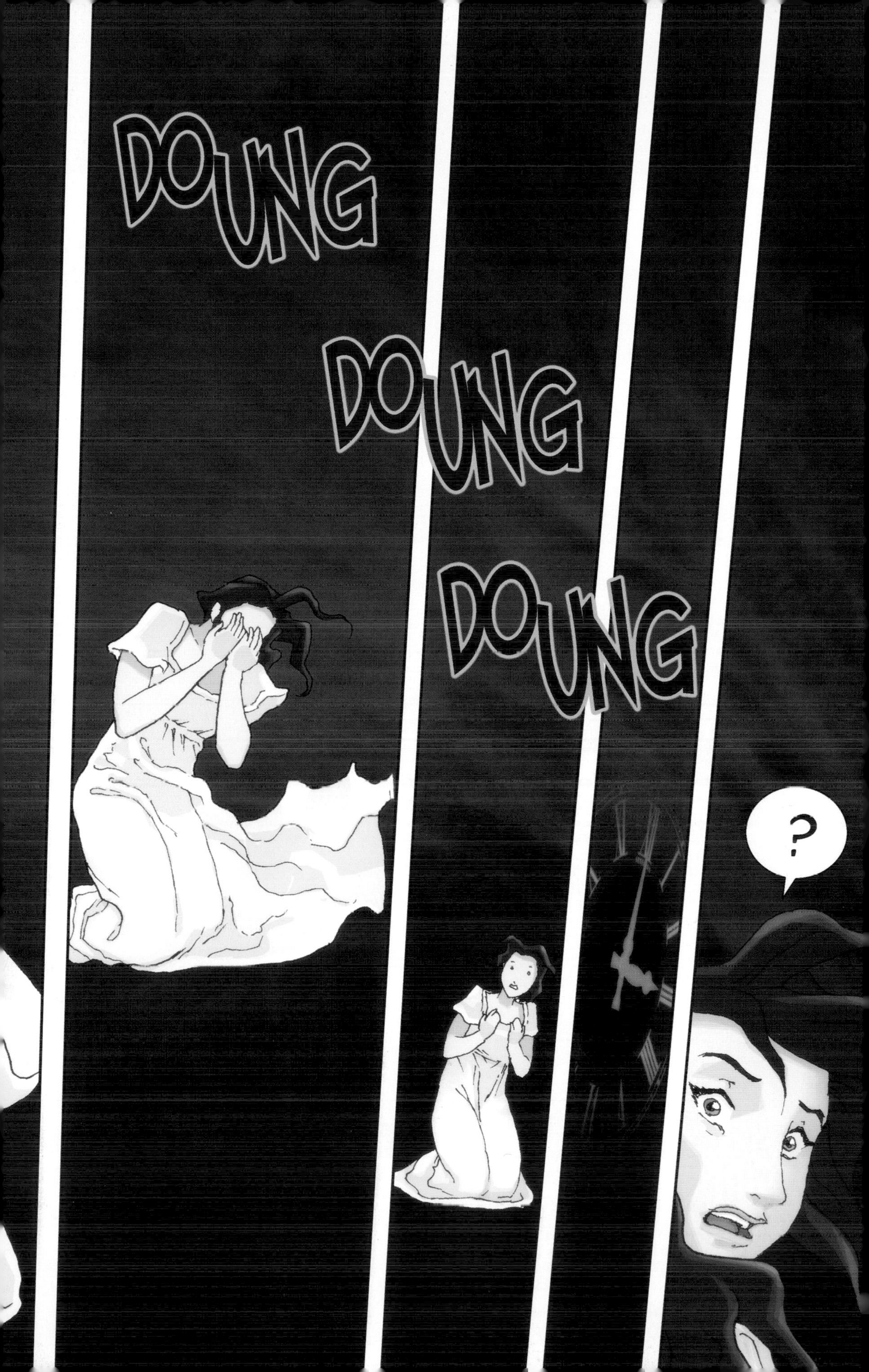
DOUNG
DOUNG
DOUNG
?

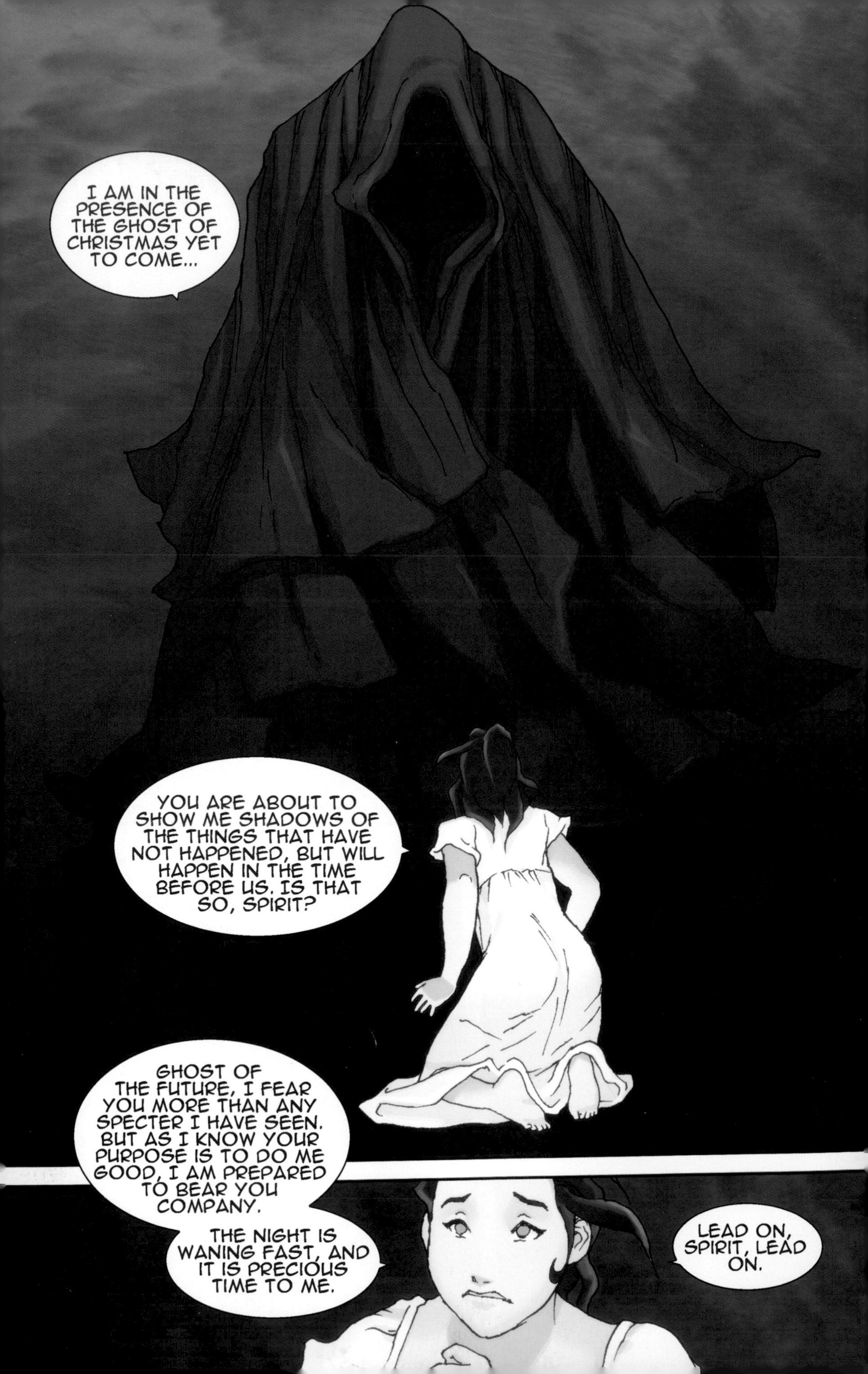
I AM IN THE PRESENCE OF THE GHOST OF CHRISTMAS YET TO COME...
YOU ARE ABOUT TO SHOW ME SHADOWS OF THE THINGS THAT HAVE NOT HAPPENED, BUT WILL HAPPEN IN THE TIME BEFORE US. IS THAT SO, SPIRIT?
GHOST OF THE FUTURE, I FEAR YOU MORE THAN ANY SPECTER I HAVE SEEN. BUT AS I KNOW YOUR PURPOSE IS TO DO ME GOOD, I AM PREPARED TO BEAR YOU COMPANY.
THE NIGHT IS WANING FAST, AND IT IS PRECIOUS TIME TO ME.
LEAD ON, SPIRIT, LEAD ON.

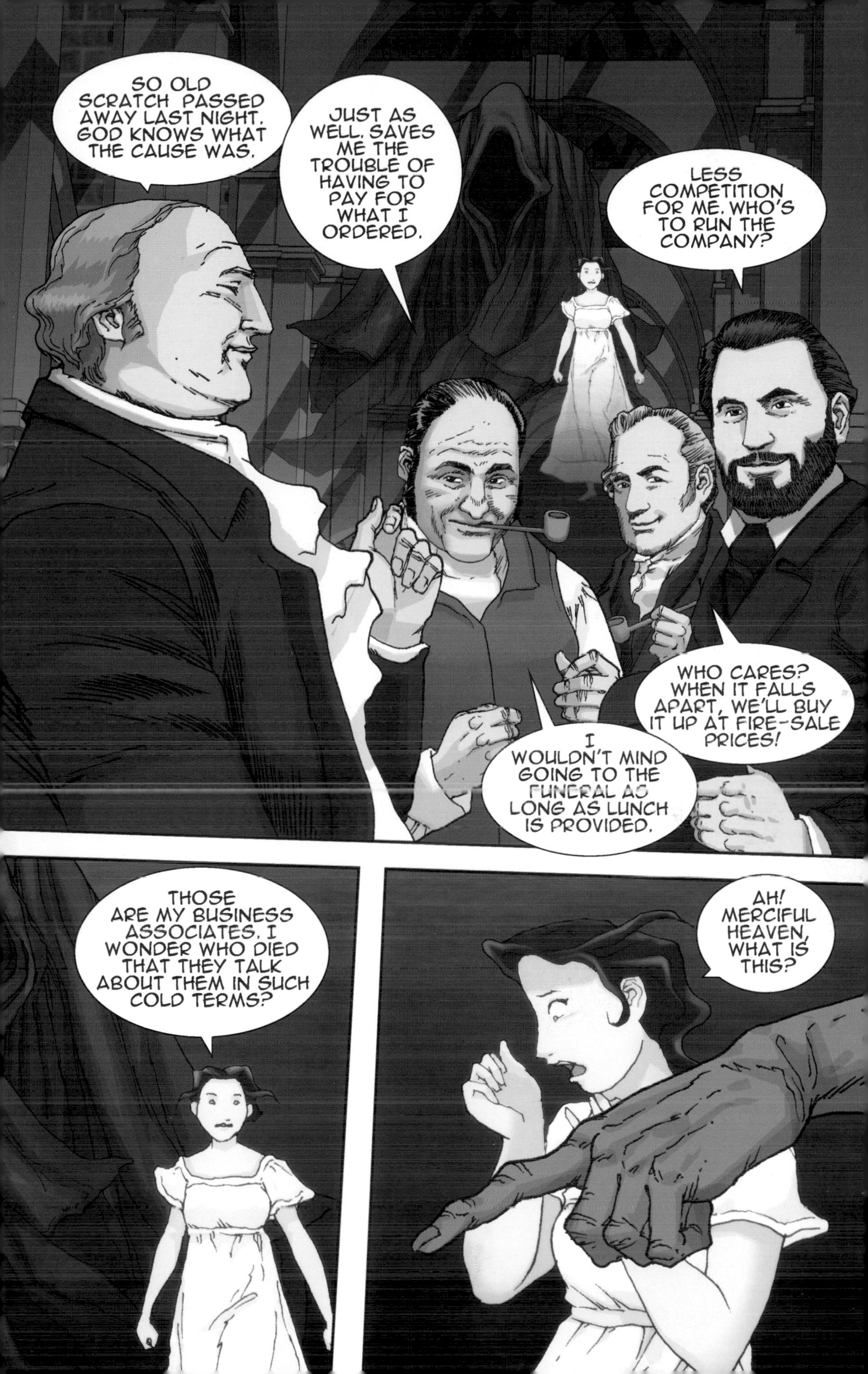
SO OLD SCRATCH PASSED AWAY LAST NIGHT. GOD KNOWS WHAT THE CAUSE WAS.
JUST AS WELL. SAVES ME THE TROUBLE OF HAVING TO PAY FOR WHAT I ORDERED.
LESS COMPETITION FOR ME. WHO'S TO RUN THE COMPANY?
WHO CARES? WHEN IT FALLS APART, WE'LL BUY IT UP AT FIRE-SALE PRICES!
I WOULDN'T MIND GOING TO THE FUNERAL AS LONG AS LUNCH IS PROVIDED.
THOSE ARE MY BUSINESS ASSOCIATES. I WONDER WHO DIED THAT THEY TALK ABOUT THEM IN SUCH COLD TERMS?
AH! MERCIFUL HEAVEN, WHAT IS THIS?

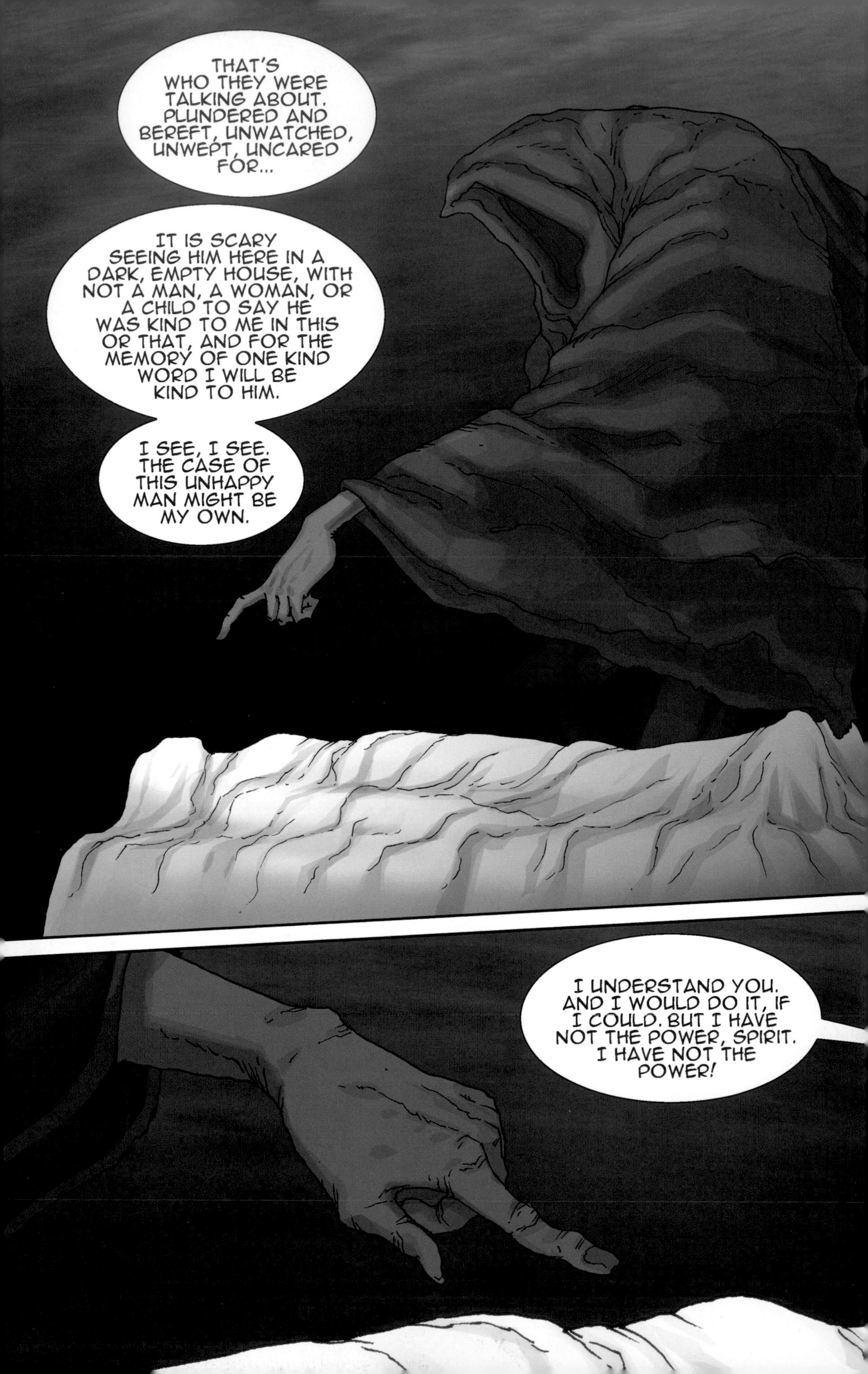
THAT'S WHO THEY WERE TALKING ABOUT. PLUNDERED AND BEREFT, UNWATCHED, UNWEPT, UNCARED FOR...
IT IS SCARY SEEING HIM HERE IN A DARK, EMPTY HOUSE, WITH NOT A MAN, A WOMAN, OR A CHILD TO SAY HE WAS KIND TO ME IN THIS OR THAT, AND FOR THE MEMORY OF ONE KIND WORD I WILL BE KIND TO HIM.
I SEE, I SEE. THE CASE OF THIS UNHAPPY MAN MIGHT BE MY OWN.
I UNDERSTAND YOU. AND I WOULD DO IT, IF I COULD. BUT I HAVE NOT THE POWER, SPIRIT. I HAVE NOT THE POWER!

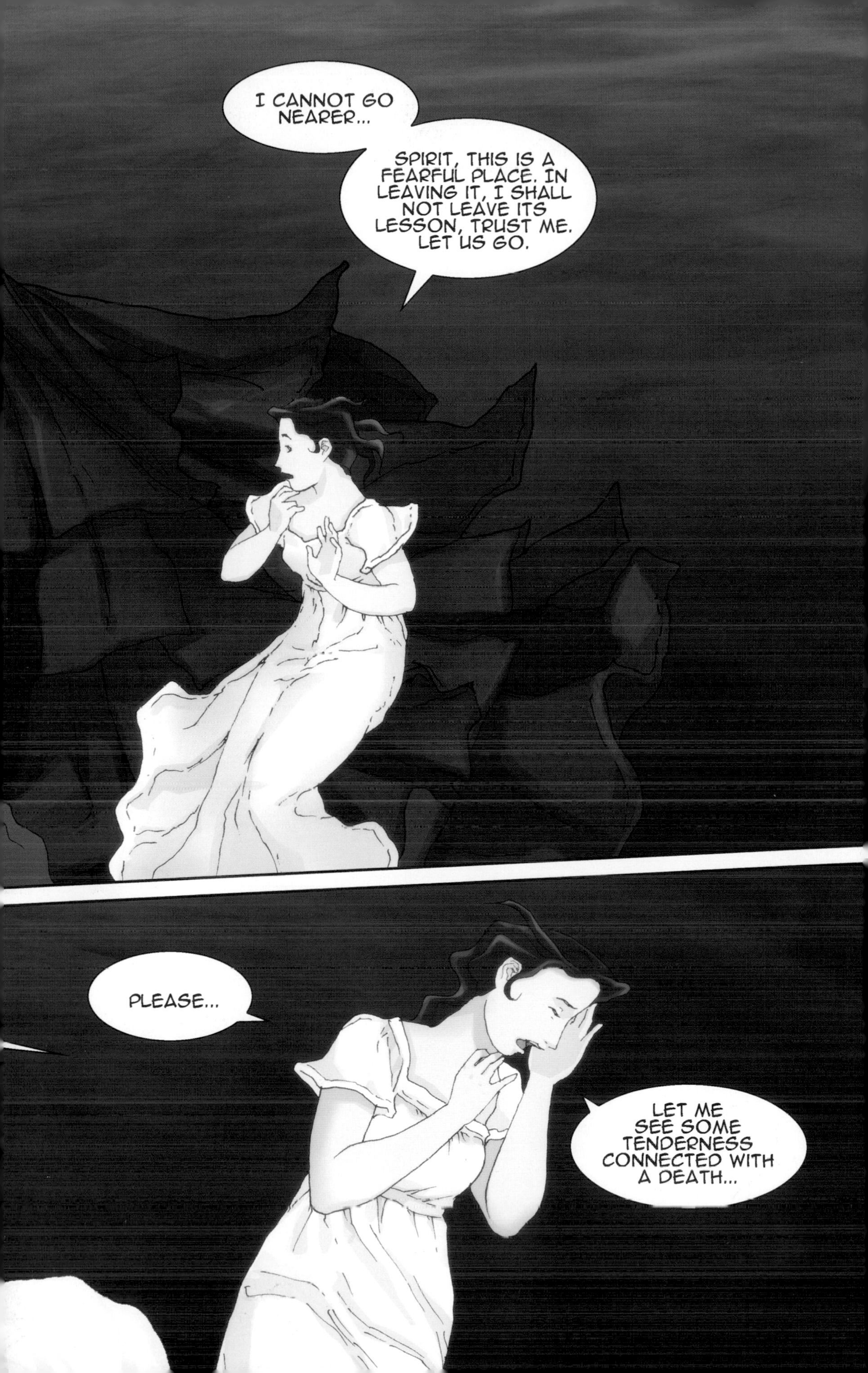
I CANNOT GO NEARER...
SPIRIT, THIS IS A FEARFUL PLACE. IN LEAVING IT, I SHALL NOT LEAVE ITS LESSON, TRUST ME. LET US GO.
PLEASE...
LET ME SEE SOME TENDERNESS CONNECTED WITH A DEATH...

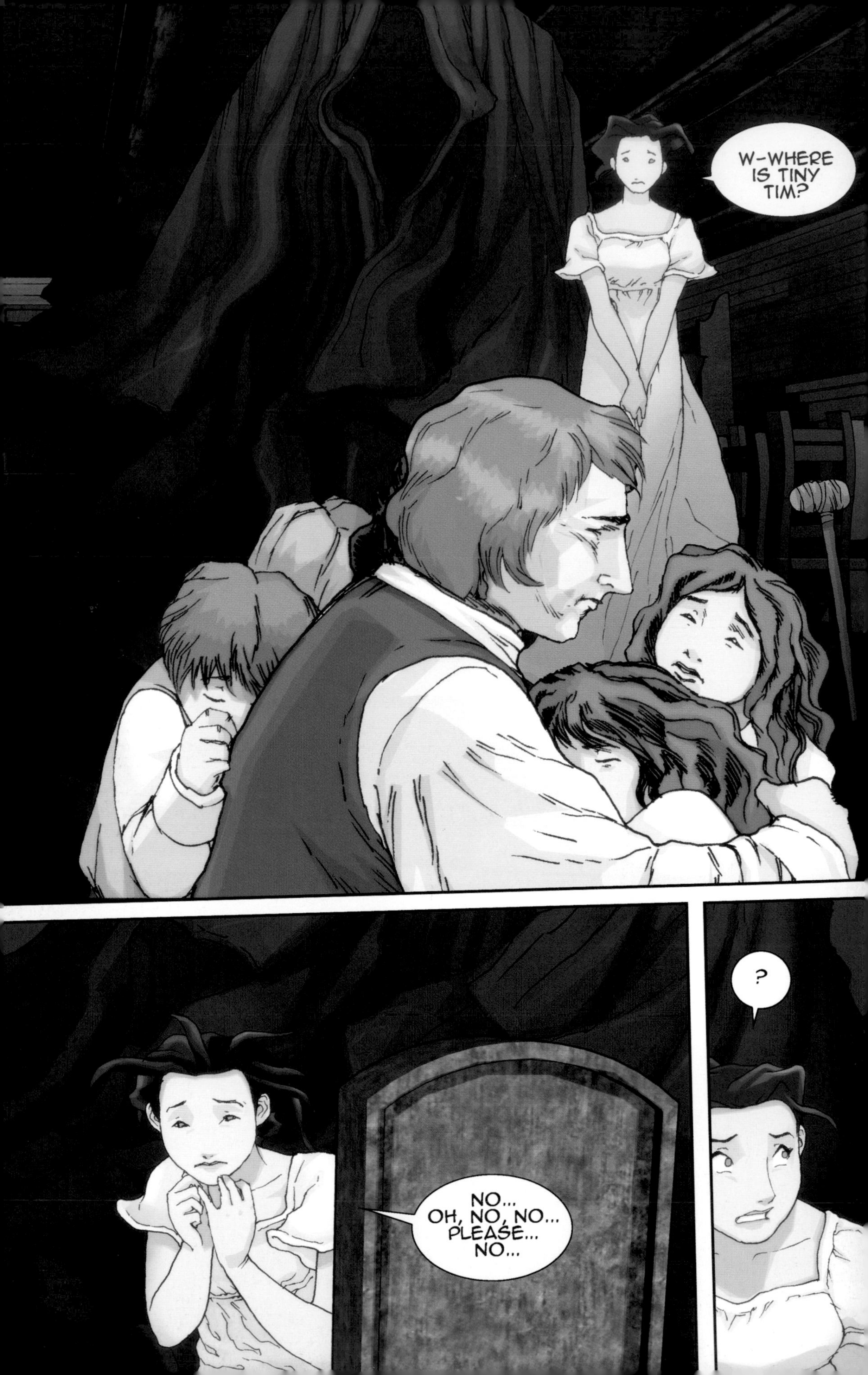
W-WHERE IS TINY TIM?
?
NO... OH, NO, NO... PLEASE... NO...

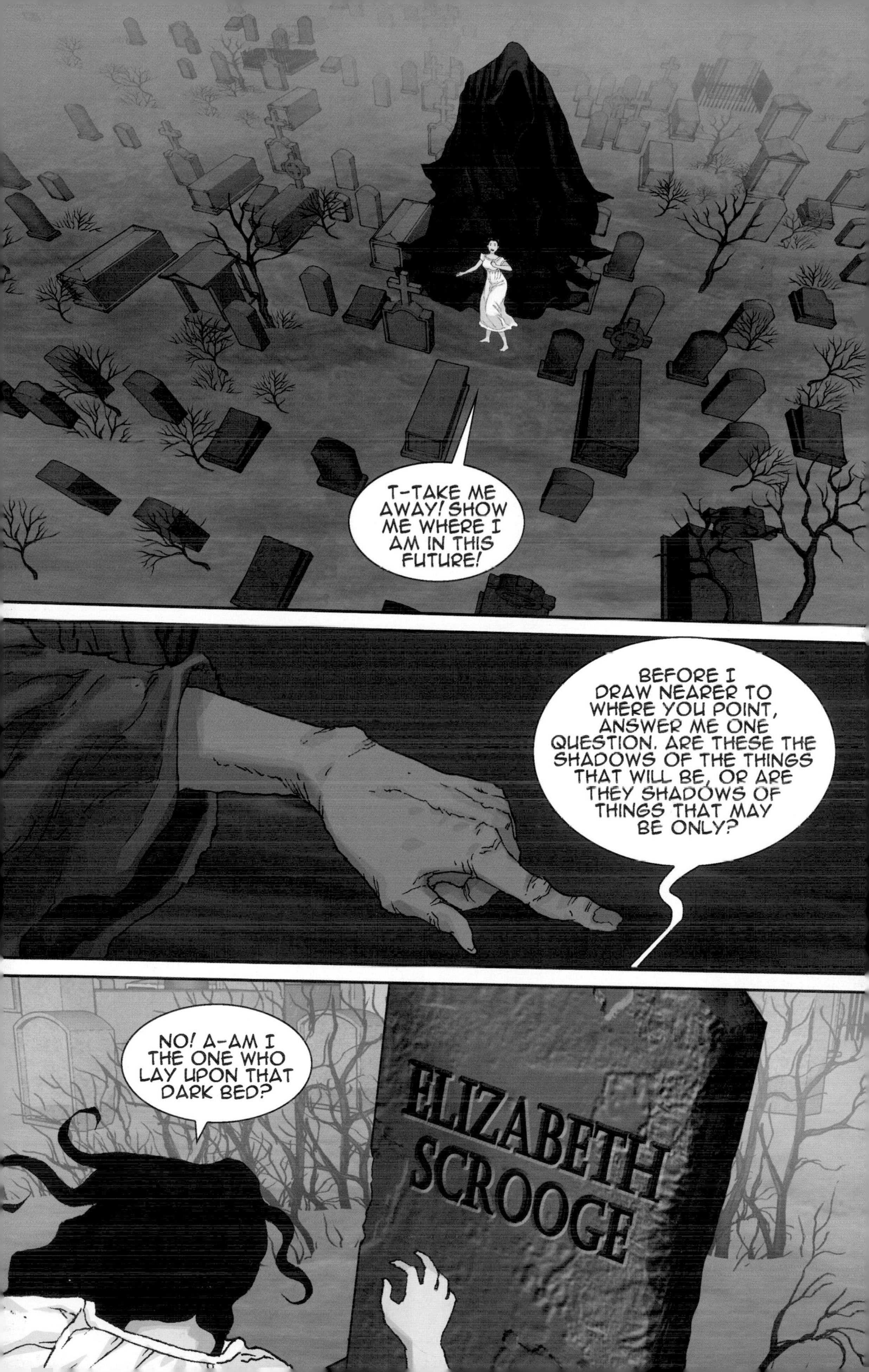
T-TAKE ME AWAY! SHOW ME WHERE I AM IN THIS FUTURE!
BEFORE I DRAW NEARER TO WHERE YOU POINT, ANSWER ME ONE QUESTION. ARE THESE THE SHADOWS OF THE THINGS THAT WILL BE, OR ARE THEY SHADOWS OF THINGS THAT MAY BE ONLY?
NO! A-AM I THE ONE WHO LAY UPON THAT DARK BED?
ELIZABETH SCROOGE

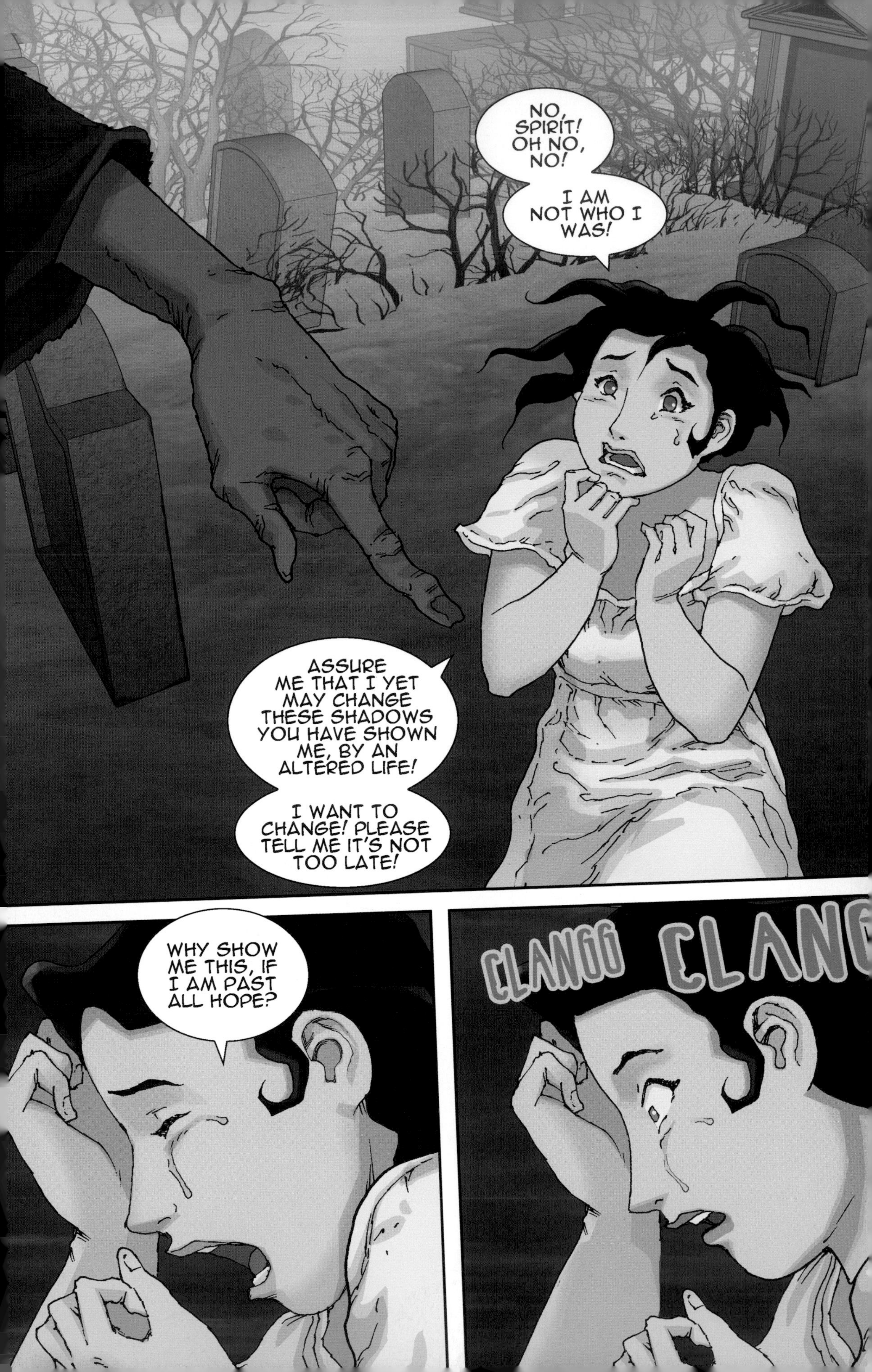
NO, SPIRIT! OH NO, NO!
I AM NOT WHO I WAS!
ASSURE ME THAT I YET MAY CHANGE THESE SHADOWS YOU HAVE SHOWN ME, BY AN ALTERED LIFE!
I WANT TO CHANGE! PLEASE TELL ME IT'S NOT TOO LATE!
WHY SHOW ME THIS, IF I AM PAST ALL HOPE?
CLANGG CLANG

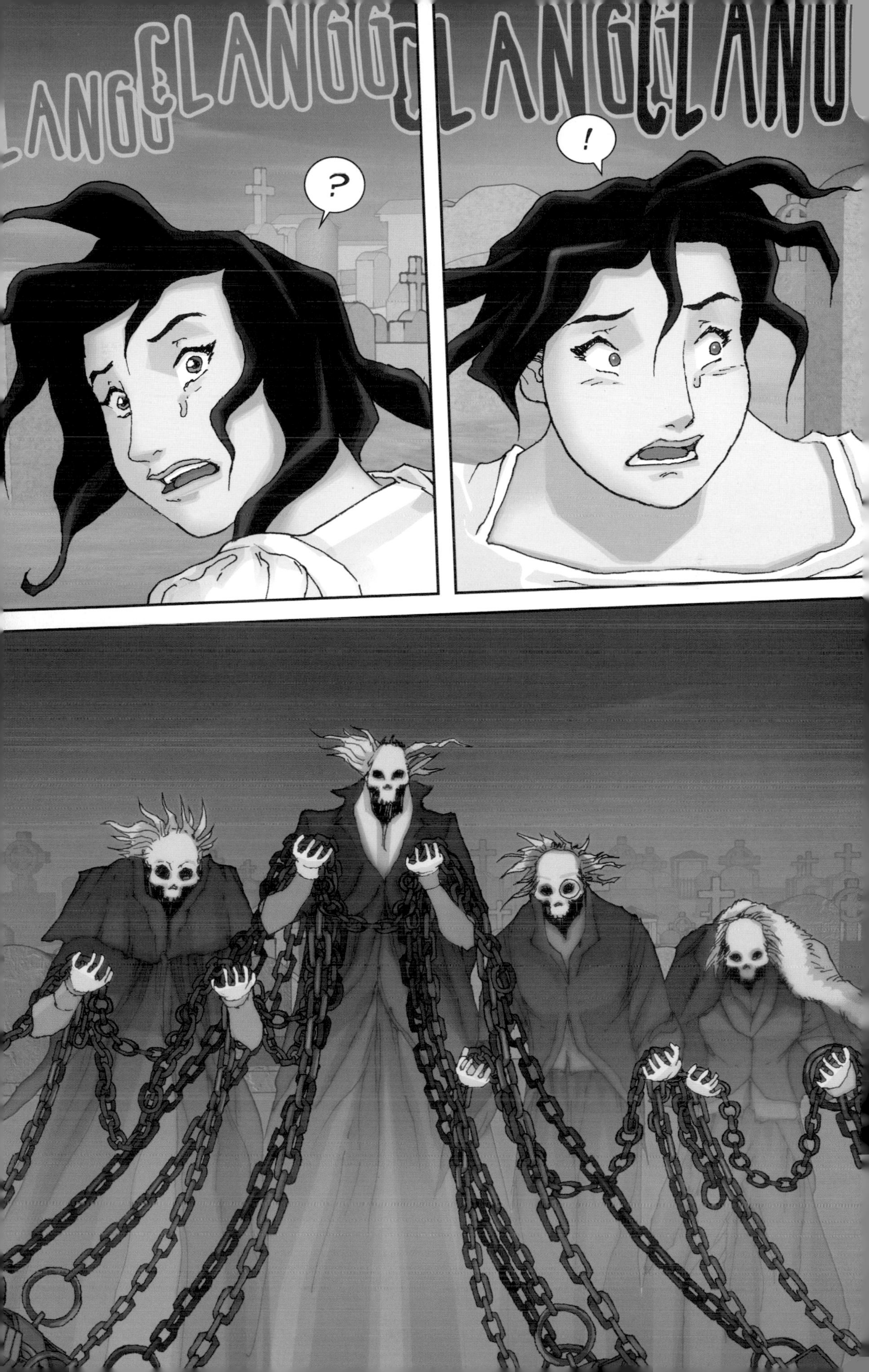

CLANG CLANG CLANG
?
!

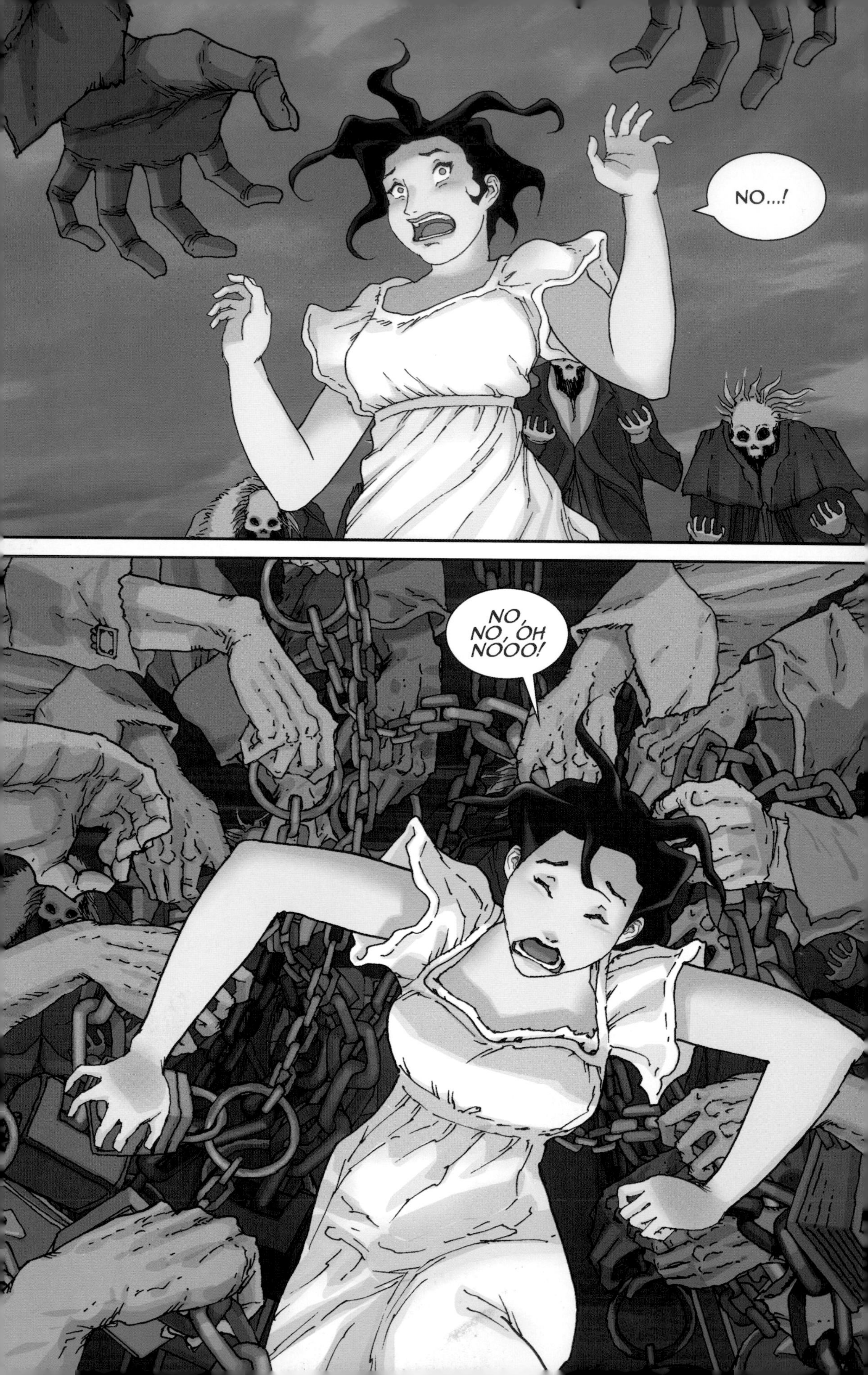
NO...!
NO, NO, OH NOOO!

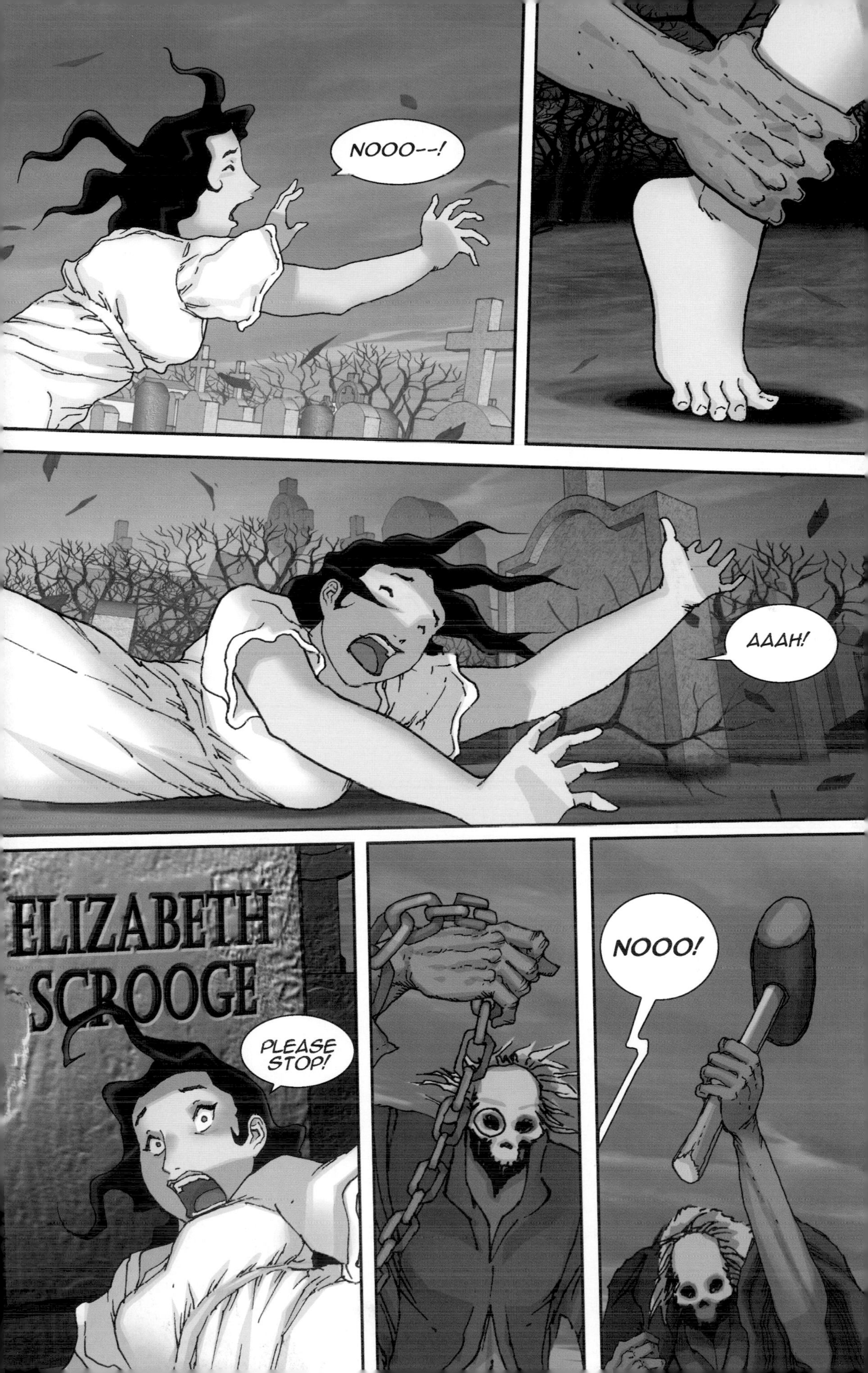
NOOO--!
AAAH!
ELIZABETH SCROOGE
PLEASE STOP!
NOOO!

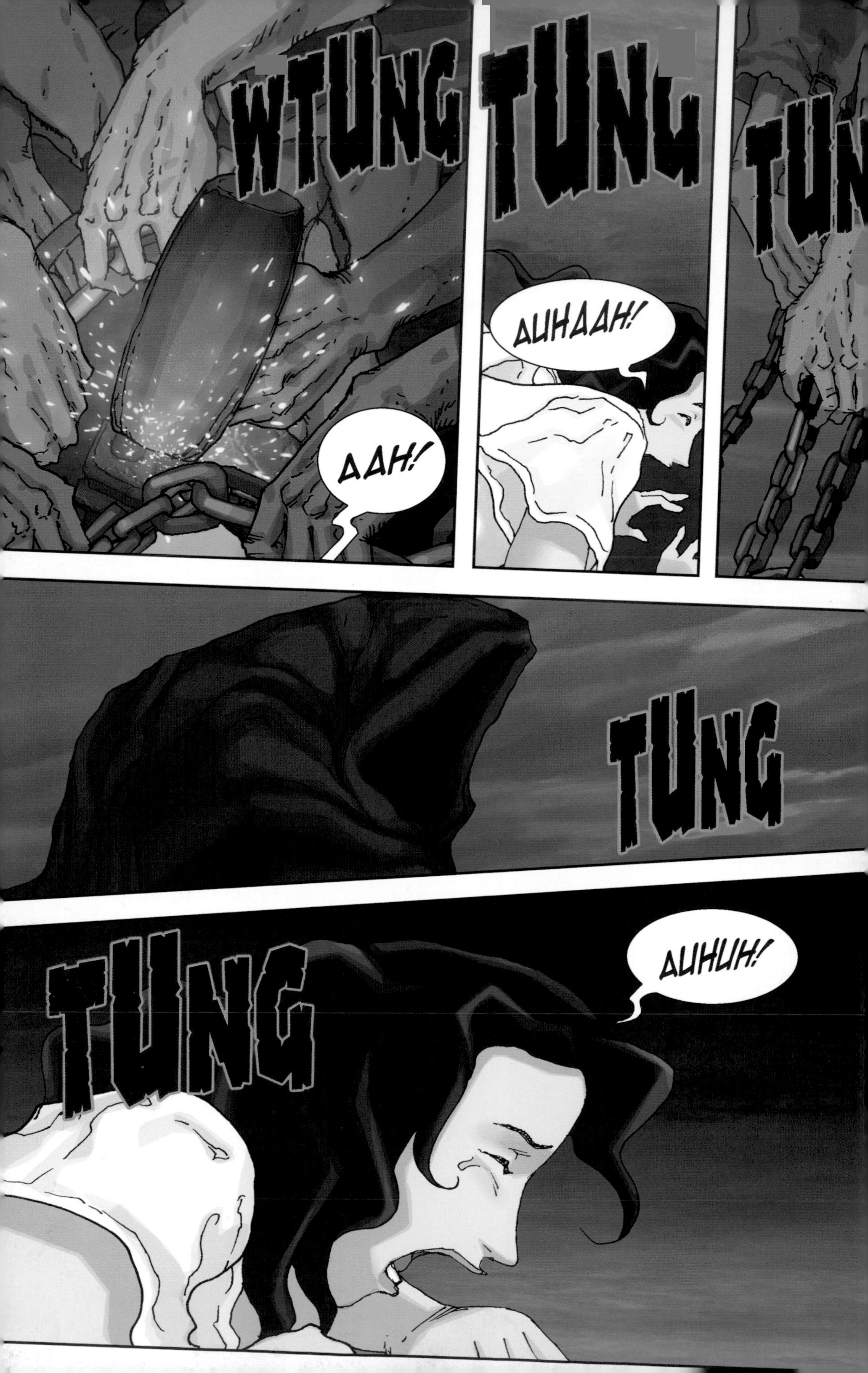
WTUNG
TUNG
AUHAAH!
AAH!
TUN
TUNG
TUNG
AUHUH!

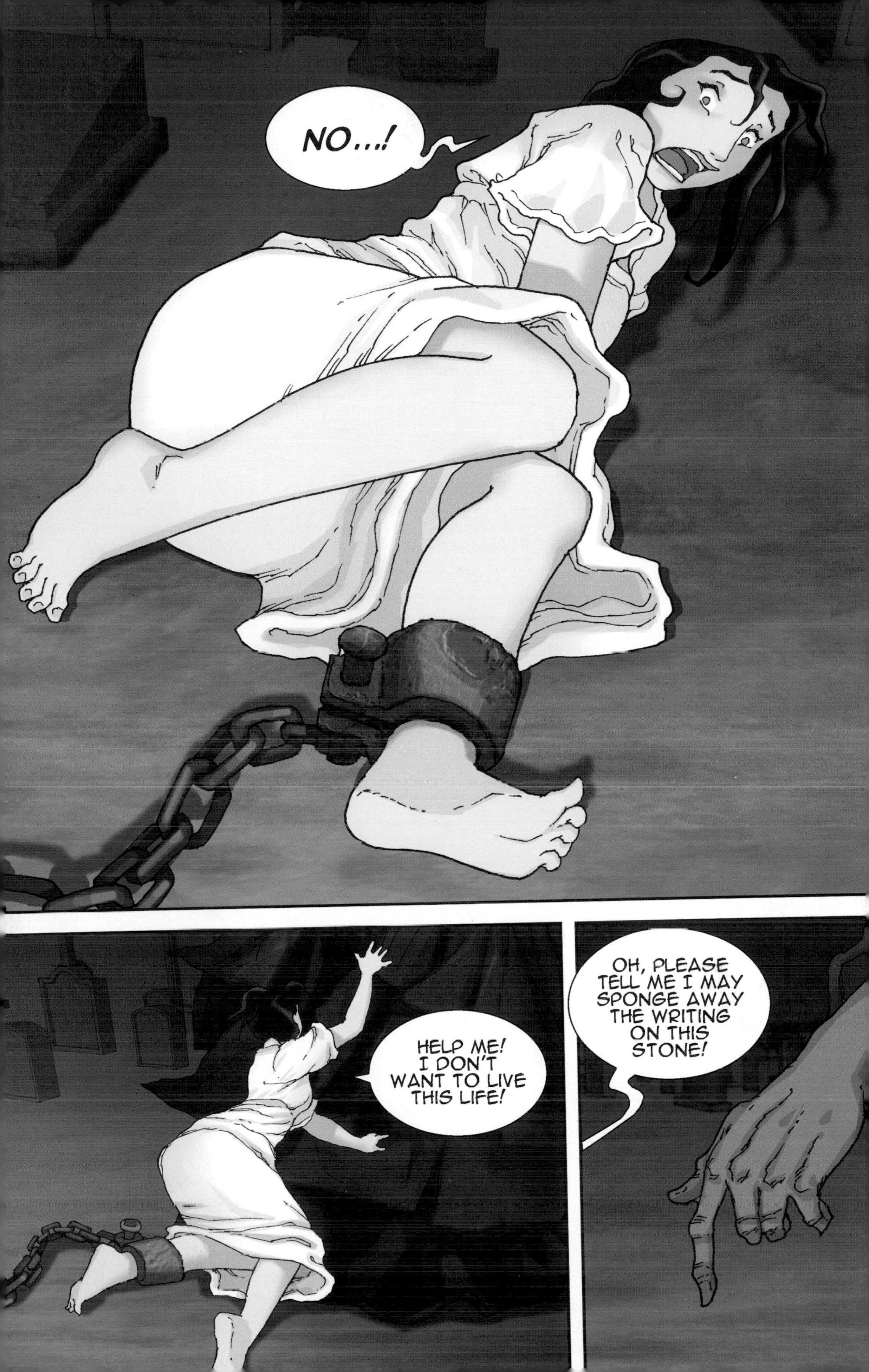
NO...!
HELP ME! I DON'T WANT TO LIVE THIS LIFE!
OH, PLEASE TELL ME I MAY SPONGE AWAY THE WRITING ON THIS STONE!

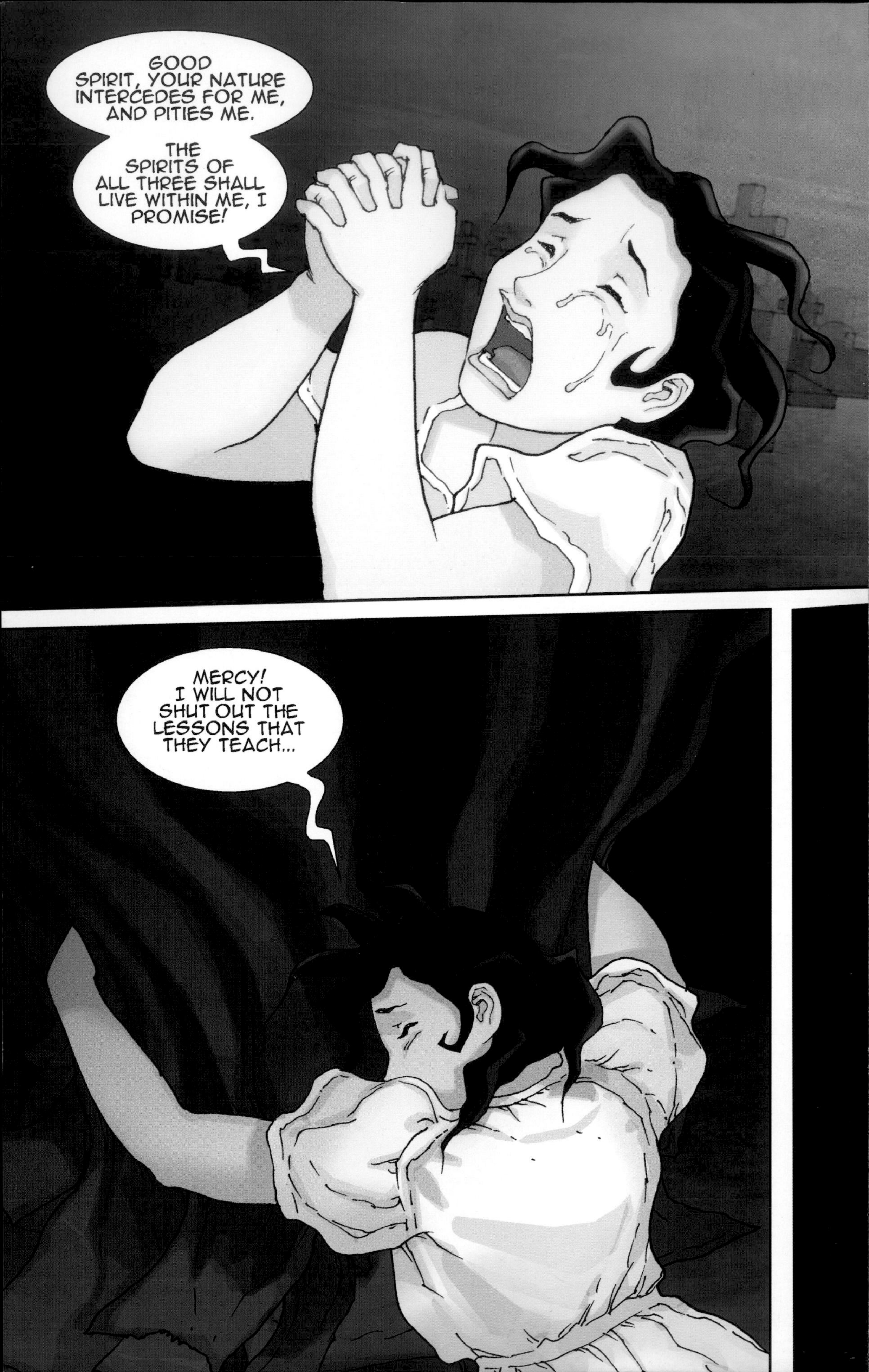
GOOD SPIRIT, YOUR NATURE INTERCEDES FOR ME, AND PITIES ME.
THE SPIRITS OF ALL THREE SHALL LIVE WITHIN ME, I PROMISE!
MERCY! I WILL NOT SHUT OUT THE LESSONS THAT THEY TEACH...

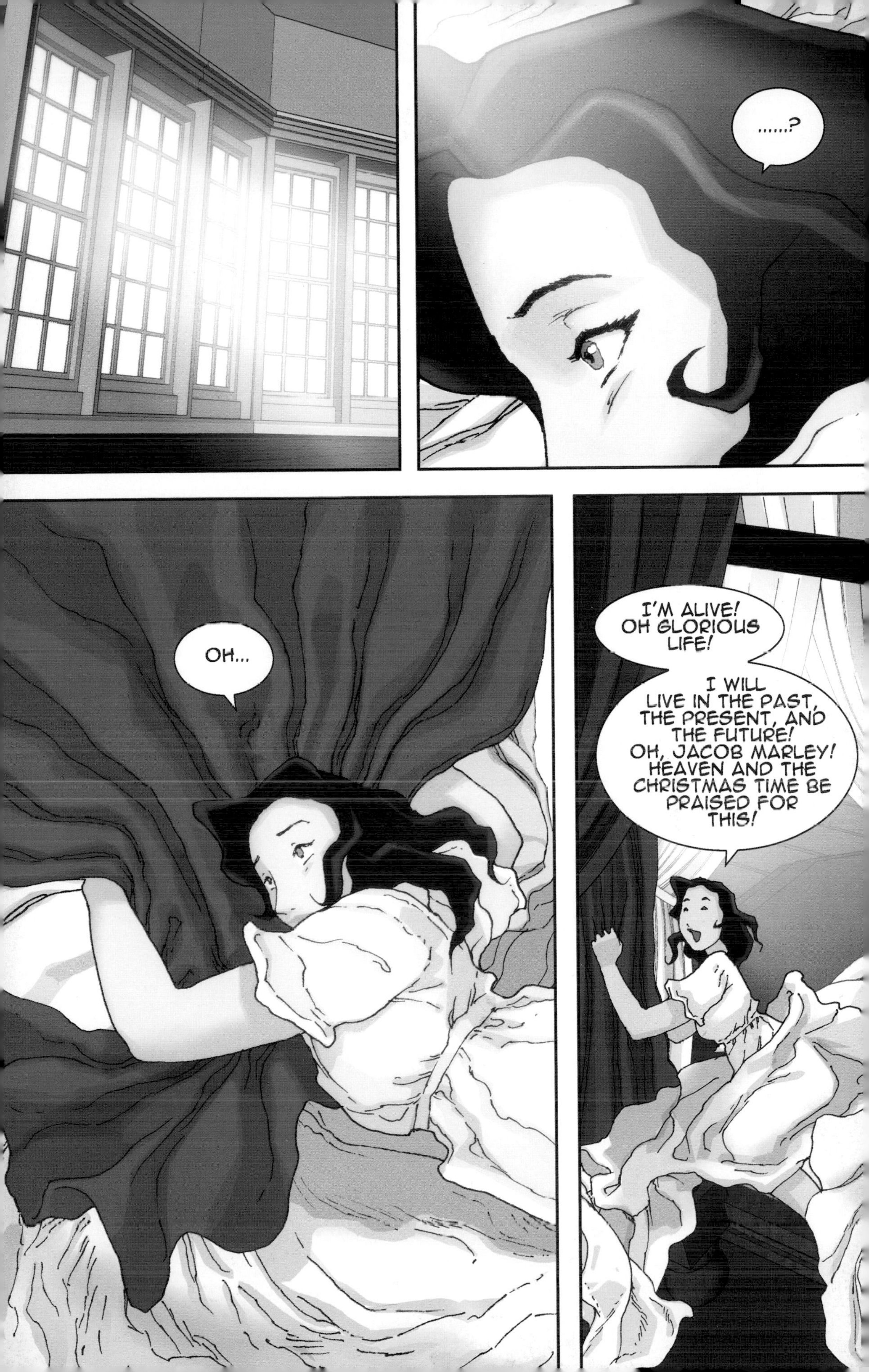
......?
OH...
I'M ALIVE! OH GLORIOUS LIFE!
I WILL LIVE IN THE PAST, THE PRESENT, AND THE FUTURE! OH, JACOB MARLEY! HEAVEN AND THE CHRISTMAS TIME BE PRAISED FOR THIS!

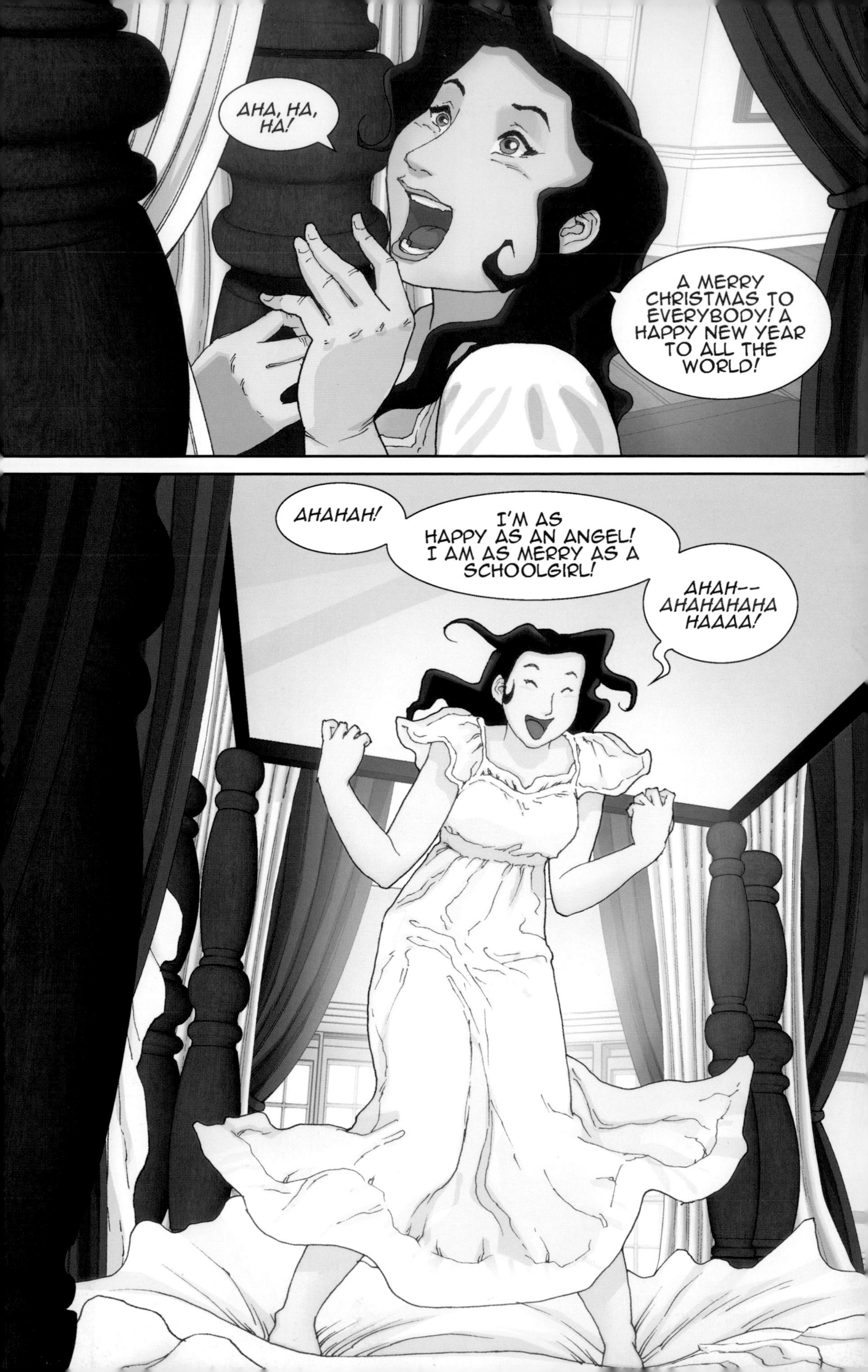
AHA, HA, HA!
A MERRY CHRISTMAS TO EVERYBODY! A HAPPY NEW YEAR TO ALL THE WORLD!
AHAHAH!
I'M AS HAPPY AS AN ANGEL! I AM AS MERRY AS A SCHOOLGIRL!
AHAH-- AHAHAHAHA HAAAA!

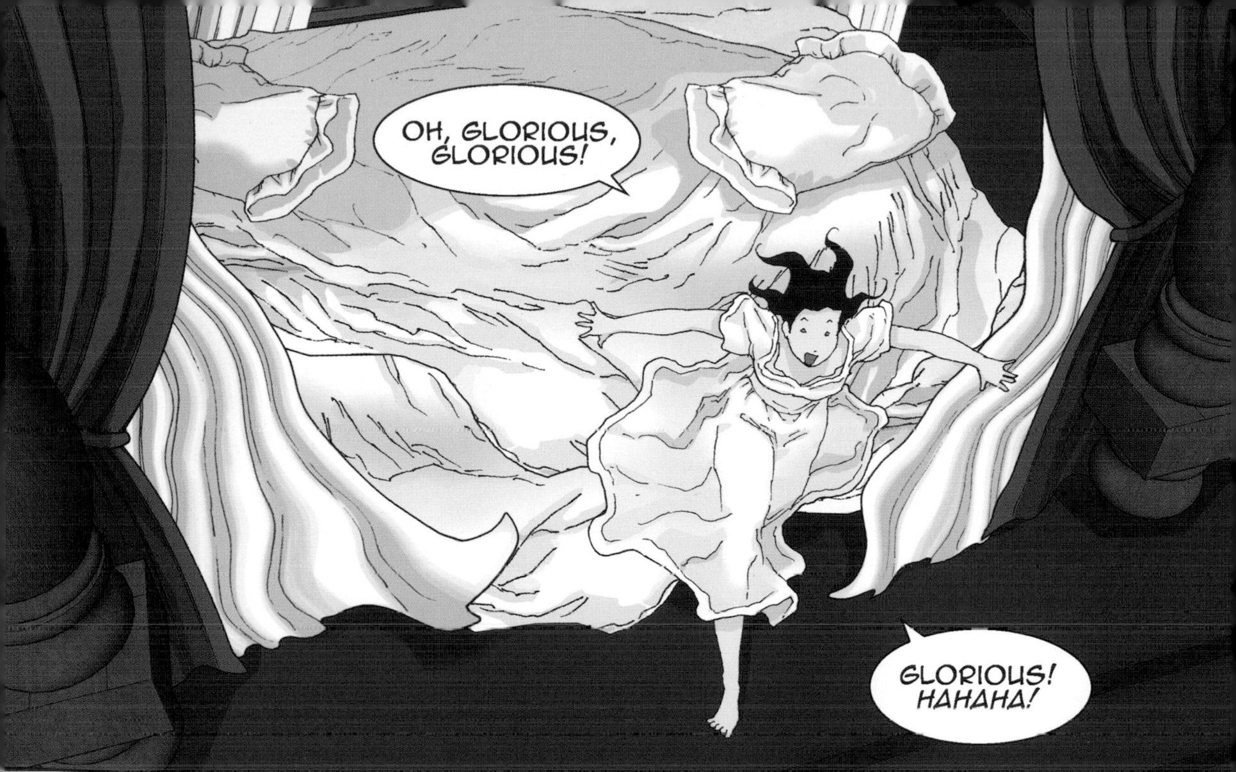
OH, GLORIOUS, GLORIOUS!
GLORIOUS! HAHAHA!
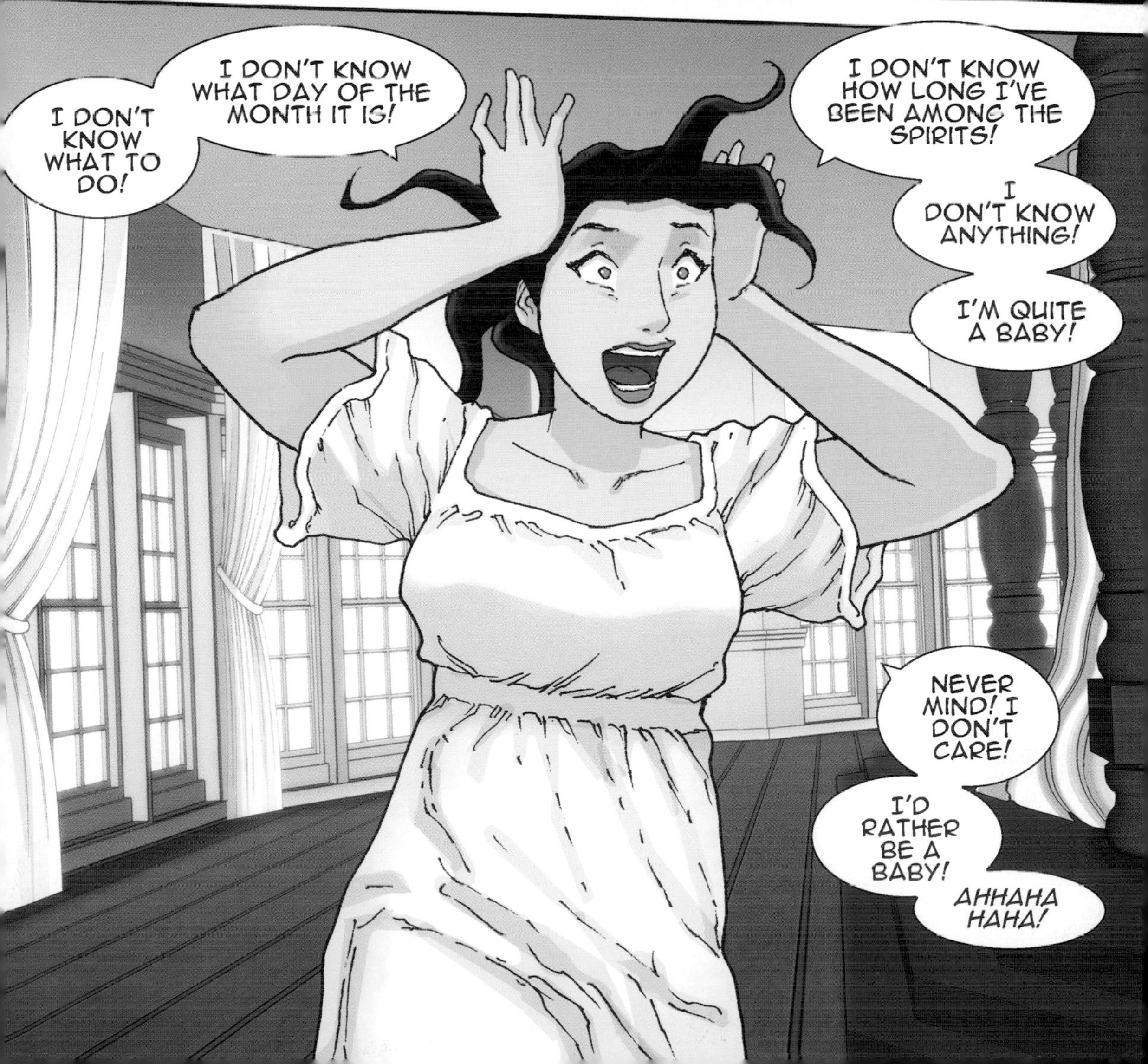
I DON'T KNOW WHAT TO DO!
I DON'T KNOW WHAT DAY OF THE MONTH IT IS!
I DON'T KNOW HOW LONG I'VE BEEN AMONG THE SPIRITS!
I DON'T KNOW ANYTHING!
I'M QUITE A BABY!
NEVER MIND! I DON'T CARE!
I'D RATHER BE A BABY!
AHHAHA HAHA!

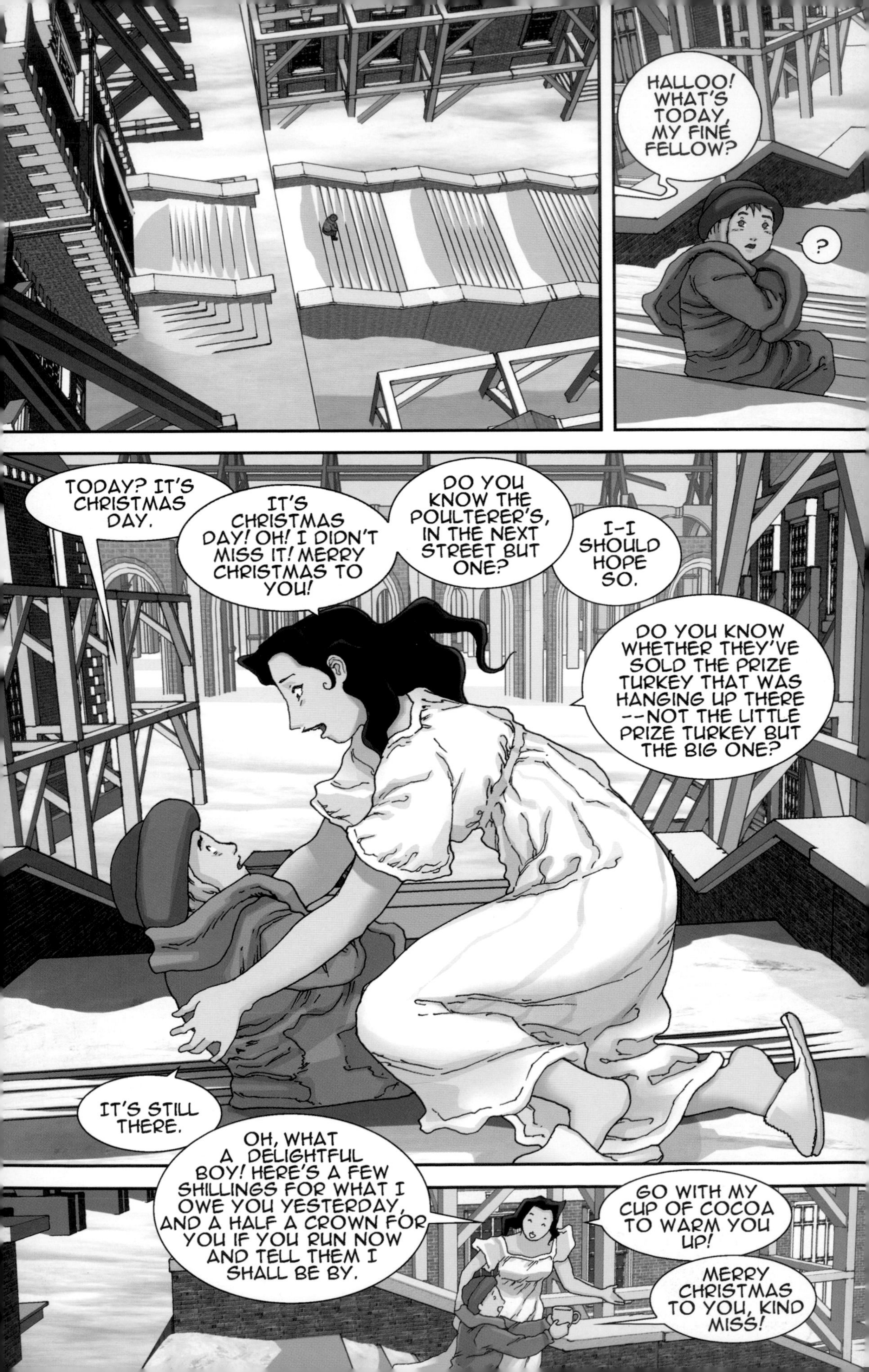
HALLOO! WHAT'S TODAY, MY FINE FELLOW?
?
TODAY? IT'S CHRISTMAS DAY.
IT'S CHRISTMAS DAY! OH! I DIDN'T MISS IT! MERRY CHRISTMAS TO YOU!
DO YOU KNOW THE POULTERER'S, IN THE NEXT STREET BUT ONE?
I-I SHOULD HOPE SO.
DO YOU KNOW WHETHER THEY'VE SOLD THE PRIZE TURKEY THAT WAS HANGING UP THERE --NOT THE LITTLE PRIZE TURKEY BUT THE BIG ONE?
IT'S STILL THERE.
OH, WHAT A DELIGHTFUL BOY! HERE'S A FEW SHILLINGS FOR WHAT I OWE YOU YESTERDAY, AND A HALF A CROWN FOR YOU IF YOU RUN NOW AND TELL THEM I SHALL BE BY.
GO WITH MY CUP OF COCOA TO WARM YOU UP!
MERRY CHRISTMAS TO YOU, KIND MISS!

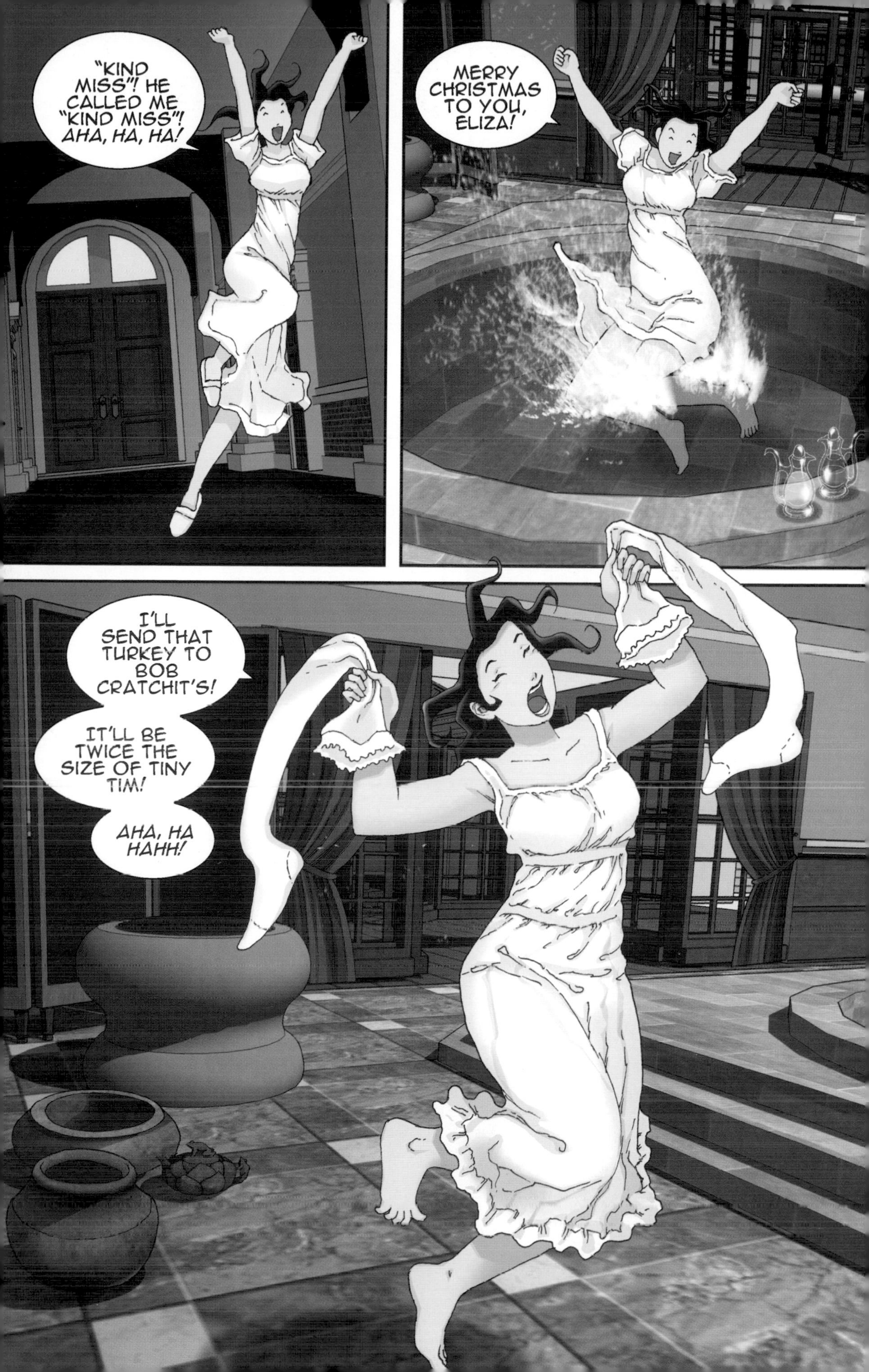
"KIND MISS"! HE CALLED ME "KIND MISS"! AHA, HA, HA!
MERRY CHRISTMAS TO YOU, ELIZA!
I'LL SEND THAT TURKEY TO BOB CRATCHIT'S!
IT'LL BE TWICE THE SIZE OF TINY TIM!
AHA, HA HAHH!

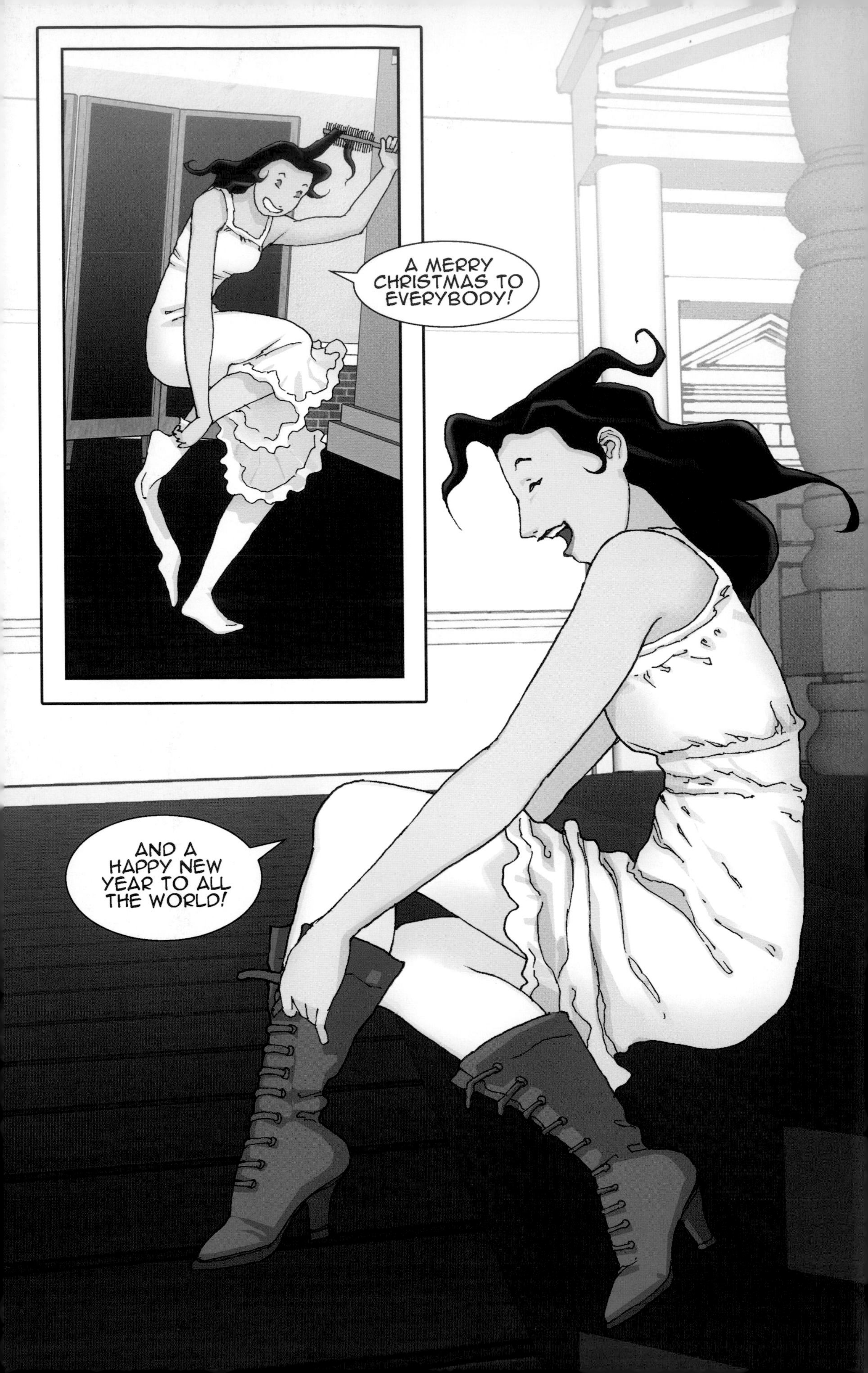
A MERRY CHRISTMAS TO EVERYBODY!
AND A HAPPY NEW YEAR TO ALL THE WORLD!

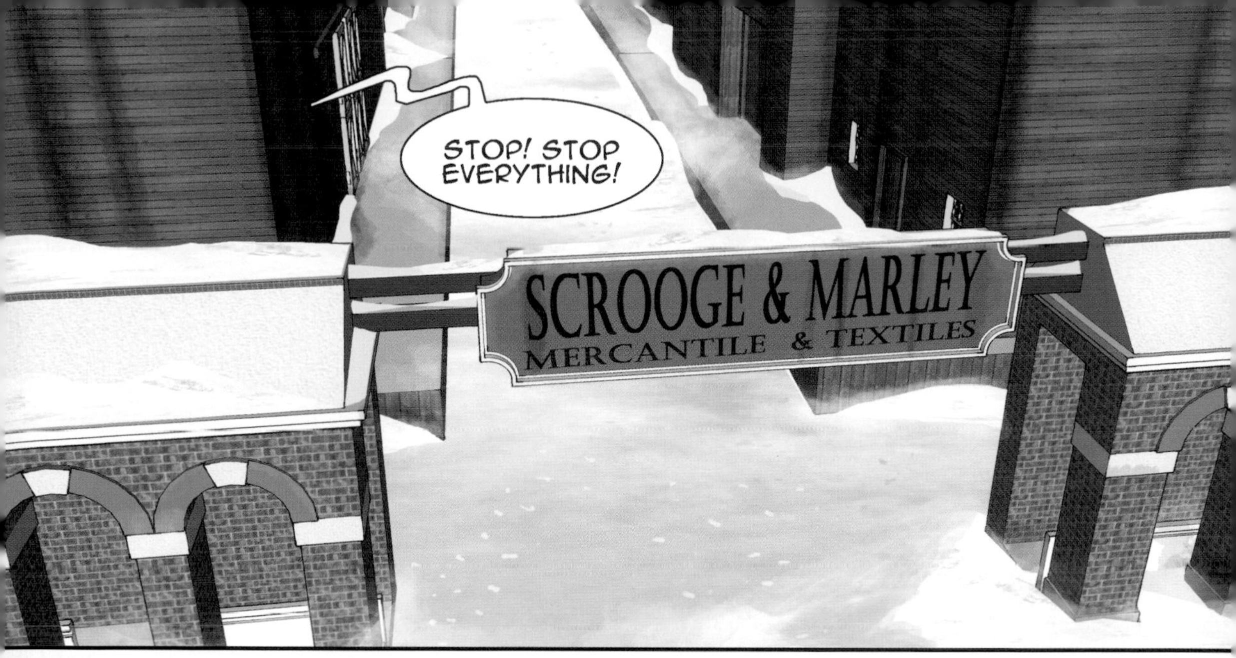
STOP! STOP EVERYTHING!
SCROOGE & MARLEY
MERCANTILE & TEXTILES
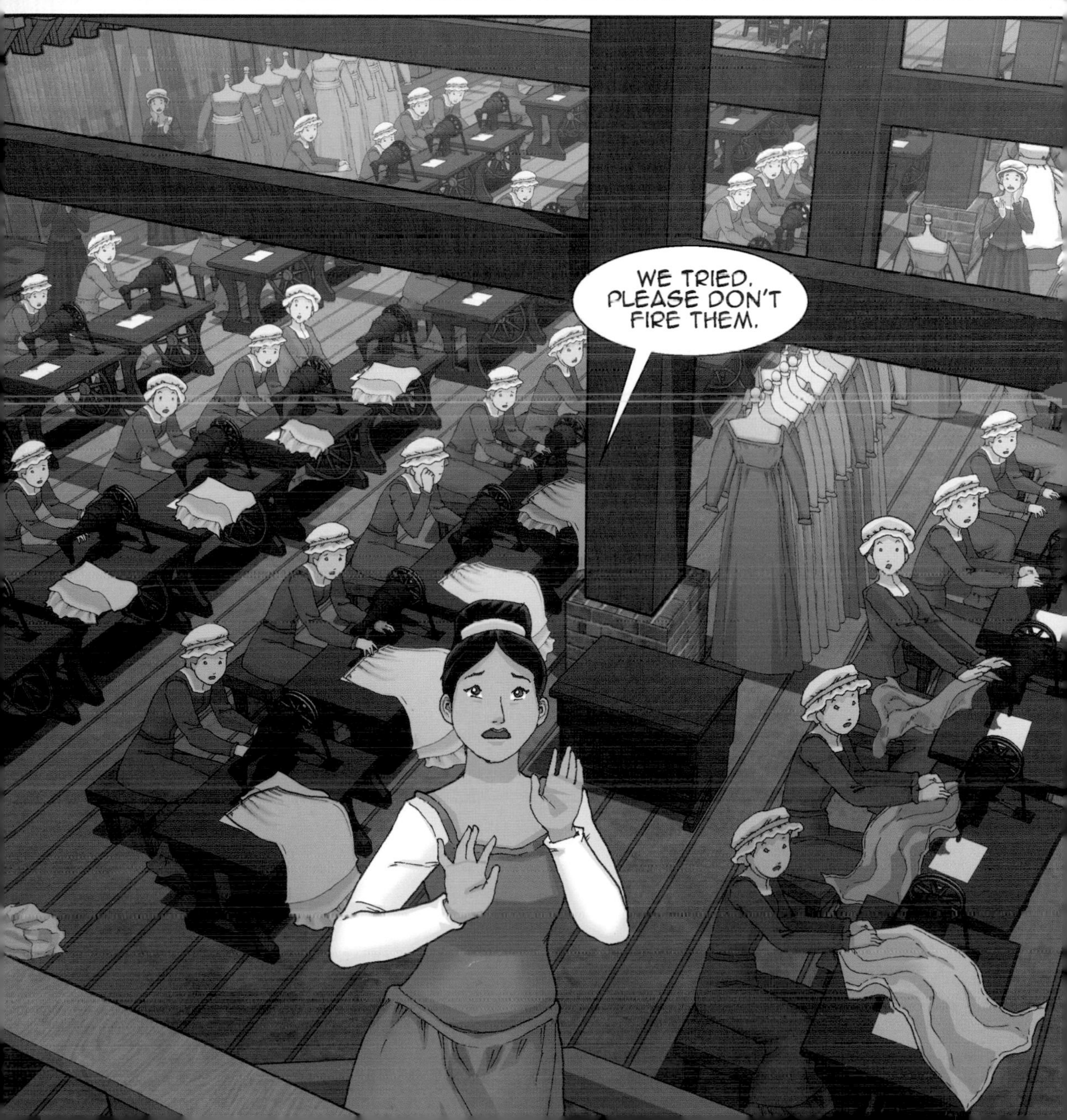
WE TRIED. PLEASE DON'T FIRE THEM.

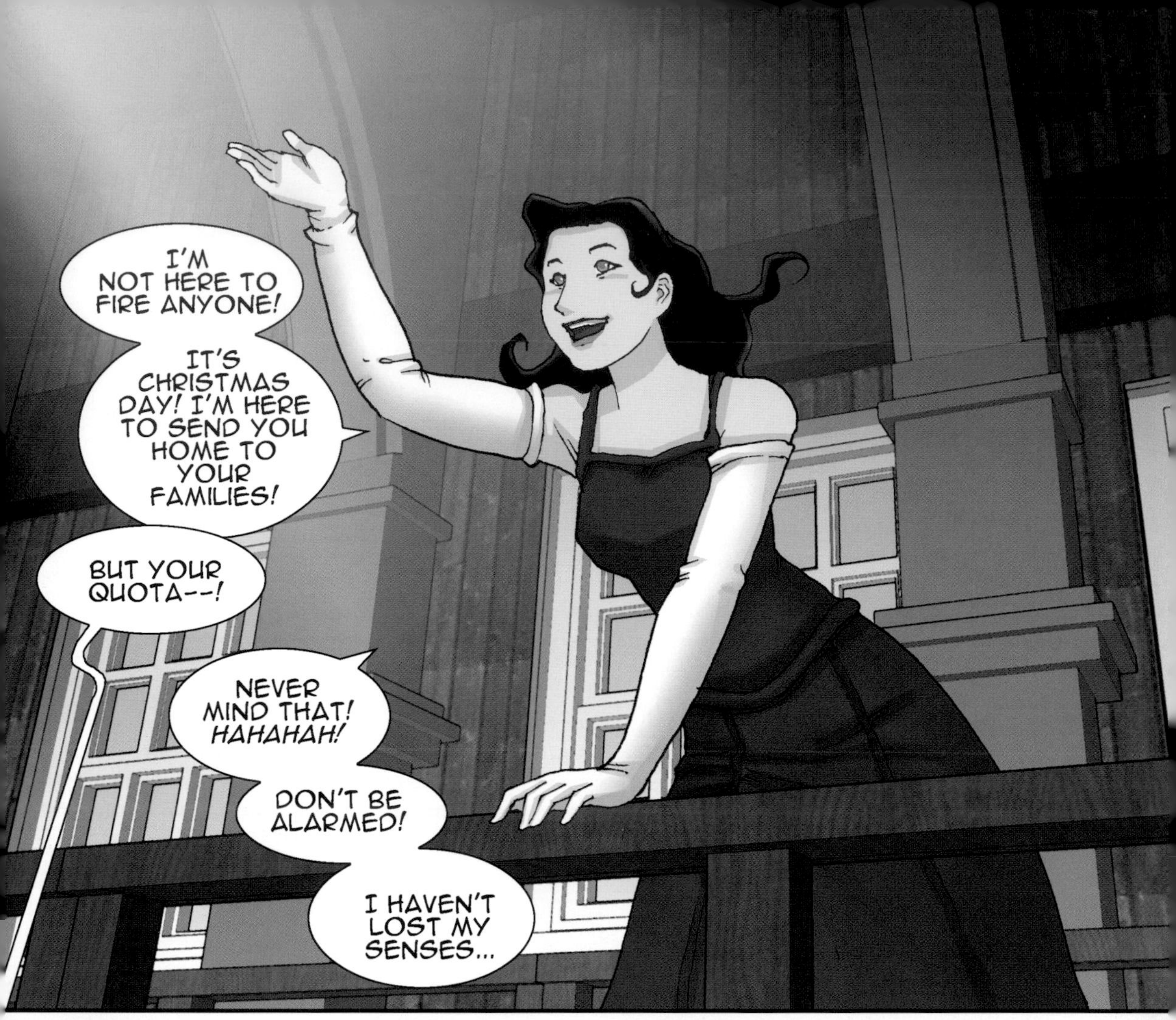
I'M NOT HERE TO FIRE ANYONE!
IT'S CHRISTMAS DAY! I'M HERE TO SEND YOU HOME TO YOUR FAMILIES!
BUT YOUR QUOTA--!
NEVER MIND THAT! *HAHAHAH!*
DON'T BE ALARMED!
I HAVEN'T LOST MY SENSES...

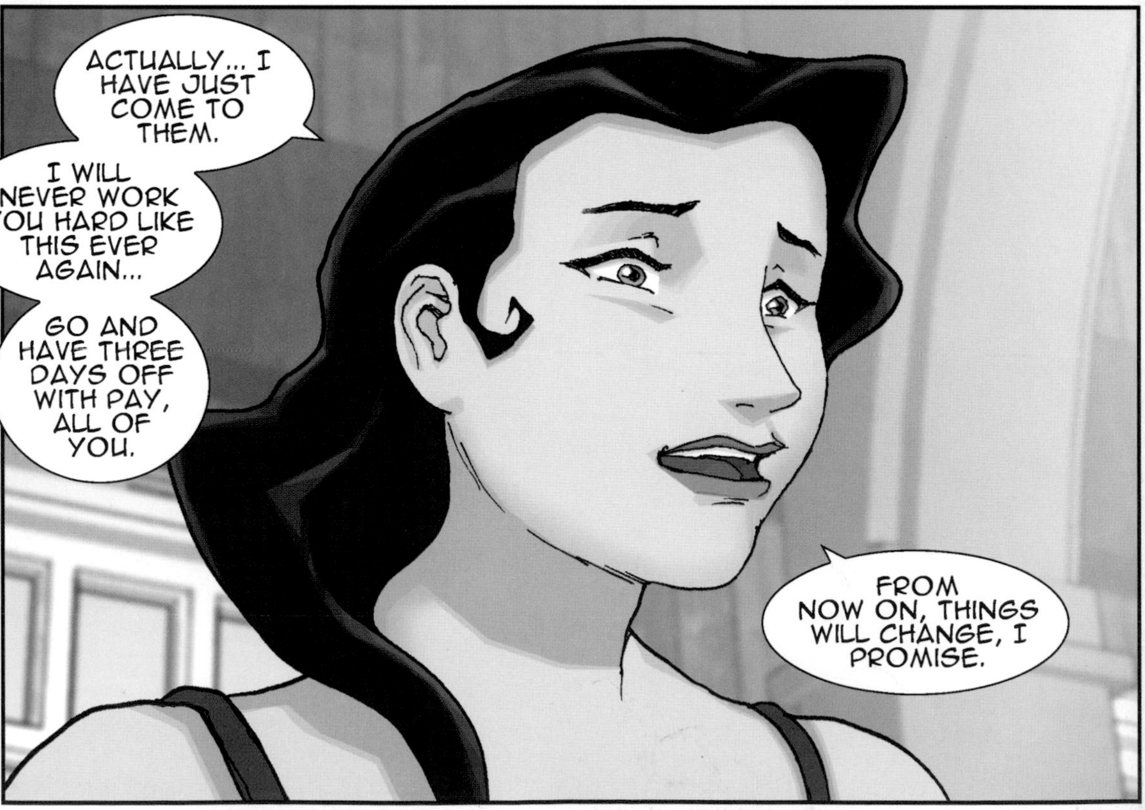
ACTUALLY... I HAVE JUST COME TO THEM.
I WILL NEVER WORK YOU HARD LIKE THIS EVER AGAIN...
GO AND HAVE THREE DAYS OFF WITH PAY, ALL OF YOU.
FROM NOW ON, THINGS WILL CHANGE, I PROMISE.

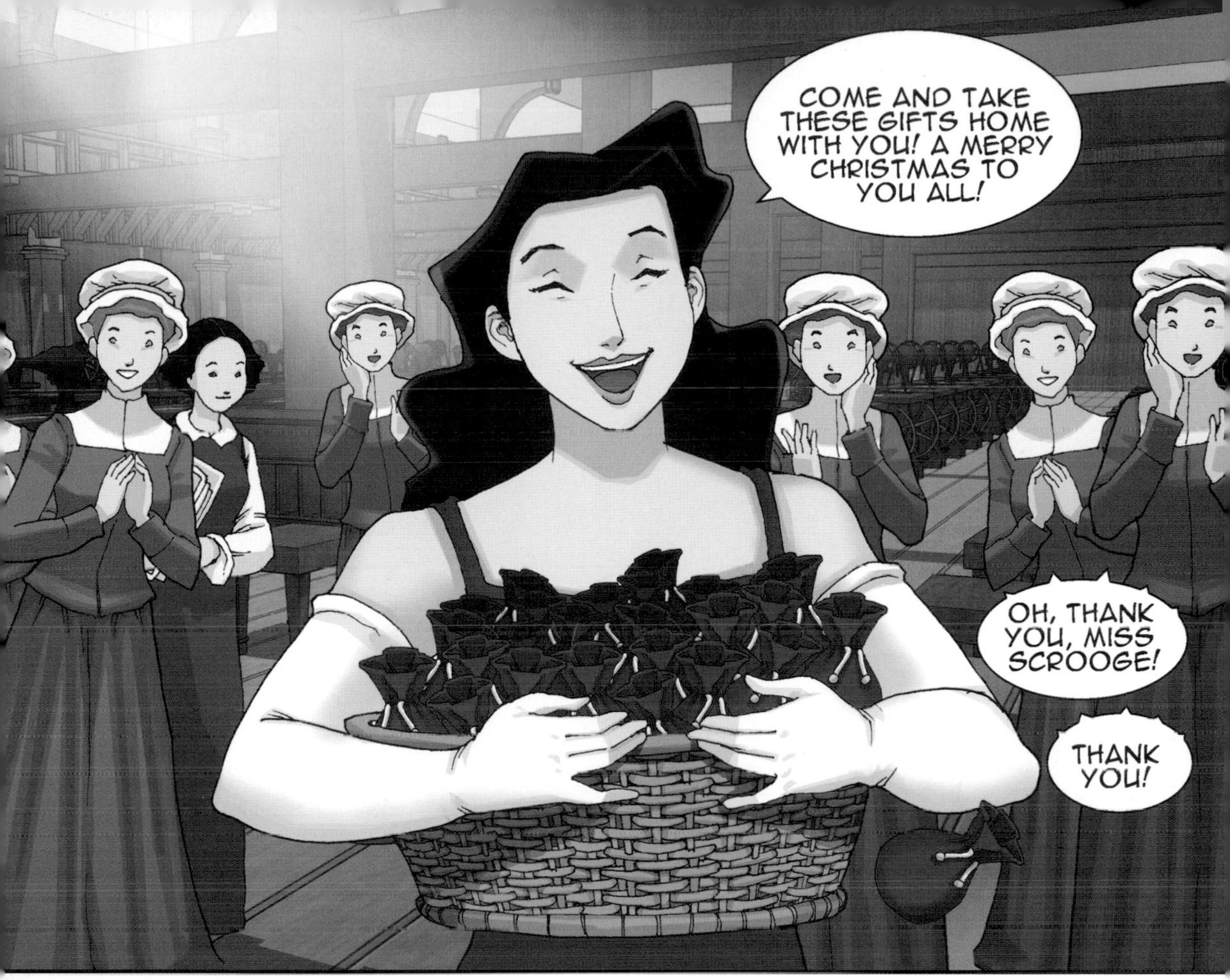
COME AND TAKE THESE GIFTS HOME WITH YOU! A MERRY CHRISTMAS TO YOU ALL!
OH, THANK YOU, MISS SCROOGE!
THANK YOU!

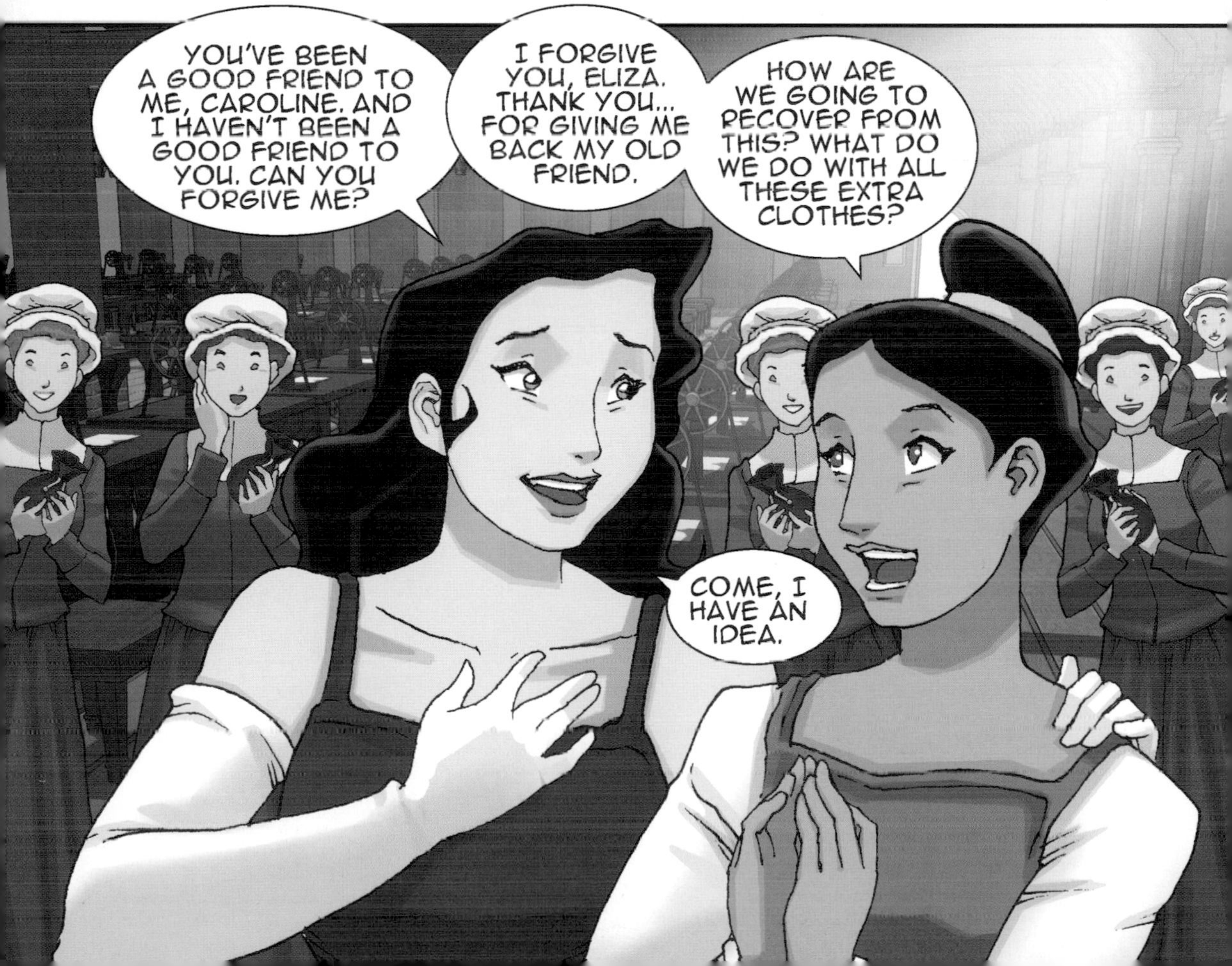
YOU'VE BEEN A GOOD FRIEND TO ME, CAROLINE. AND I HAVEN'T BEEN A GOOD FRIEND TO YOU. CAN YOU FORGIVE ME?
I FORGIVE YOU, ELIZA. THANK YOU... FOR GIVING ME BACK MY OLD FRIEND.
HOW ARE WE GOING TO RECOVER FROM THIS? WHAT DO WE DO WITH ALL THESE EXTRA CLOTHES?
COME, I HAVE AN IDEA.

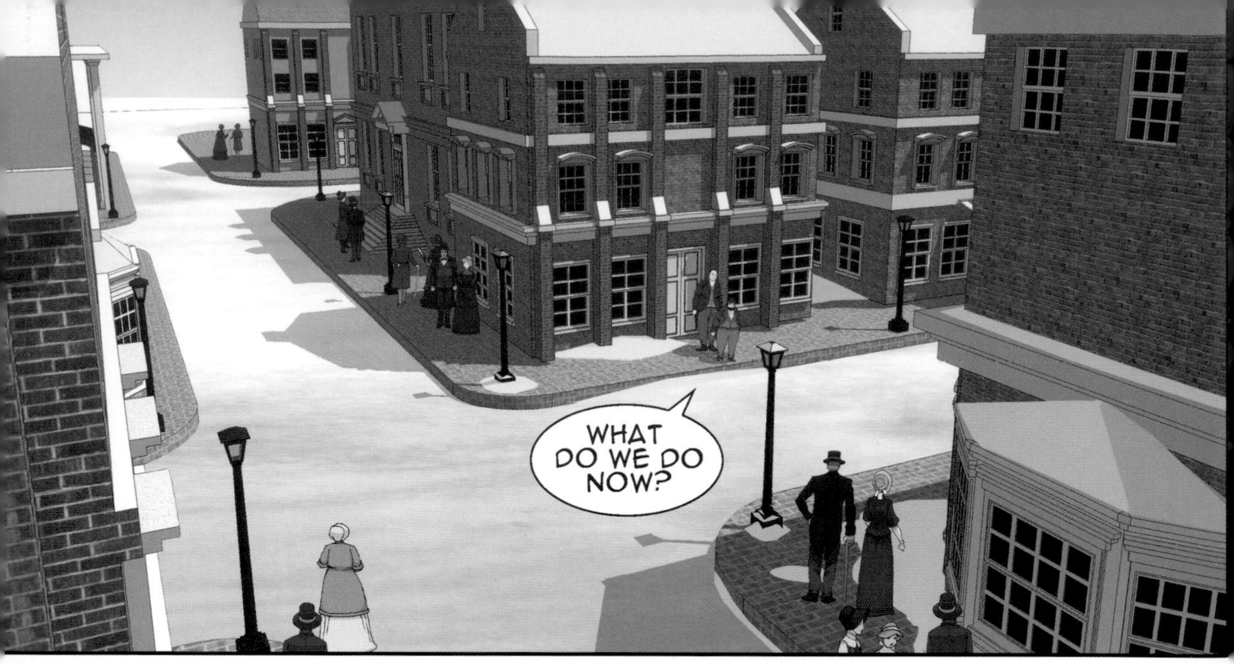
WHAT DO WE DO NOW?

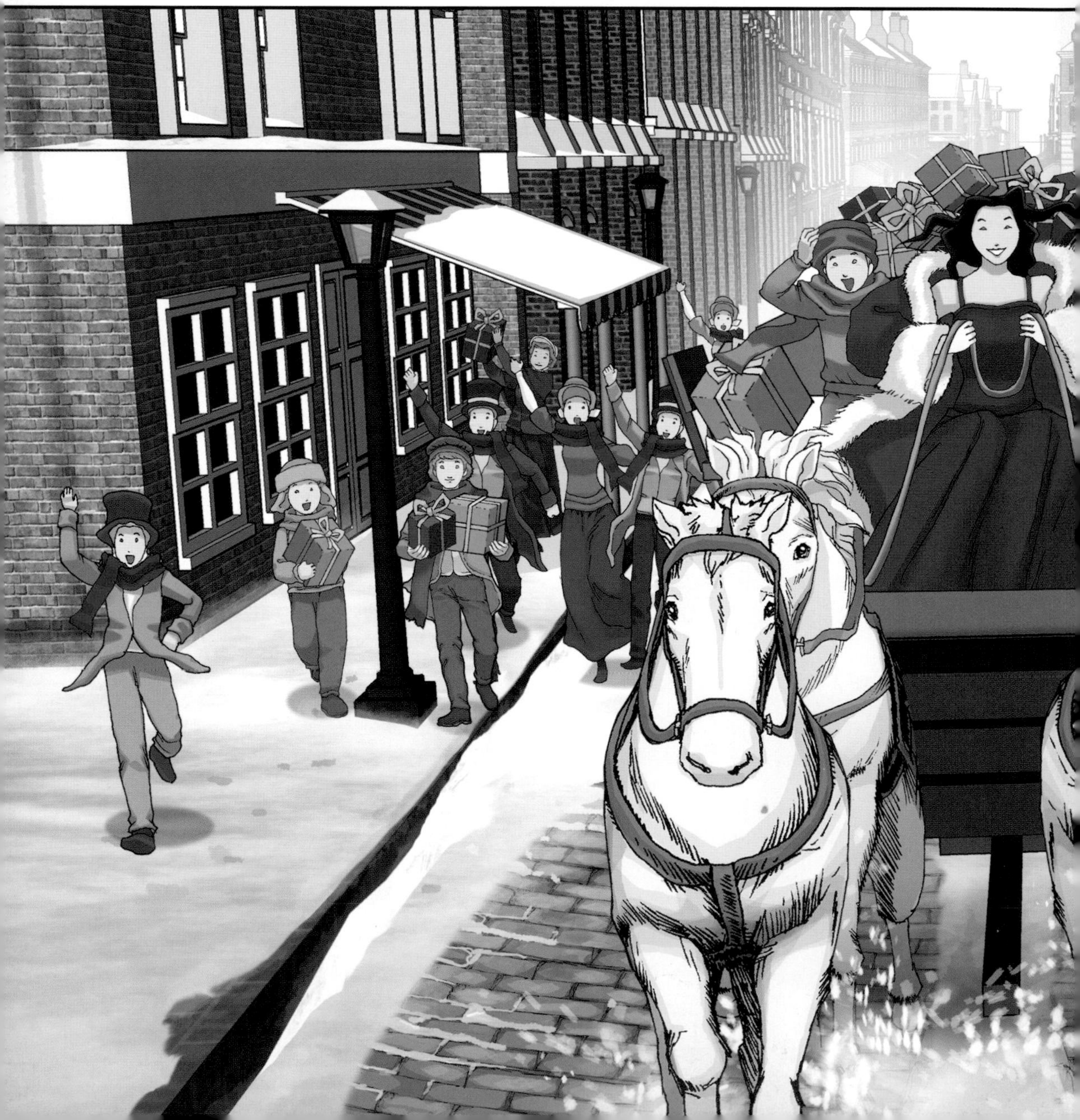

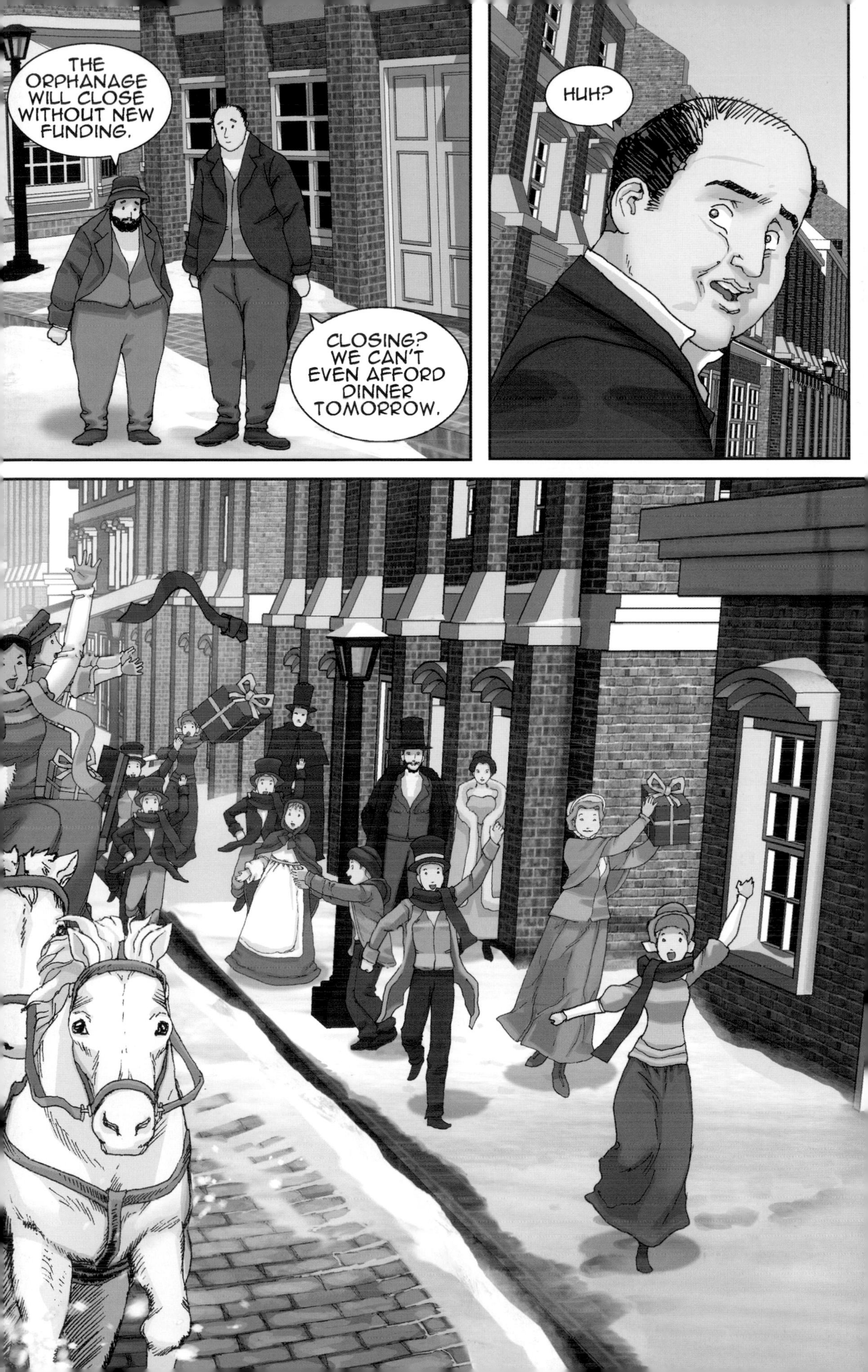
THE ORPHANAGE WILL CLOSE WITHOUT NEW FUNDING.
CLOSING? WE CAN'T EVEN AFFORD DINNER TOMORROW.
HUH?

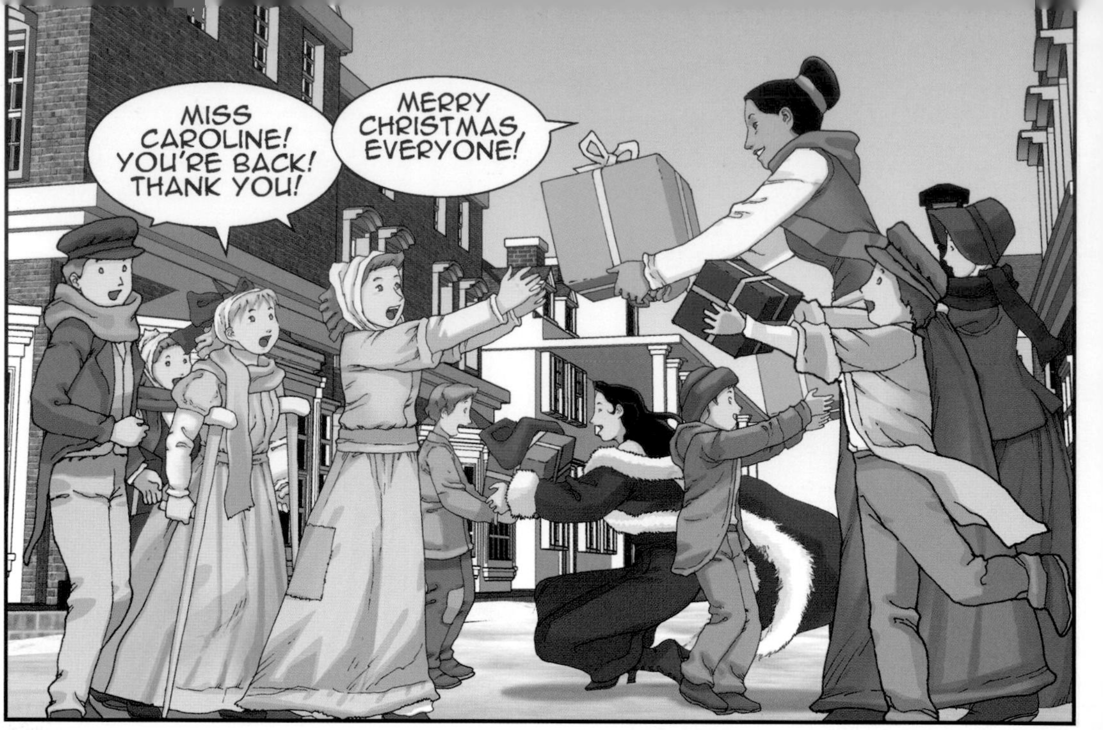
MISS CAROLINE! YOU'RE BACK! THANK YOU!
MERRY CHRISTMAS, EVERYONE!

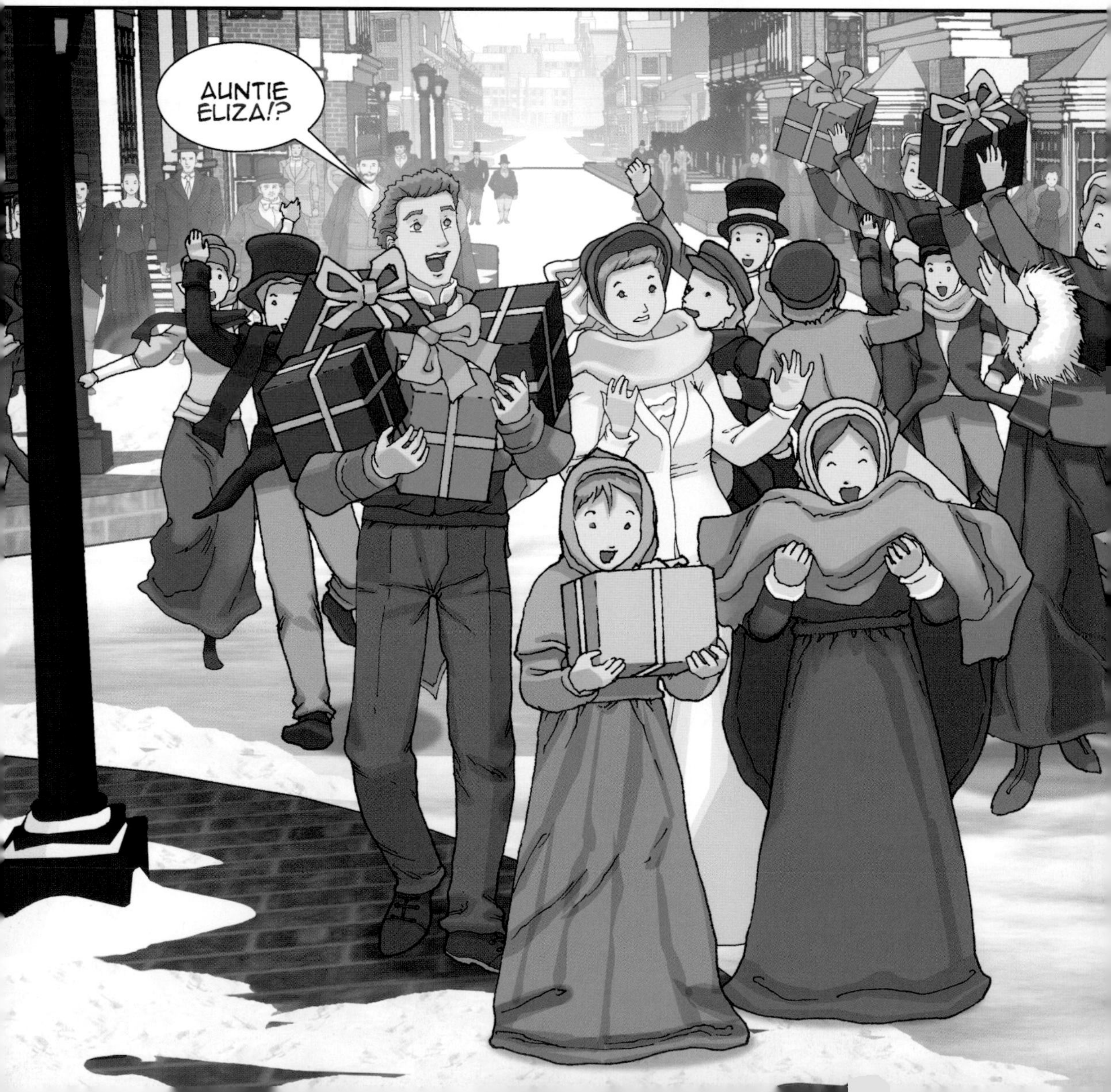
AUNTIE ELIZA!?

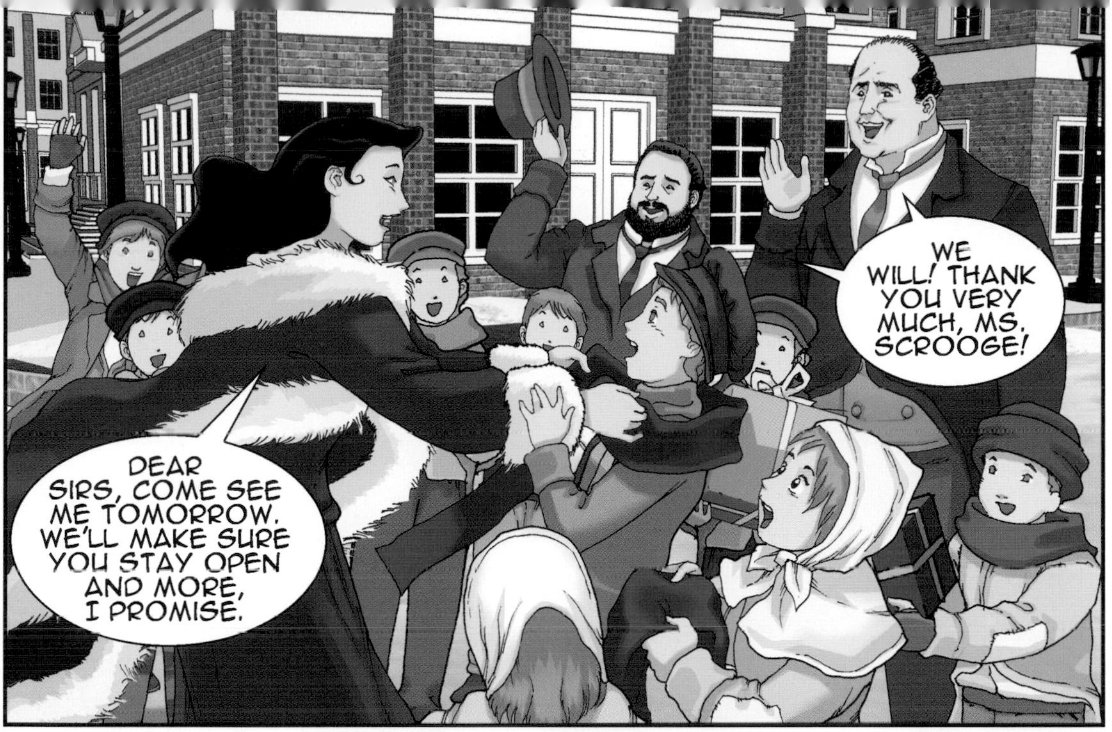
DEAR SIRS, COME SEE ME TOMORROW. WE'LL MAKE SURE YOU STAY OPEN AND MORE, I PROMISE.
WE WILL! THANK YOU VERY MUCH, MS. SCROOGE!

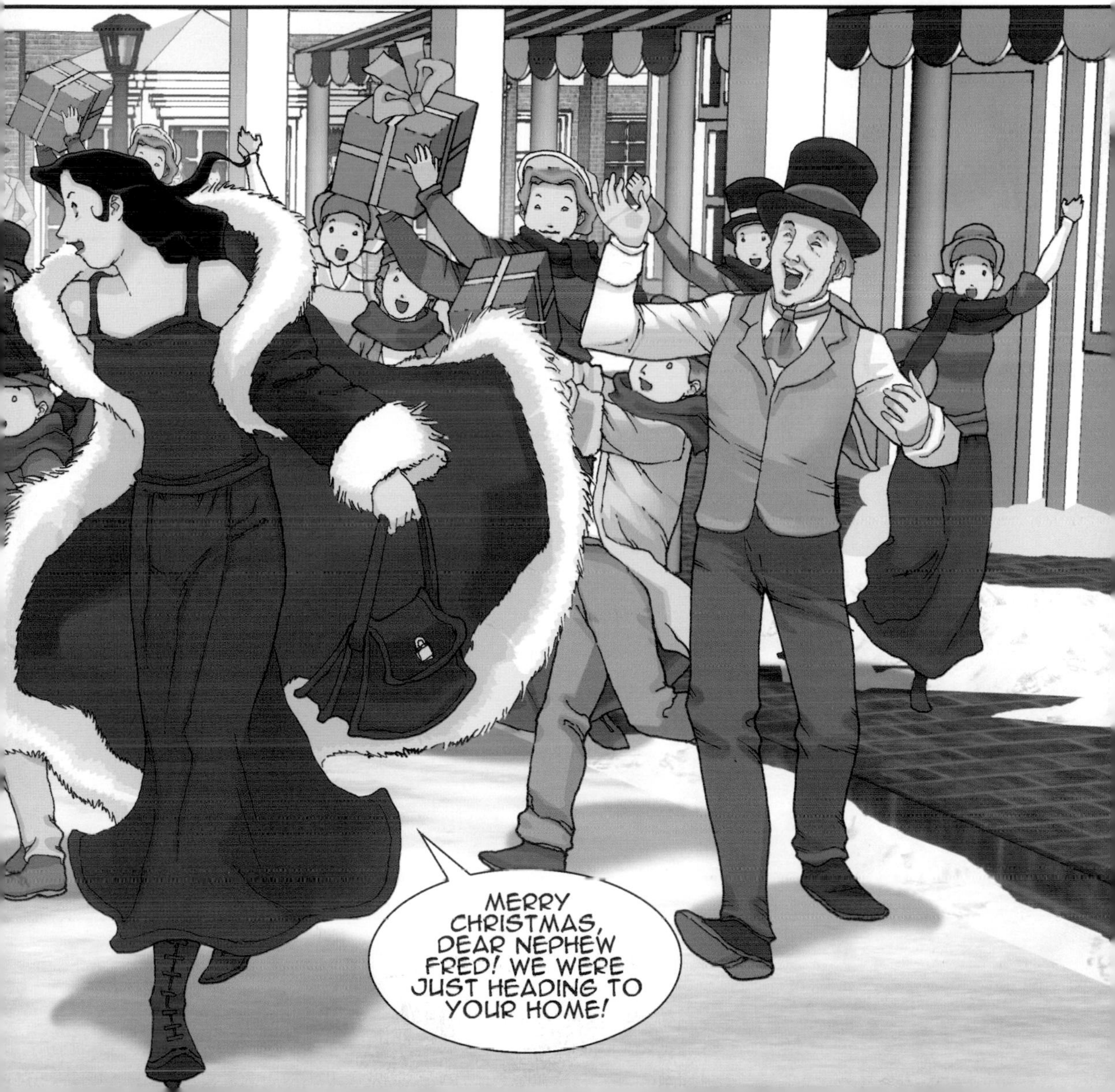
MERRY CHRISTMAS, DEAR NEPHEW FRED! WE WERE JUST HEADING TO YOUR HOME!

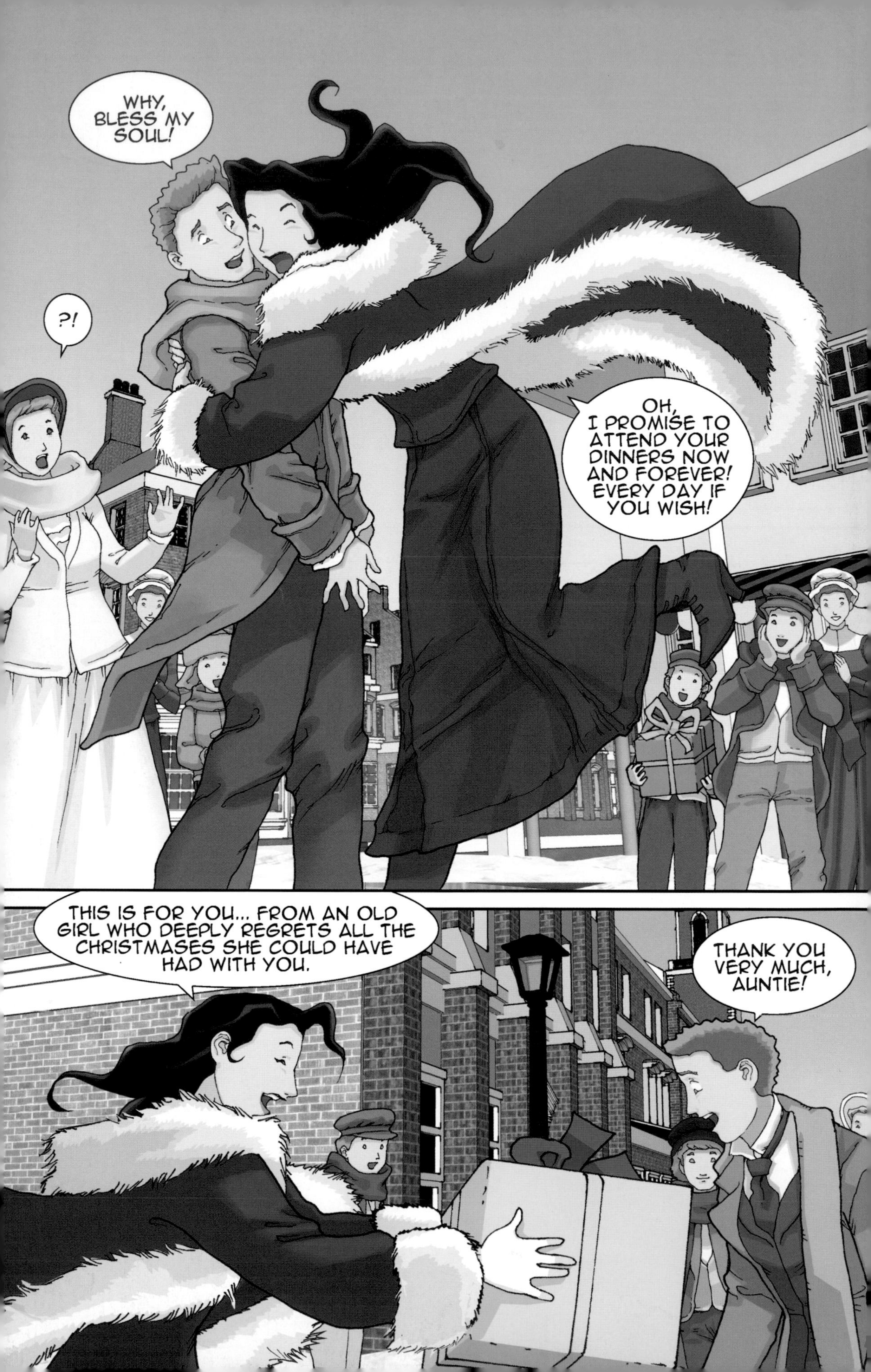
WHY, BLESS MY SOUL!
?!
OH, I PROMISE TO ATTEND YOUR DINNERS NOW AND FOREVER! EVERY DAY IF YOU WISH!
THIS IS FOR YOU... FROM AN OLD GIRL WHO DEEPLY REGRETS ALL THE CHRISTMASES SHE COULD HAVE HAD WITH YOU.
THANK YOU VERY MUCH, AUNTIE!

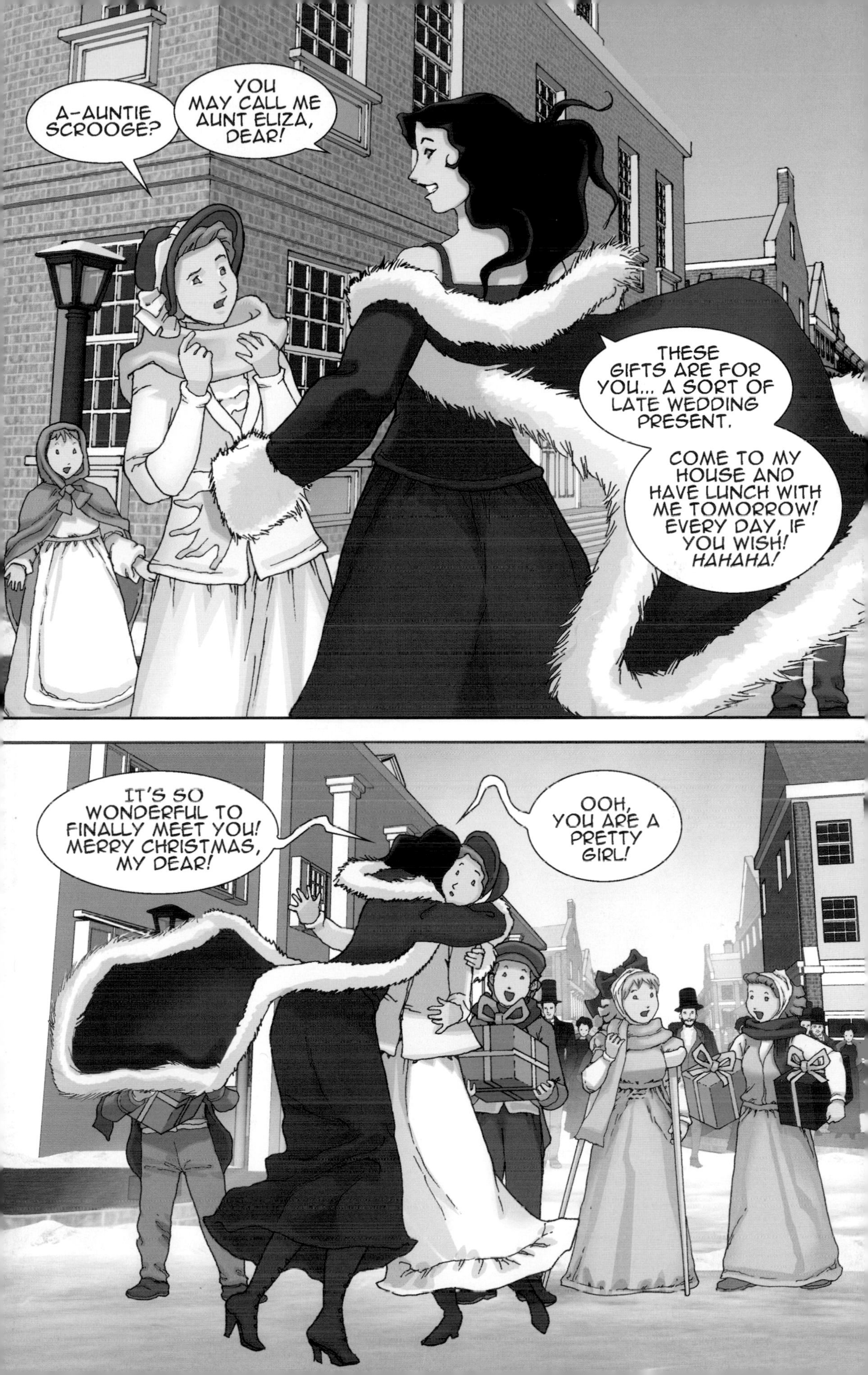
A-AUNTIE SCROOGE?
YOU MAY CALL ME AUNT ELIZA, DEAR!
THESE GIFTS ARE FOR YOU... A SORT OF LATE WEDDING PRESENT.
COME TO MY HOUSE AND HAVE LUNCH WITH ME TOMORROW! EVERY DAY, IF YOU WISH! *HAHAHA!*
IT'S SO WONDERFUL TO FINALLY MEET YOU! MERRY CHRISTMAS, MY DEAR!
OOH, YOU ARE A PRETTY GIRL!

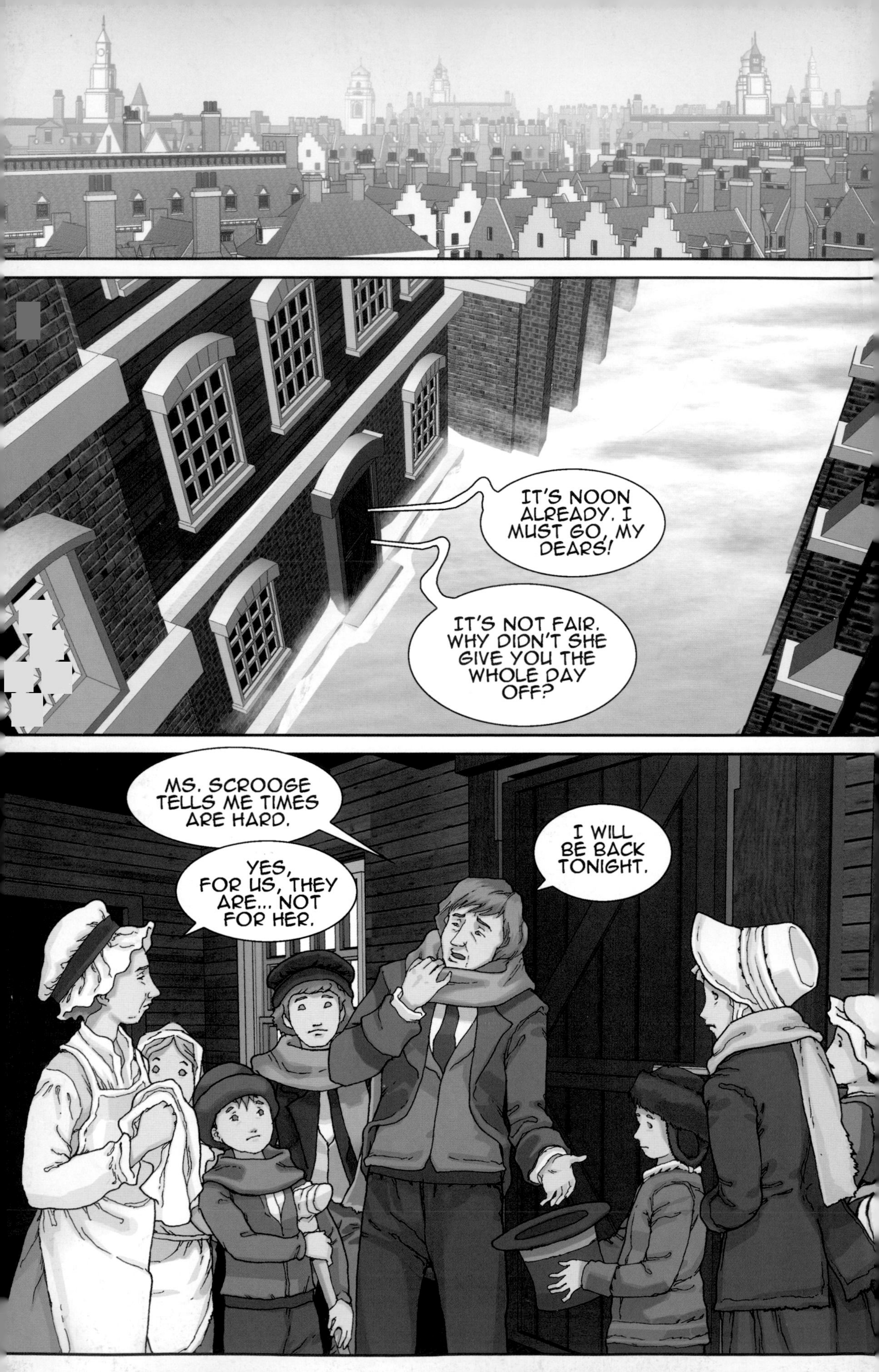
IT'S NOON ALREADY. I MUST GO, MY DEARS!
IT'S NOT FAIR. WHY DIDN'T SHE GIVE YOU THE WHOLE DAY OFF?
MS. SCROOGE TELLS ME TIMES ARE HARD.
YES, FOR US, THEY ARE... NOT FOR HER.
I WILL BE BACK TONIGHT.

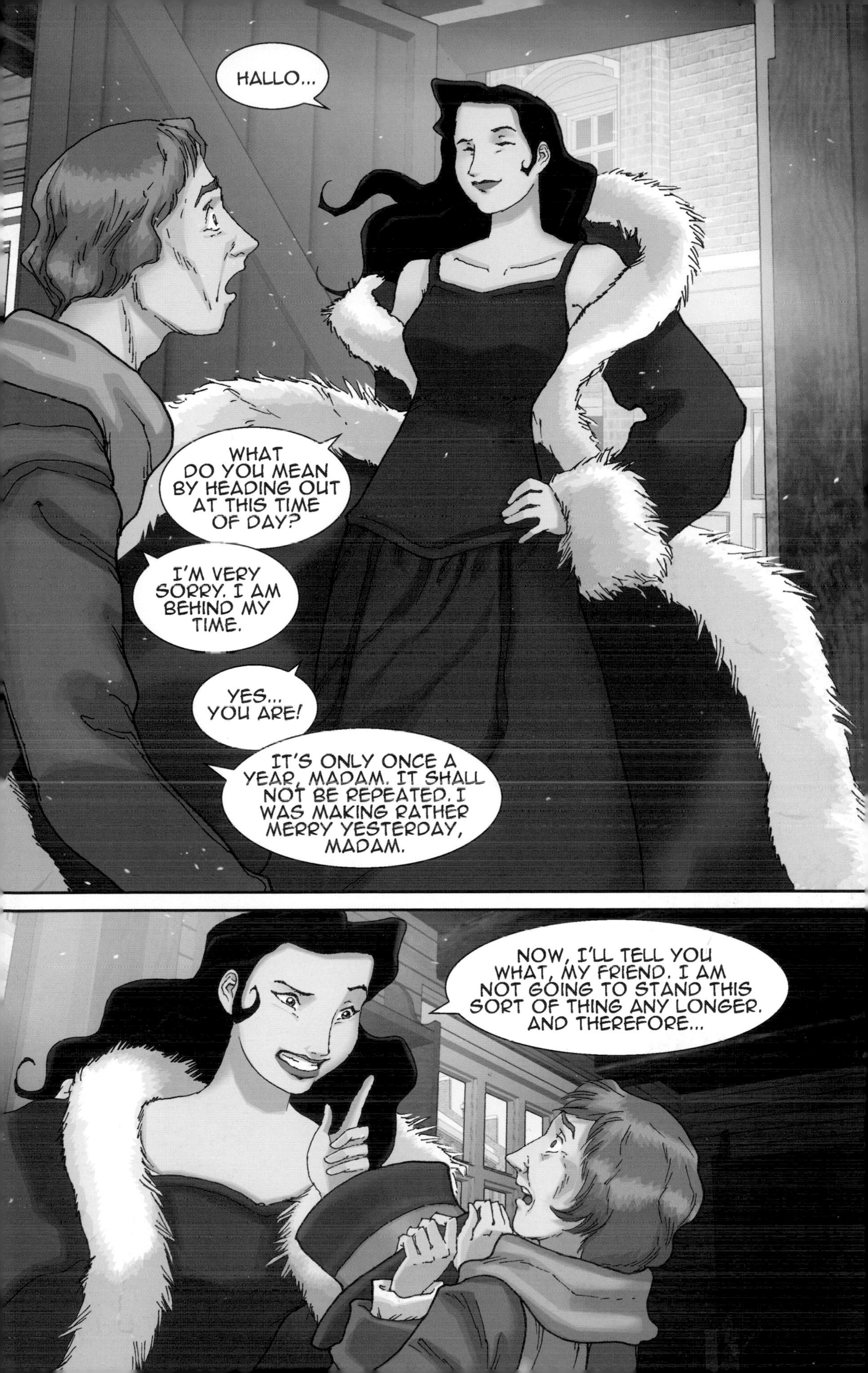
HALLO...
WHAT DO YOU MEAN BY HEADING OUT AT THIS TIME OF DAY?
I'M VERY SORRY. I AM BEHIND MY TIME.
YES... YOU ARE!
IT'S ONLY ONCE A YEAR, MADAM. IT SHALL NOT BE REPEATED. I WAS MAKING RATHER MERRY YESTERDAY, MADAM.
NOW, I'LL TELL YOU WHAT, MY FRIEND. I AM NOT GOING TO STAND THIS SORT OF THING ANY LONGER. AND THEREFORE...

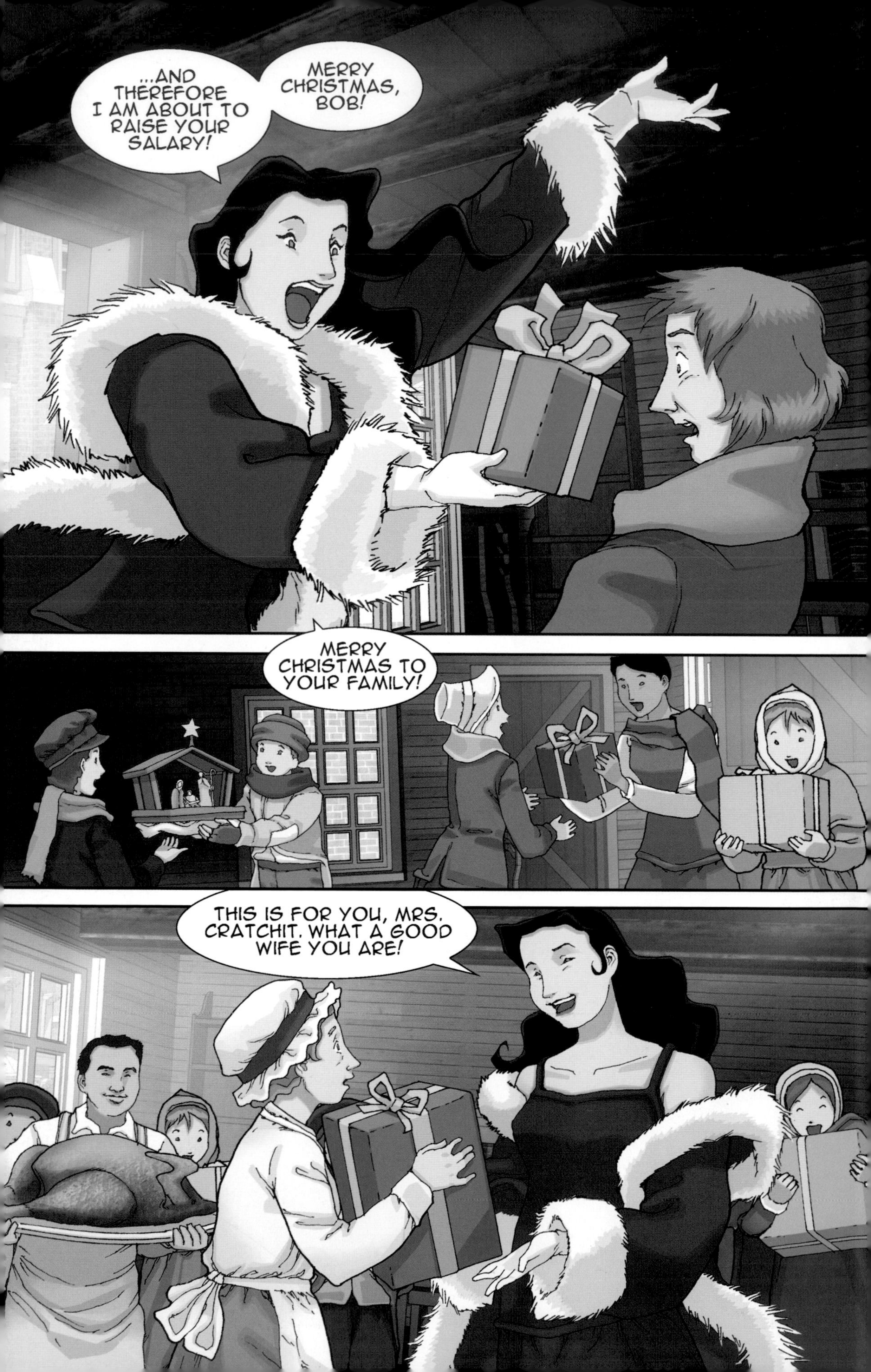
...AND THEREFORE I AM ABOUT TO RAISE YOUR SALARY!
MERRY CHRISTMAS, BOB!
MERRY CHRISTMAS TO YOUR FAMILY!
THIS IS FOR YOU, MRS. CRATCHIT. WHAT A GOOD WIFE YOU ARE!

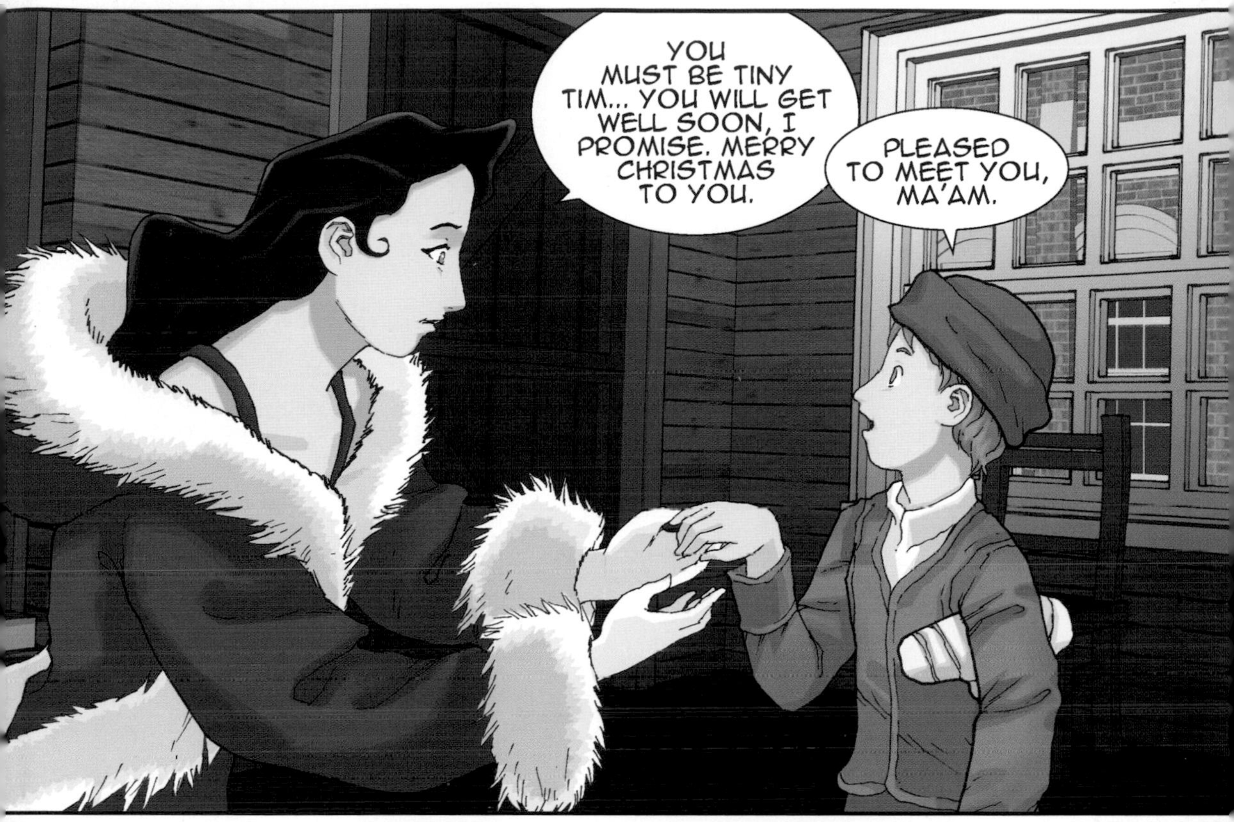
YOU MUST BE TINY TIM... YOU WILL GET WELL SOON, I PROMISE. MERRY CHRISTMAS TO YOU.
PLEASED TO MEET YOU, MA'AM.

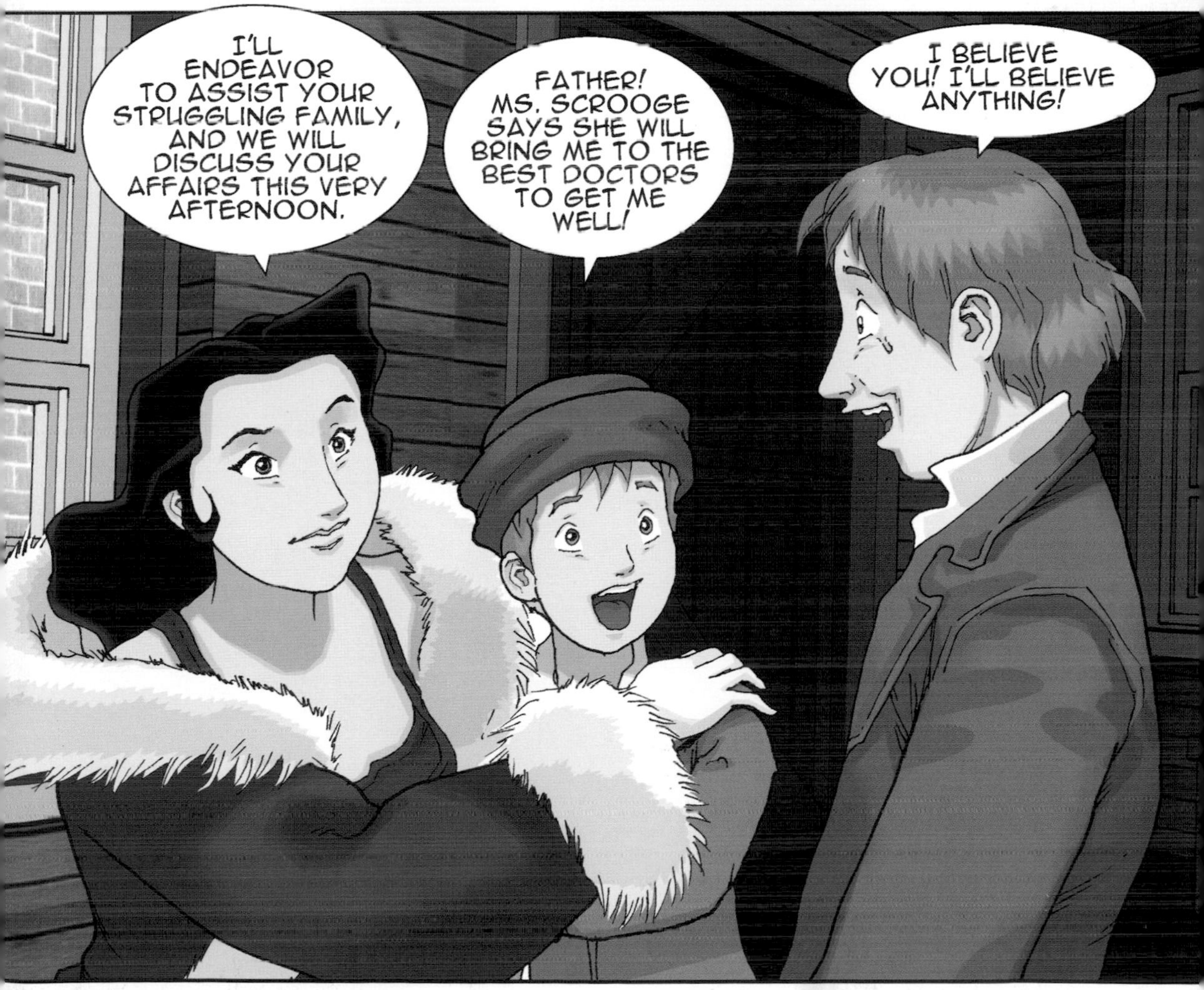
I'LL ENDEAVOR TO ASSIST YOUR STRUGGLING FAMILY, AND WE WILL DISCUSS YOUR AFFAIRS THIS VERY AFTERNOON.
FATHER! MS. SCROOGE SAYS SHE WILL BRING ME TO THE BEST DOCTORS TO GET ME WELL!
I BELIEVE YOU! I'LL BELIEVE ANYTHING!

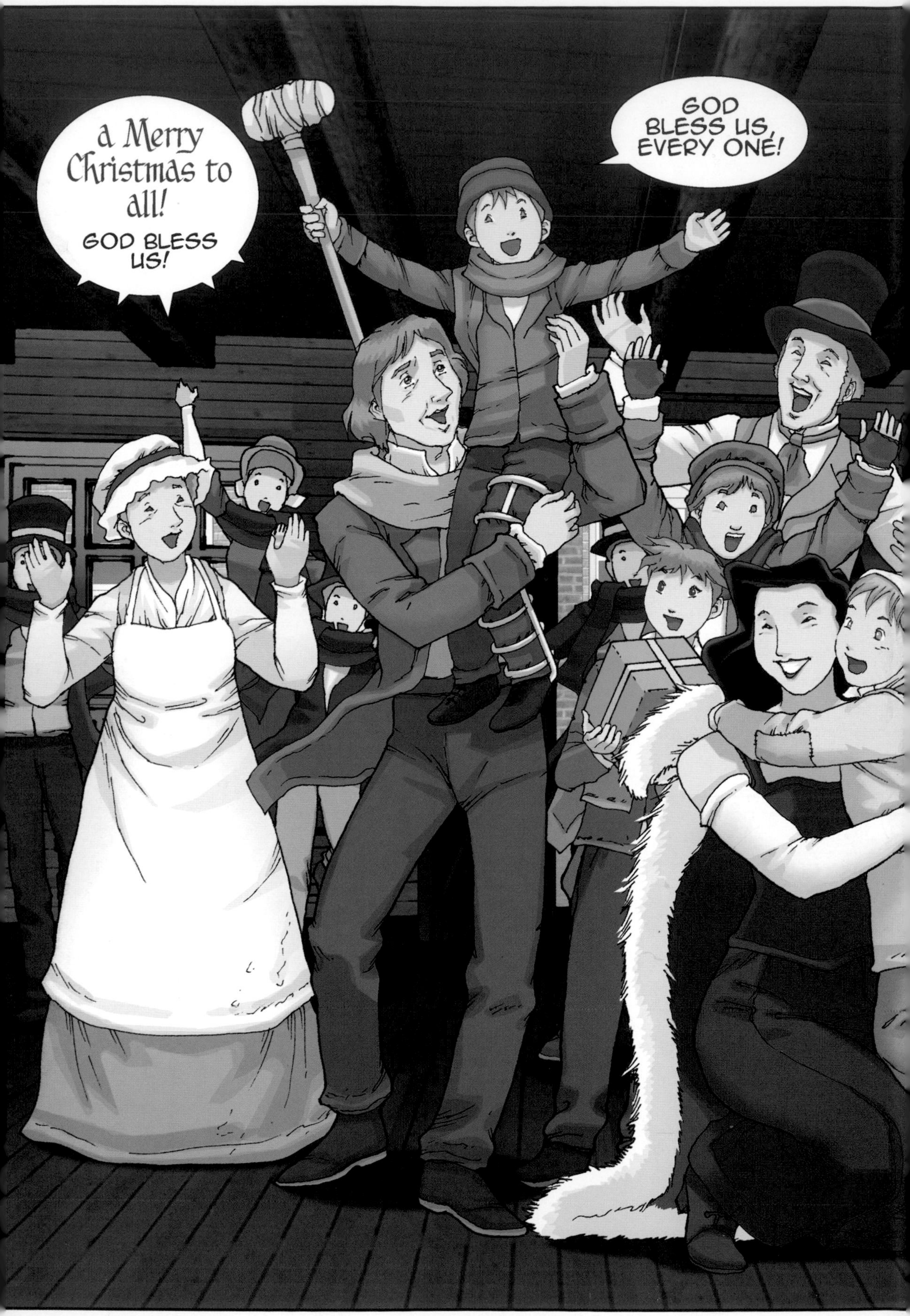
a Merry Christmas to all!
GOD BLESS US!
GOD BLESS US, EVERY ONE!

Merry Christmas!
Rod Espinosa
2009

THE END

president and publisher
MIKE RICHARDSON

executive vice president
NEIL HANKERSON

chief financial officer
TOM WEDDLE

vice president of publishing
RANDY STRADLEY

vice president of book trade sales
MICHAEL MARTENS

vice president of business affairs
ANITA NELSON

vice president of product development
DAVID SCROGGY

vice president of information technology
DALE LAFOUNTAIN

senior director of print, design, and production
DARLENE VOGEL

general counsel
KEN LIZZI

senior director of marketing
MATT PARKINSON

editorial director
DAVEY ESTRADA

senior managing editor
SCOTT ALLIE

senior books editor
CHRIS WARNER

executive editor
DIANA SCHUTZ

director of print and development
CARY GRAZZINI

art director
LIA RIBACCHI

director of scheduling
CARA NIECE

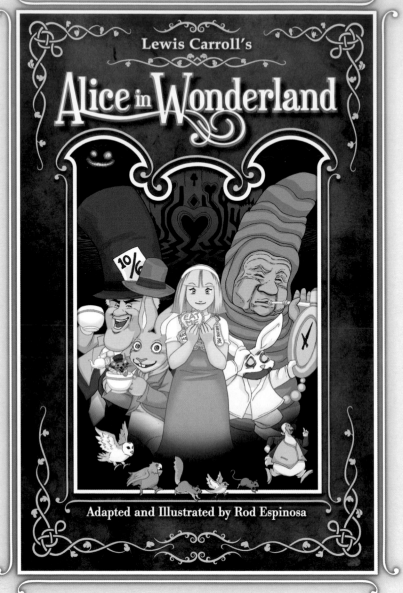

The Courageous Princess™

Written and illustrated by Rod Espinosa

Once upon a time, a greedy dragon kidnapped a beloved princess . . . but if you think she just waited around for some charming prince to rescue her, then you're in for a surprise!

Princess Mabelrose may not be the fairest of the land, but she has enough brains and bravery to fend for herself in a fantasy world of danger and adventure!

ISBN 978-1-59307-719-8 | $14.95

THE POP WONDERLAND SERIES

A new line of children's storybooks, the POP Wonderland series
is rendered in a friendly pastel palette and an engagingly modern
style. With words by Michiyo Hayano and illustrations by POP,
a well-known manga artist and anime designer in Japan, these
books bring familiar fairy tales to life in a brand-new way!

Alice's Adventures in Wonderland
ISBN 978-1-59582-266-6 | $16.99

Cinderella
ISBN 978-1-59582-269-7 | $16.99

Little Red Riding Hood
ISBN 978-1-59582-267-3 | $16.99

Thumbelina
ISBN 978-1-59582-268-0 | $16.99

Available at your local comics shop or bookstore!
To find a comics shop in your area, call 1-888-266-4226
For more information or to order direct: • On the web: DarkHorse.com
E-mail: mailorder@darkhorse.com Phone: 1-800-862-0052
Mon.–Fri. 9 AM to 5 PM Pacific Time

DARK HORSE BOOKS
DarkHorse.com